The Use of Humor
in Psychotherapy

The Use of Humor in Psychotherapy

Edited by
Herbert S. Strean

JASON ARONSON INC.
Northvale, New Jersey
London

This book was set in 10 point Garamond by Lind Graphics of Upper Saddle River, New Jersey, and printed and bound by Haddon Craftsmen of Scranton, Pennsylvania.

Library of Congress Cataloging-in-Publication Data

The use of humor in psychotherapy / edited by Herbert S. Strean.
    p. cm.
  Includes bibliographical references and index.
  ISBN 1-56821-084-1 (softcover)
  1. Wit and humor—Therapeutic use. 2. Psychotherapy. I. Strean, Herbert S.
  [DNLM: 1. Wit and Humor. 2. Psychotherapy—methods. WM 420 U835 1994]
RC489.H85U84   1994
616.89′14—dc20
DNLM/DLC
for Library of Congress   93-25547

Manufactured in the United States of America. Jason Aronson Inc. offers books and cassettes. For information and catalog write to Jason Aronson Inc., 230 Livingston Street, Northvale, New Jersey 07647.

To the memory of
JEROME BEN ROSEN
A creative analyst able to understand and
utilize the healing power of humor

Contents

II PRACTICE CONSIDERATIONS

III INNOVATIVE APPLICATIONS

Preface

The human being is the only organism on earth that has the ability to laugh. No other animal has this capacity. Furthermore, it is a virtual truism that it is the relatively mature and emotionally healthy individual who laughs frequently and enjoys it. Mental health professionals tend to agree that an absence of a sense of humor indicates that the person is suffering from emotional conflicts and is probably depressed.

The other emotional response that is uniquely human is crying. The absence of tears, when they are expected, like the absence of laughter, also indicates unconscious emotional conflict.

Although laughing and crying are two basic, inborn emotional reactions, psychoanalysts and psychotherapists have been much more interested in the phenomenon of crying than laughing. In contrast to the many clinical papers in the professional literature that deal with the patient's inability to cry and mourn, there are very few that discuss the dynamics of the patient's inability to laugh. When wit, humor, and laughter are used by the patient, most professional commentators on the subject have pointed to this behavior as a means of acting out, a way of resisting, a sign of a regressive transference, a maladaptive response, and frequently a disguised way of expressing hostility.

Until very recently, the use of humor by the clinician has been viewed very negatively. It is breaking the frame, a misalliance, a clear sign of counterresistance, and definite acting out on the part of the therapist. Humor in the therapeutic situation has been both decried and demeaned.

The strong resistance by professionals to viewing humor as a positive dimension of the therapeutic situation is quite surprising when we consider that the founder of psychoanalysis and psychotherapy very much appreciated wit and humor. Sigmund Freud was an active joke teller and used wit in many of his interactions with patients and nonpatients. Furthermore, he carefully subjected the many facets of jokes, humor, and wit to psychoanalytic investigation. He demonstrated, for example, that humor reflects a part of the superego that looks upon the ego with the warmth and understanding of an empathetic parent. Freud showed that the superego tries to console the ego by means of humor and attempts to protect it from suffering. He also pointed out that humor has a forgiving nature and is a way we accept reality with a little more equanimity and less pain.

Despite Freud's affirmative orientation to humor and his freedom to appreciate it in his patients and himself, it has taken mental health professionals over six decades to permit the master's perspective on humor to take the effect it might have in our work with patients in psychoanalysis and psychotherapy.

The writers of the chapters in this anthology are unique individuals! They have had the courage to investigate a most controversial issue that has been shrouded in secrecy, and have stated their findings with clarity, openness, and creativity. Although often disagreeing with one another on the place of humor in the treatment situation, they share a strong interest in the metapsychology of wit, humor, and jokes and how it affects the treatment process, for better or worse

In preparing this book, I undertook a computer search of some of the major characteristics of the psychoanalytic and psychotherapeutic processes. I found that there were close to 600 entries for hate, hostility, and rage in psychotherapy and psychoanalysis, but there were only thirty-eight for humor, laughing, or jokes in the treatment situation. After reviewing the thirty-eight entries carefully, I wrote to about twenty authors who had something important to say about humor in therapy and who said it in readable and clarifying language. Almost all of the twenty responded enthusiastically to my invitation to participate in this anthology and their papers are reproduced herein.

In addition, several of my colleagues who are faculty members of the New York Center for Psychoanalytic Training (Robert Barry, Louis Birner, Richard Friedman, Joe Richman, Norman Shelly, and Margot Tallmer) wrote chapters specifically for this anthology. These colleagues were all friends of the late Jerome Rosen, to whom this volume is dedicated. Jerry, a year before his death in 1989, had the idea of putting together a volume on the use of humor in treatment and it was the aforementioned colleagues who responded to his call. I am very grateful to them and to Jerry's wife, Dorothy Lander, for working with me so that Jerry's dream could come true. He always wanted therapists to appreciate the use of humor in the treatment situation, whether it be the patient's or the therapist's.

In the tradition of Sigmund Freud, who viewed humor as an expression of maturity and love, our lead chapter in this anthology by Warren Poland, "The Gift of Laughter: On the Development of a Sense of Humor in Clinical Analysis," mirrors Freud's sentiments. Dr. Poland convincingly demonstrates that a good analysis will help the patient's sense of humor become richer and more constructive. Concluding his chapter, he poignantly states, "The facilitating of the development of the patient's capacity for mature humor is one of the happiest and proudest effects of clinical analysis."

If therapists and patients are more human than otherwise, then it would follow that as the clinician matures, he or she will be freer to use humor in the treatment situation discriminately. Dr. Michael Bader in "The Analyst's Use of Humor," shows how his own use of humor with two patients tended to promote the analytic process. With both of the patients he describes in his chapter, painful affects were released and the transference neurosis could be examined in more breadth and depth when Dr. Bader used well-timed and well-phrased humor.

Bader's point of view seems similar to that of Dr. Richard Friedman who show us that humor can be used to resolve certain intractable resistances. In his chapter, "Using Humor to Resolve Intellectual Resistances," Dr. Friedman suggests that for obsessive patients who use interpretations to become even more obsessive, humor can activate latent affects and help foster a better working alliance.

Both Drs. Bader and Friedman infer that a humorless patient (or a humorless therapist) is an individual who needs help in overcoming some suffering. However, to help through humor an individual who is in emotional pain, the treating professional has to be very discriminating. Like any helpful intervention, the choice of the humor, its type, and the timing must show empathy and understanding.

All dynamically oriented therapists who subscribe to the notion that there is an unconscious mind and that all children go through specific psychosexual stages recognize that jokes, wit, and humor have unconscious meaning to the teller and the listener. We know individuals who particularly like, for example, anal jokes. Others get much pleasure from phallic jokes. Since much humor expresses what is often taboo, many forbidden impulses such as voyeurism, exhibitionism, sadism, and masochism become the major themes in the humor. In "The Oral Side of Humor," Jule Eisenbud finds that in all jokes there is a strong connection between laughter and the nursing situation.

In contrast to what has been a phobic attitude toward humor in the treatment situation, Dr. Robert Barry shows us that humor is always present in the transference–countertransference relationship. In his thoughtful chapter, "Recognizing Unconscious Humor in Psychoanalysis," Dr. Barry demonstrates that an appreciation of humor by the therapy's participants enhances the therapy. He concludes, "Not acknowledging the humor replicates the terrifying parent's inability to tolerate ridicule."

Humor can be used to muffle anxiety and both therapist and patient can use it for this purpose. As clinicians we have to be sensitive to our own anxiety and its meaning as well as to the anxiety of our patients. In "Anxiety and the Mask of Humor," Norman Shelly shows us how the patients' use of humor can be used productively in the analysis so that the meaning of the anxiety can be determined and eventually used in the service of the patients' self-understanding and emotional growth.

Not only is humor always present somewhere in the therapeutic relationship, as Barry shows, but the telling of and listening to jokes have many similarities to the therapeutic situation. This is the conclusion of Dr. Louis Birner's interesting chapter, "Humor and the Joke of Psychoanalysis."

This anthology would be incomplete if it did not include some of the caveats on the use of humor in treatment and a consideration of some of its limitations when used in therapy. Dr. Lawrence Kubie's paper on "The Destructive Potential of Humor in Psychotherapy" is reproduced as is Dr. Ned Marcus's article on "Treating Those Who Fail to Take Themselves Seriously: Pathological Aspects of Humor." Dr. Marcus, using a cognitive approach, highlights some of the defensive aspects of humor but demonstrates how the therapist can use the patient's humor to help him or her overcome dysfunctional behavior. Similarly, Dr. Bernard Saper suggests that laughter is not always the best medicine and that much more research needs to be conducted before clinicians can really be sure using humor has the therapeutic effects some of its proponents claim. This is similar to Dr. Robert Pierce's point of view in "Use and Abuse of Laughter in Psychotherapy."

But, humor has its place in psychotherapy if used discriminately, as Dr. Warren Poland advises us in "The Place of Humor in Psychotherapy." Dr. Frank Prerost shows us that by incorporating imagery procedures, humor can be extremely useful in resolving personal conflicts and lessening individual stress. Prerost's "Humor as an Intervention Strategy" offers sage advice on planning how to engage the patient in order to bring more joy into his or her life. This is also the attempt of Dr. Daniel Malamud in "The Laughing Game: An Exercise for Sharpening Awareness of Self-Responsibilty." Groups are used by Dr. Malamud and they are also the modality of choice of Dr. Shura Saul and Dr. Sidney Saul in their work with the elderly. Their chapter, "The Application of Joy in Group Psychotherapy for the Elderly,'' is a touching description of how humor can enhance the psychosocial functioning of the elderly.

Humor can be utilized in many ways and clinicians need to give this issue much thought. This is the message in "Humor as Metaphor" by Dr. Don-David Lusterman. It is also one of the messages in Dr. Margot Tallmer's chapter written with Dr. Joseph Richman, "Jokes Psychoanalysts Tell." Drs. Tallmer and Richman imply that clinicians do have a sense of humor and most of us believe that this is good news!

Although the use of humor in psychoanalysis and psychotherapy has been endorsed by several mainstream Freudians such as Warren Poland, Michael Bader, and others who appear in this anthology, including all of my colleagues from the the New York Center for Psychoanalytic Training, Dr. Roberta Satow takes the position that the use of humor is more compatible with an object relations perspective coupled with an interest in self psychology. In her chapter, Classical, Object Relations, and Self Psychological Perspectives on Humor," Dr. Satow concludes that "how we understand and deal with humor, laughter, and jokes in treatment is based on our general theoretical perspective . . ." Although few will question this proposition, we may also want to add that the use of humor in treatment is based on many factors, among which are the transference–countertransference relationship, the working alliance, the therapist's maturity and flexibility, and the patient's ego functions or lack thereof, particularly his or her unique defenses.

Following Dr. Satow's perspective is a short chapter by Dr. Harry A. Olson, "The Use of Humor in Psychotherapy," reflecting an Adlerian approach to humor.

Many individuals who appreciate humor like to leave others laughing. This is the intent of this editor. "Therapeutic Laugher: What Therapists Do to Promote Strong Laughter in Patients" by Drs. Gervaize, Mahrer, and Markow, and "Strong Laughter in Psychotherapy" by Drs. Mahrer and Gervaize are attempts to demonstrate that laughter can be a very welcome and therapeutic event in treatment.

The Use of Humor in Psychotherapy is, I believe, the first book on the subject. I am very grateful to Dr. Jason Aronson for proposing the idea, admiring of my colleagues, the authors of the papers herein, for their creative contributions, and pleased that this anthology will probably serve as a stimulus to other clinicians to reflect further on humor in treatment.

BASIC
CONSIDERATIONS

The Gift of Laughter: On the Development of a Sense of Humor in Clinical Analysis

Warren S. Poland

"He was born with a gift of laughter and a sense that the world was mad." Sabatini's opening words describing Scaramouche (1912, p. 3) sketch the portrait of someone we turn to with delight, someone enough at peace with himself to keep alive warmth and humor in the face of frustration and pain.

Rare are those who by nature fit Sabatini's description. Yet the capacity for humor linked to wisdom about the world is available in varying degrees to all of us, and one of the special delights of clinical analysis is seeing the liberation and development of such humor in the course of a patient's analytic work. My interest here is in the realization of such a capacity for humor during the course of and through the process of analysis. I shall first try to make clear that particular developed, perhaps mature, humor that Sabatini described and to which I refer. I shall also address the phrase "the gift of," the implications of the word "gift." I will look at some clinical considerations, and a sampling of the range of the development of such a sense of humor, in practice. Finally, I will offer some thoughts on technical questions these matters imply.

THE MATURE SENSE OF HUMOR

The varieties of senses of humor are vast: lesser and greater, drier and broader, sharper and gentler, and so forth. Many sorts of laughter, such as the cruel, the sardonic, and the sadistic, are strongly colored by aggression, while other sorts are markedly charged with sexuality. Such conflictual jokes are familiar in our daily analytic work. They are not, however, what we have in mind when we speak of "the gift of laughter." Rather, we refer to a capacity for sympathetic laughter at oneself and one's place in the world. Humor of this sort does not imply pleasure in pain but reflects a regard for oneself and one's limits despite pain. With such humor there is an acceptance of oneself for what one is, an ease in being amused even if bemused. This humor exposes a mature capacity to acknowledge inner conflict and yet accept oneself with that knowledge, even when it is the knowledge of one's narcissistic limits. Such humor, often linked to an appreciation of irony, requires a self-respecting modesty based on under-lying self strength and simultaneous recognition of and regard for others.

As I proceed, I shall refer to these specific aspects of what might be called sublimated or instinctually neutralized humor when I speak of the gift of laughter. Such a sense of humor implies sufficient skills of mastery for at least a partial taming of drive urgency, together with a moderation of the narcissistic demands of vanity, a respect for the authenticity of others, and a realization of the grander scale of reality beyond oneself. The quality is of acknowledgment and even acceptance of pain and loss without resignation to depressive hopelessness and hatred.

What I try to define is a *quality* of humor, a way of accepting oneself and the world with neither undue guardedness nor pretentious standing on high places. As with any human functioning, the qualities cannot be known simply from considering manifest behavior. There is no brand of humor or style of wit that in its manifest expression can proclaim itself as integrated and mature. The meanings and the uses of humor within the individual's psychic world, not the outside form, determine the type of humor. Both the appearance and the deeper meanings are always individual and unique.

There likely is a line of development of the sense of humor, one that parallels both psychosexual development and the development of maturity of object relationships. From the child's earliest smile on being satisfied, through sadistic delight in manipulating others, on to the flourishing of pleasure in recognizing the limits of words yet the ability to play with words in riddles and puns, to the aggressive and sexual jokes of adoles-cence, and so on—the line of development is determined by constitutional drive pressures and by maturing capacity to appreciate otherness, finite-ness, and the limits of reality. The adult gift of laughter, as I shall be using the phrase, refers to the relatively mature capacity to acknowledge urges and frustration, hopes and disappointments, with a humor in which bitterness is tamed but not denied.

This is a flower we all recognize on sight even though we have difficulty describing it botanically. Immature and conflictual jokes are familiar to us all. For illustration (and not as a prototypical model) I offer an example of mature humor. Robert Bak, highly regarded for his analytic skills, was known as a man dedicated to the good life. A former analysand of Bak's recalled with warmth a time in his analysis when he had been bemoaning the losses that come with disillusionment. After reviewing them in sad detail, the man had sighed, "There is no Santa Claus." Referring to the then preeminent restaurant in town, Bak answered in a sympathetic tone, "There *is* no Santa Claus . . . but there's always Lutèce!"

It is not a perfect world or an ideal world, but we deal with it as best we can and even find delight in that. Such a mature level of delight is the quality now addressed as the gift of laughter.

Freud (1905) considered *jokes* at the same early time in his development that he first considered dreams. Later, after he had moved on to appreciation of the structural implications of inner conflict, he returned to take a look at *humor* (Freud 1927). He then addressed the ego's assertion of invulnerability in humor, even while acknowledging the trauma confronting the person. An extreme can be seen in the instance of the rogue on the gallows early Monday morning saying, "Well, this week's beginning nicely." In all uses of humor there is, as Freud (1927, p. 162) said, a "triumph of narcissism." Clearly, such an aspect must be present whenever one says, "I can continue to look at myself and the world even in the face of my own destruction." Narcissism itself is at the same time acknowledged and ridiculed with such humor.

Such "triumph of the ego," one of

the great series of methods which the human mind has constructed in order to evade the compulsion to suffer, . . . possesses a dignity . . . by means of which a person refuses to suffer, emphasizes the invincibility of his ego by the real world, victoriously maintains the pleasure principle— and all this, in contrast to other methods having the same purposes, *without overstepping the bounds of mental health.*" [Freud 1927, p. 163, italics added]

Freud made the point that the ability of humor to view danger as tolerable is like that of the parent who reassures the child by saying, " 'Look! here is the world, which seems so dangerous!' It is nothing but a game for children—just worth making a jest about!" (p. 166). The internalization of such a parental view lies in the superego, consoling and protecting the ego, the legacy of benevolent parents.

Roustang (1987) noted that laughter reveals suffering as human, containing the possibility of respect. He linked humor to uncertainty and its toleration, to time, and to anguish."Whereas, according to Kierkegaard, anguish is the kind of freedom which is imposed as an unavoidable possibility, laughter is freedom's possibility to escape from itself" (p. 711).

Chasseguet-Smirgel (1988) addressed humor by considering its links to depression. Agreeing with Kris (1938), she felt that the greatest accomplishment of humor was that of banishing the terror of loss of love. She drew attention to Freud's carrying the roots back to the smile of the "infant at the breast when it is satisfied and satiated and lets go of the breast as it falls asleep" (Freud 1905, p. 146, n. 2). For Chasseguet-Smirgel, "the humorist is a person trying to be his own loving mother" (1988, p. 205).

The Gift of Humor

Discussion of the early good parents reminds us that we have spoken of the *gift* of laughter. For Sabatini, the gift was a God- or nature-given gift, an endowment at birth. Could anyone doubt the existence of a variety of natural endowments, the variable capacities present at birth? It may be too simple even to think of an underlying attribute called a capacity for humor. Rather, an entire range of attributes and functions may have to coalesce to determine both the style and the range of ultimate sensibilities. These attributes include the innate strength of drives, the strength of capacities for self-taming and frustration tolerance, activity/motility styles, and the capacities for symbol formation and for a range of play with ideas. Yet, as in all other aspects of life, how a natural endowment is realized, indeed whether it even has the opportunity to become actualized, is determined by experience and fate.

Freud, too, called this a gift, "a rare and precious gift" (1927, p. 166). But Freud was emphasizing what was given through experience as the underlying capacities matured and were shaped by the actualities of an individual's life. He thus implied a question that extends to our clinical work: Can this capacity for detached amusement be given by one person to another? In asking this, I do not minimize the individual's constitution. Freud remarked that "many people are even without the capacity to enjoy humorous pleasure that is presented to them" (1927, p. 166). Perhaps there are some whose humorlessness is beyond repair. Fortunately, clinical analysis most often leads to the appearance of some degree of humor, endowment and experience uniting for humor to flower.

We are in no position dogmatically to divide this much as constitutional and that much as experiential. Staying respectful of the limits of what is inborn, what is by inheritance given, we still can turn our attention to the more approachable, to what can be changed, that is, how experience can modify the actualization of what is given.

Experience is internalized; the ego grows around precipitates of identifications. A woman known for her wit had a young daughter just learning to speak. The 16-month-old child walked into the living room, bent over, put a piece of bread on her foot, looked up at the adults present, announced "Shoe," and burst out laughing. She not only knew a word and what it represented, but she was able to play with the idea, mocking the reality. Hearing the story retold, friends replied, "She comes by it naturally. She has her mother's humor."

No doubt "her mother's humor" includes an inherited constitutional capacity. But equally certain is the importance of identification. We used to speak of primary autonomous spheres of the ego, areas like the capacity for walking and talking, which develop free of conflict. But no child grows outside the human world, and children walk and talk in the manner of those who raise them. So it seems, too, with humor. A child's humor, or lack of humor, reflects the child's level of development, but it is also expressed in the idiom of the private world in which the child has grown.

Also, it is important to notice that this instance does not seem to be a function of the child's internalizing a comforting mother at a moment of pain. Rather, what has been internalized, what has been identified with, is the way the mother's mind works. The clever little girl has a way of playing with words that is a small replica of the way her mother plays with words. Adding her own talents and freedom, she becomes a new, improved version, not merely a second-hand copy.

The role of identification is sufficiently clear that we even speak of cultural differences in humor, of national styles of humor. We talk of a dry British humor, a pained Jewish gallows humor, an irreverent French humor. (Though unknown to me, there may even be a Swiss fashion of humor.) Prejudice is present along with generalization when we speak in terms of such large groups, yet the underlying recognition of cultural patterns confirms the role of identification and shared experience in the development of brands of humor.

THE PATIENT'S HUMOR

What does this have to do with clinical analysis? Let us move from vast groups to that small and private two-person group, the clinical analytic dyad. What can an analysis do, what does it do, in terms of the gift of laughter? Might the analytic process not only be a freedom road that liberates from the slavery of inhibition and repetition but also be a technique that fosters new ways of viewing oneself, resulting in new uses of humor?

Consideration of the development of a sense of humor during analysis does not suggest that the analytic experience is a laughing matter. Engagement in relentless self-investigation with and before another person demands courage in the face of terrors and uncertainties. Shengold (1981) demonstrated the value of humor even as he emphasized the essentially painful nature of psychoanalytic work. He compared the journey to insight with Freud's tale of a poor man who stowed himself without a ticket on the fast train to Karlsbad. The man was repeatedly caught and repeatedly thrown roughly off the train each time tickets were inspected. At one of the stations near the end of his traumatic trip he met a friend who asked where he was going. "To Karlsbad," he replied, "if my constitution can stand it."

Moments of humor arise during the analytic journey. When they do, they are as multiply determined as are all other associations: their unconscious and instinctually charged aspects demand analytic attention. However, there are times when the humor appears like unexpected clearings in internal conflicts, moments not mainly defensive but rather exposing new understandings and integrations.

A markedly guarded patient, long crippled by overriding shame, reflected when once he was able to view himself more respectfully that he previously "only opened my mouth to change feet." He had been self-depreating for very long. His new way of expressing his self-observation revealed both pain and respectful sympathy for himself in conflict. His humor, a sign of strength, was a secondary reward from his arduous labor.

There are people whose natural wit becomes inhibited by the development of an acute neurosis, such as depression. Working through the current pathology then exposes a humor already present. Here, analysis does not significantly contribute to developing a capacity for humor. Rather, it clears an interference, exposing what had always been present but temporarily hidden.

Another brief instance was evident in work with a patient who for years had been severely constricted, appearing publicly like a socially proper automation. After much struggle to understand this quality as it appeared in the transference, she exposed an earlier unseen humor. Begrudgingly acknowledging an interest in our collaborative analytic work, she said, "All right, I'll look at reality, but only as a tourist." A remarkable capacity for subtle wit had been hidden, buried under the rubble of the psychic warfare of her development.

The ability to tolerate uncertainty and ambiguity and the ability to integrate into one's view of oneself and the world the vast mix of contradictory urges, feelings, and ideas are accepted goals of successful character analysis. They are, at the same time, the requisites for the gift of laughter. Mature humor is a reflection of analytic work successfully done.

Before considering the relative impact of the patient's analyzing position, such as the loosening of associations, and of the place of the analyst as a new person in the patient's analyzing experience, let us turn to a few clinical samples, instances intended to be illustrative of a range rather than all-inclusive.

First Illustration—An Initial Unwitting Joke

A first dream of a beginning analytic patient offers a fitting beginning illustration of the development of humor, especially apt because the humor that struck me, as the listener, was at the time of the dream unknown to the patient. He was a young musician, bright and cultured, but something of a snob. Racked by envy and disdain, he was tortured by having a place in his social and professional worlds that was distressingly junior to the position he felt properly his due.

The sense of the dream was of his receiving news of the birth of the son of a colleague. The content of the dream was the name printed on the birth announcement card: Montgomery Fink.

Grandeur and abasement, exposed side by side. Although I then remained quiet, I remember finding the name then, as now, funny. Pride and humiliation, naked and condensed.

These were the major themes of our subsequent work together. At that first moment I was able to see as humorous what had already been impinging on me in the conflicting currents of the transference. As time went on, and with it very much work, the patient himself came to see many of his own tendencies with increasing acceptance, coming to find his own humor in such circumstances.

This man's dream was at once symptomatic and witty. It was a condensation that was clearly structured like an elegant joke, one that aided the development of distance and increased understanding, an early analytic step in his development of his own mastery and, secondarily, his own sense of humor.

Second Illustration—Freeing of an Already Evident Capacity for Humor

Formal, perfectionistic, rigid obsessional patients often seem humorless, though some reveal a contemptuous sarcasm. Such patients are familiar to us.

There are at times, however, patients who expose from the start a natural humor and wit, but who consider such capacities symptoms rather than strengths. One young reporter came for analysis paralyzed by indecisiveness. His need for absolutes, his inability to integrate mixed feelings, left him frozen in the face of needed life decisions. It was with embarrassment that his humor was revealed. He felt it to be "silly," the inane humor of a little boy, a humor that showed him as cute but not an adult among adults. At first, the "silly humor" was presented as a symptom to be removed.

As oedipal conflicts were analyzed, as the patient was able to venture beyond his clinging to juniority, was able to be a man among men, he began to value his native wit and whimsy, enjoying rather than squelching them. With his father away at war he had been raised by a mother who did not seem responsive to his budding masculinity. His humor, like his sexuality, was taken as a sign of smallness, weakness, qualities to be overcome. Now, feeling more respectful of himself and more secure in the world of adults, he became able to expose his humor in both professional and social circles. He was no longer ashamed of the childlike aspects of his whimsy, and his increased freedom for fantasy allowed him a humor that was often creative.

In this instance, analysis did not so much facilitate the development of an unformed humor; rather, it liberated a sense of humor already substantially developed.

Third Illustration—Growth of Previously Undeveloped Humor

In the second illustration, above, the patient's humor, though at first defensively devalued had been present from the start. There are others whose capacities for comfortable humor had never had the freedom to develop, those with depressed characters unable to realize their native humor. What wit that does show through is often bitter. Analysis of the depression, both working through superego pressures and allowing opportunity for mourning when necessary, may reveal an underlying potential for humor atrophied by fixation. With the following woman, the humor that broke through her depression was mainly sadistic. Analysis both helped expose her wit and aided in mastering the conflicts that kept that wit caustic.

A widow of many years consulted me at the time her youngest child was going off to college. She was militantly depressed. She was convinced she would end as a bag lady walking the streets. She ate and slept only with great difficulty, was withdrawing from her limited earlier social contacts, and led a life of isolation. She considered killing herself.

As analytic work progressed, first signs of humor had the quality of biting acerbic wit. For instance, she spoke of the House of Ruth (a local charity for abused women) as the House of Medea. As another instance, after mentioning M.A.D.D. (Mothers Against Drunk Driving), she said her own preferred charity was D.A.M., initials she said stood for Mothers Against Dyslexia.

Through analytic work, in which the direct analysis of such humor played only a minor role, her underlying character structure was explored. The youngest child, she had been conceived to cure her mother's depression. The prescription had failed. During childhood she had used a sharp tongue to protect herself against cutthroat competition with two older brothers and also to handle the excitement of over stimulation, discharging and warding off sexual urges.

She married a controlling and withholding husband who seemed to her to repeat the ungiving qualities of her mother and the stimulating but unavailable aspects of her brothers. When he died young, she gave over her life to raising the three children she was left. She did not become involved with any new men and, by her account, did not masturbate. Despite loneliness and sexual frustration, the years she had her children to herself were generally happy ones.

Sharp-tongued wit was the first face she showed of her humor, but as the analytic work went on, the harshness softened. Increasingly, new openings in the work were announced by jokes. When erotic feelings first made their way into the transference, she signaled the fact by telling the story of two elderly nursing home residents in adjoining wheelchairs. An old woman insisted she could tell an old man's age despite his skepticism. She challenged him to let her prove her ability. When he finally agreed to let her try, she said she first had to hold his penis. After fondling it several minutes, she announced the man was 87 years old. He was astonished by her accuracy and asked how she could tell. "Easy," she answered, "you told me last week."

The humor served to bridge conflicts from displaced areas to the transference. Telling the joke had in it the wish to elicit a sexual effect in me. The patient's charged use of humor served as an introduction to and enactment of her sexual and aggressive concerns in the transference. Its analysis made what had been implicit now explicit: whether with me in the transference or with her brothers while growing up, her sexual curiosity and sexual wishes arose in *her*. They were her own.

Indeed, the grace with which the patient could use her wit with me was itself seductive. That is, the use of humor, above and beyond the contents of any specific instance, enacted the patient's subtle enticement. Analysis of the sexual nature of the transference, revealed through such humor, exposed underlying sadistic fantasies and impulses, with terrors of helplessness lying behind both.

By the time of termination, the patient not only was no longer depressed but had a broadened social life. She was increasingly known by her friends for her uncommon wit and good humor, which were now generally put to the use of opening herself in life rather than closing herself off. The patient herself, however, knew how easily her humor could fall back to sadistic biting. She came to use that knowledge as a valuable signal for introspection when such regression appeared. Old conflicts no longer interfered with her ability to take and to give pleasure.

The analysis of this woman evidenced the important links between depression and humor focused on by Chasseguet-Smirgel (1988). This woman indeed used humor as a way of becoming her own loving mother.

Fourth Illustration—A Moment of Humor in the Progressive Unfolding of the Transference

The third illustration, above, demonstrated the broad movement of the patient's sense of humor over the length of an analysis. In this example I would like to turn to a more narrow moment in the midst of an analysis to demonstrate a shift of identifications in the transference related to the patient's humor.

A 35-year-old writer, whose great social charm was used in the service of intense self-aggrandizing narcissism, came for analysis because of dissatisfaction with his life. After a long period of work it became apparent that he went about his seemingly lighthearted social life in a deadly earnest manner to protect himself against a sense of body fragility, which he experienced as dangerously disintegrative.

Early in our work the patient happened across a brief paper I had written defending the therapist's use of humor (Poland 1971). As he belittled and resented his father, he competitively resented my having written, and he belittled my published view as not that of a real or strong analyst. All my efforts to address his narcissism and his competitiveness were long repudiated for implying vulnerability in him or competent strength in me.

Nonetheless, gradually and with undeniable courage, the patient confronted the power of his own vanity. Careful of his appearance, he looked ten years younger than his actual age. Now he admitted that socially he pretended to an age many years younger than he was, trying to cling to an image of idealized youth. By this time, his egotism had given way to recognition of and beginning regard for the otherness of others. Now his charming seductive humor could leave room for early evidences of humor about himself.

During one session he bemoaned the length of analysis and wondered of what use integration would prove to him if it were not obtained until he was 45 years old. Then with a laugh he added, "Because for me, when *I* am 45, I'll actually be 70!" It was apt that his humorous self-observation served to announce his readiness to give up the social facade of eternal youth. This was one of the first times he had been able to laugh at his own foibles.

The complexities of multiple determination make seeming clarities in analysis dangerous. I believe what I have described captures accurately a significant shift in the analysis. However, what serves the resolution of one conflictual level can simultaneously serve the defensive side of a deeper and, one hopes, emerging, conflictual level in the transference. There was a ring of truth in his witty introspection, but there also seemed a beginning effort to identify with me, as in a defensive and detoxifying identification with the aggressor.

The joke expressed both a new insight and a new level of defense. The capacity to look at himself and at his vanities was a major accomplishment for this man. In part, the use of humor manifested an effort to observe himself, perhaps even to identify with my analyzing functions. On the other hand, the process involved a narcissistic bribe to me in order to gain approval and relief from further free association. In the hierarchy of movement in the analytic process, what was worked out on one level served simultaneously to defend against, and thus implicitly expose, what was coming next.

My effort, then, was to respect the genuineness of the self-observation and the creativity of the humor while at the same time questioning the implied appeal for me to like him because he would be, presumably, like me. Attention to the latter proved fruitful, leading to a world of fantasies and memories about the patient's seduction of and by his mother. But the partial mastery evidenced in his half-mocking self-reflection was neither diminished nor undone by the simultaneous effort to turn a partial insight to defensive use.

THE DEVELOPMENT OF HUMOR IN CLINICAL ANALYSIS

These vignettes have been selected to give a taste of patients' gradual transitions from humorlessness or conflicted humor to more mature senses of humor. Yet the special nature of humor, and particularly the question of "the gift of laughter," may allow us to focus specifically on some aspects of the analytic process. Humor implies in its very nature the presence of an other. Certainly, no drive can exist in actuality outside the context of an implied object; and, just as certainly, no object conceptualization has useful meaningfulness outside the context of drives. The transference presents our model: intrapsychic forces are manifest and open to examination as they become evident in a special and unique dyadic field.

Freud attended from the beginning to both dreams and jokes. Dreams took precedence of attention because they truly seem to offer a"royal road to the unconscious." They seem a very model of intrapsychic processing. Though the significance of dreaming as a form of communication within a transference relationship has been recognized, still dreams maintain their centrality as an inner dynamic whether or not others appear immediately involved.

Jokes, a developmentally early level of humor, are different. While wit and mature humor can be private, that is, with oneself as one's own private audience, the origin always implies others. There is an other made to laugh, and private humor has merely developed to the point where parts of oneself can serve as both originator and observer. Unlike dreams, humor cannot be conceived of without uniting both inner forces and intended or imagined impact on others.

Transference is a way of relating: relating as telling, as in associations, and relating as connecting, as in attempting to elicit a feeling or a reaction. The very words used in the talking cure also carry both levels, the content and the emotional action. Humor in the clinical situation inevitably partakes of this double path, the patient's story as a tale told and as an effort to elicit and engage the analyst-other in an enactment. Although in actuality the two are facets of an experiential unity, for convenience we can consider each aspect separately.

The Nature of Words and the Patient's Development of Humor

The analytic situation fosters free association with resulting loosening of rigidities of word meanings and broadening of abilities to play with words. Interpretations open new levels of meaning, extending the previous range of understanding of what was thought and said. Such relaxation of constricted patterns of relating to words, to ideas and fantasies, to reality in general, leads to greater freedom of play of thoughts and feelings and greater ease in seeing both oneself and the world for what they are.

The nature of words as exploited by the nature of analytic listening offers the first push to a developing sense of humor. In listening to both words and music, analysts are particularly alert to the multiple meanings of words. This is no more than another way of saying that they listen for unconscious implications in the manifest messages of patient associations.

As Freud (1905) made clear in his study of the relation of humor to the unconscious, the experience of humor derives significantly from the economic discharge of tension. We also know that transference is manifest on many levels, not only from past to present and from others to analyst, but centrally within the mind transference involves passage of energy from one level to another and from one symbol to another (Loewald 1960). When we hear and interpret any condensation, any displacement, any symbol, we help free energy in the patient's mind.

Words not only make a statement, they also reveal what is hidden behind the statement. The role of metaphor is crucial in clinical communication. The literature is large, but Sharpe (1940) provided an exemplary instance in her attention to biological meanings structured in metaphor. When the analyst hears the implications of puns or of metaphorical meanings of which the patient is not aware and interprets those to the patient, the analyst draws a part of the patient a step away from the experience of the moment into a split position, one of both experiencing and noticing. In making this split (Sterba 1934), patients move to a position of being able to notice conflicts and paradoxes, even ironies. They have the start of the ability to laugh at parts of themselves.

Certainly, our common experience is that words give this ability. We groan when we hear simple puns, but the groan, I think, is a sign of great familiarity, even, at times, of affectionate familiarity. The little girl learning to speak, mentioned earlier, was playing with nascent humor when she recognized that "bread" and "shoe" were different, that the words for those two were not the same as the things spoken of, and that the words could in play be interchanged. The play, the sense of pleasure, comes from the sense of mastery. Hearing and speaking of the different forces united into single names in the patient's words gives a similar pleasure of mastery, along with the singular delight that comes from making the unspeakable speakable. As a result, when working analytically, even the most staid analyst with abstinent technique and sober style contributes to patients' developing sense of humor by recognizing the implications of multiple meanings of words, the presence of puns.

The principle of multiple determination has led us to recognize and respect the presence of compromise formation behind any manifest mental function. Freud spoke of "dream work" in his early examination of compromise formation regarding dreams. Paralleling that model, the phrase "word work" has been used to consider factors involved in the compromise formations behind choices of words (Poland 1986). Increasing understanding of the power and limits of words, strengthened by their being heard by the analyst as tentative associations rather than immutable ultimate facts, leads to the ability to play with words. Toying with the motives behind the compromise formations involved in the processing, the choosing of words, a person is then able to play with words. "Word work" speaks of the compromise formation structured behind words used. As those forces are increasingly recognizable, a person is increasingly able to move to "word play," the economical discharge of mental energy by freer mobility and freer use of words themselves.

The Analyst as an Other in the Analytic Process and the Patient's Development of Humor

When patients learn over time how the analyst's comments reflect an openness of hearing and thinking, when they notice new attentiveness to multiple meanings, when they learn to listen similarly in their own private scanning of their minds, the new looseness and ease of thought can become manifest as a broadening sense of humor. Where beyond the use of words is the analyst in relation to "the gift" of laughter?

A sense of humor, like insight, cannot simply be given. It is not available on prescription. But when transference evocations do not call forth the reaction the patient expected and instead elicit an unexpected reaction such as an interpretation, then the analyst inevitably comes to function as a model for increased freedom for mental play. Thus the analytic process of transference crystallization and exploration contributes as much as does the structure of words to the capacity for humor.

There are structural similarities between the development from jokes to humor on the one hand and the development of transference in the analytic dyad on the other hand that may allow each to cast some light on the other. (For this comparison from a different slant, see also Weber [1982].)

Let us first look at jokes. Freud (1905) emphasized the object relationship implicit in jokes. Focusing on "dirty jokes," he considered their telling to be like the seduction of a woman in the presence of a third person. In this structure he saw the joke teller as a first person with the listener as third. The listener "laughs as though he were the spectator of an act of sexual aggression" (p. 97), the seduced woman serving as absent but implied second person.

The success of such a joke is measured by the listener's reaction, the laughter. Thus, not only are the skill of the telling and the gratification potential of the content essential to the joke's success, also the psychology of the listener is a crucial factor. (That, certainly, is something we all know first-hand, having told jokes with great success to some, only to find the same stories falling flat with others.)

The third person, the listener, must approach the listening from a position of some degree of propriety. He must also be able to share delight in transgressing a prohibition; otherwise he would not find pleasure in the joke. That is to say, he must have a mind that can be both shocked and also illicitly pleased by the urges expressed in the joke. As regards the possible shock, he represents a superego that threatens the joke teller's underlying anxiety, that of unsuccessfully violating taboos. And as regards the possible pleasure, he must have an ego sufficiently integrated to admit to pleasures, even illicit ones, when recognized as "only in a joke," that is, only played in words, not enacted in outer reality.

The teller tells the story and by wit captures the listener into sharing emotionally in the forbidden enactment. When the teller is successful, the listener laughs. In contrast to the joke, mature humor involves taming and internalizing both parts of this process. There is an implicit telling oneself a joke, plus the ability to see the humor in it, whether or not the joke is shared with others.

In the analytic situation patients, the first persons, come to tell the analyst, the third person, about themselves and their relationships with the characters of their life events, the second persons. Simple telling does not an analysis make. Freud remarked that you cannot execute a man by hanging him in effigy: inner conflicts cannot be known and mastered simply by the intellectual discussion of them. If not from the first moment, then very soon the patient tries to lure the analyst transferentially, that is, the patient tries to lure the analyst into participating emotionally in the patient's characteristic patterns of relating.

Both joke teller and patient start out as if to offer their listeners the manifest content of stories. And both joke teller and patient work to engage their listeners, trying to draw them actively into the experience of participating and reacting, into sharing forbidden wishes and mutually confirming the badness of authorities feared and flaunted.

If the listener is too rigid to tolerate mental play about a taboo, there can be no humorous effect. If the analyst is too rigid to tolerate trial identification, a partial tasting of the patient's processes, similarly there can be no analytic process. Also, if joke listener or analyst is too identified with the views of the tellers, humor and analytic process are lost.

In an analysis, the patient attempts to elicit the supposedly gratifying reaction, akin to the laughter of the person told a joke. It is the frustration of that wish which, in important part, permits further regression and possible insight. Yet, for the sake of understanding, analysts must leave their minds sufficiently open to get the point, to recognize and even feel some of what their patients try to elicit.

As analysts, we put our minds to work in the service of our patients. Our own various conflicts are sufficiently mastered to allow us an integrated functioning in consideration of the reality of the moment, the analytic task with the patient. As the patient begins to regress, we respond with trial identifications as a way of maintaining a connection in the face of psychological separation (Greenson 1960). However, we respond to our personal parallel regression as to a signal, recognizing the separateness of our minds from those of our patients (Olinick et al. 1973). We utilize our understandings of what has occurred within us, both similarities and differences from the patient, as a way of enriching our understanding of what we hear from the patient (Poland 1988). Then, no matter the content of our interpretations, our words carry the implicit message, "No, I am not you nor your impulses nor your ghosts, but as a person who can know the experience of such forces, I can speak of them. Together we can find your urges and your ghosts to be speakable and identifiable. We can give them names." In the process, the patient's pull to shared enactment and the analyst's responsive pressure to merger yield to recognition of essential separateness of the two. Respectful contact across separation replaces frustrated fusion, and the patient (though not he or she alone) is changed in the process (Poland 1975).

With the successful joke, there is the tale, the invitation to enactment, and the resulting laughter, marking the listener's having been seduced or tricked into sharing the implicit forbidden expression. With the successful analytic moment, the tale and invitation to enactment are sufficiently potent to be experienced by the analyst, but inhibition of enactment permits understanding, interpretation, and insight.

The grand sweep thus summarized takes place on repeated and gradually progressive microscopic levels. This working out and working through with constant sorting out takes place in the confused uncertainties of analytic exploration (an experience belied by the clarity of even the best *post facto* case report). It is shared exploration of the dark in many preceding hours that makes the highlights of "good hours" possible. Repeatedly, behind his or her words the patient acts with a pull to "come along with me, enact with me." Repeatedly, the analyst goes a bit of the way, then steps aside to notice and ultimately to speak of what is going on.

To find a joke funny, the listener must be alert against being taken in and must simultaneously be willing to be taken in. To let the analytic process take hold, we, as analysts, must not only be alert against being taken in; we must also be open enough to be willing in our own privacy to go along emotionally a part of the way. Our fear of enactment cannot be so strong that we hold the line against experiencing emotional engagement. However, rather than offering the patient the comfort of our affective discharge (like the hearer's laughter following a joke), we offer understanding. The patient who starts to make a point can thus end by getting the point.

With each small step in and out—experiencing together, observing and distinguishing, the patient's mind strengthens and eases, allowing more room for looseness and play. In my first instance, that of the patient's early dream of a newborn child's being named Montgomery Fink, the patient presented a conflict in neurotic condensation. Coming to the patient's mind as an outside stranger, I first heard the name as a humorous condensation. I laughed to myself when I was with the patient. In the years of our work together, as I joined the patient in a collaborative effort of exploration, for a long time I no longer saw humor in such matters. As the analysis progressed, the patient came to a point where he could accept himself, and himself in his world. Instead of envy and contempt, he came to know humor. There should be no misunderstanding: the price for humor was paid with rage, discomfort, and pain.

As mentioned, the early capacity for jokes develops into the mature internalized sense of humor. This particular shift has a further relevance. In early jokes the teller invites the listener to share an overthrow of the superego. With mature humor, in contrast, taboos and frustrations are observed but dealt with with internal satisfaction. Now, instead of the collusion of an outsider, the speaker turns to an accepting part of him/herself (with or without an other), and finds comfort in the face of pain. Conflictual emotions are tamed. Jokes are steps toward mature humor. They not only express conflictual urges, they also are moments of trial mastery on the road to mature humor.

This developmental shift parallels an analytic shift. Patients present themselves for analysis for the treatment of painful conflicts. However, clinical analysis takes for itself a double goal: the relief of that pain and also the development of the capacity for self-analysis. Analysis hopes for transfer of the technique so that patients can continue exploration independently.

Mastery through the multiple slight identifications, observations, distinctions, and understandings leads not only to insight but also to a gradual internalization of the analyzing process. As transference is progressively understood and mastered, the patient develops an increasing capacity for self-analysis. As outer jokes grow into inner humor, transference neurosis gives way to self-analytic skill.

The Analyst's Own Sense of Humor and the Patient's Development of Humor

This general question cannot be set aside without at least briefly considering the matter of the place of the analyst's own humor in the course of clinical analysis. The thought of one person's exposing his or her inner world to and with another over years of intimate engagement and finding that other person throughout those years of agony and lightness to seem totally devoid of humor is, at the least, frightening. Yet, with good clinical reasons, including those implied above, the principle of abstinence substantially constricts the appropriateness of the analyst's own direct expression of humor.

What is the role of the analyst's humor? In addition to the factors discussed, can the patient's humor grow by manifest example? Does analysis work in this area exclusively by ego strengthening through insight and the analyzing experience, or are instances of the analyst's own expression of humor, such as that cited with Bak, also of value?

If, as seems likely, some degree of the analyst's humor is bound to show through in the course of an analysis, how much of the patient's burgeoning sense of humor is bound to reflect that of the analyst, with unanalyzed or even unanalyzable transferences included? And, as with insight, how much might be colored by identification with the process in the analyst but realized in the patient's own idiosyncratic style?

I do not believe the questions are answerable as posed. Rather, it is more realistic to consider the possible benefits and the dangers inherent when analysts *enact* their own humor. Speech is a form of action, especially potent in the analytic situation, and humorous speech is emotionally charged and especially potent.

The questions for the analyst are the same as they would be for the patient. Why now? What does the particular use of humor mean? What feelings and associations of the analyst are screened from experience by virtue of being discharged into action?

These questions apply to any intervention, and posing them ought not lead to paralysis, a destructive caricature of appropriate abstinence. Yet the questions demand fair consideration. If we use humor to discharge some aspect of our own conflicts, we do not help the development of the patient's insight, mastery, and humor. In that circumstance, we seriously inhibit progress.

Kubie (1971) gave thoughtful and strong warning against the clinician's use of humor, emphasizing especially the aggressive and even sadistic forces often, if not usually, carried by a seemingly funny intervention. Greenson (1973) remarked that he never said anything clever to a patient that he did not later regret.

Yet acceptance of the need for great caution in approaching the analyst's humor does not imply that all such humor is necessarily technically wrong. Rose (1969) pointed out the model of the Fool as the one who could say to King Lear what Lear could not hear from anyone else. Regardless of how much prior analysis is done of resistances, some especially painful observations can be made digestible by slight leavening. The caution is that this be in the service of opening, not of enacting and obscuring.

In addition, the analyst's words are always those of an interpretive other, not one who knows the essential truth of the patient's meanings. Thus, a humor of modesty can mitigate authoritarian tendencies while still striving to keep faith with ruthless candor. Humor is always double edged in its use. Even seeming modesty, self-deprecating humor, runs the risk of the analyst's warding off emerging negative transferences.

Respecting Kubie's important and accurate caveats, instances of integrated and fitting humor can also be considered. To round out the instances given of the patient's humor, I offer one example, previously examined, of the analyst's expression of humor (Poland 1971).

The patient, a 40-year-old professional man, was quite enthusiastic on starting his analytic work. He greatly valued his analysis, and he greatly valued me as his analyst. In the early months everything relating to the two of us was seen as good. His wife was for him then the embodiment of evil in the world. During that early period, the patient was pleased by whatever I said, even when I tried to interpret the transferential nature of such idealization.

After some months the patient's delight in me changed to its opposite. Where I had previously been ideal, I now was seen to be seriously flawed in all ways. He now seemed dedicated to the analysis of my defects. Whatever I said, including my efforts to observe the shift, was taken as further evidence of my own character flaws. Any comment I could make was of no avail in getting him to observe himself.

At one point, as he was recounting how seriously limited and disappointing I was, he reflected, "And to think, I used to hang on your every word." I am not now sure whether it was with a laugh or with an exasperated sigh that I spontaneously replied. "And now *I* hang on my every word."

My intervention reflected a moment of my acceptance and acknowledgement of my exasperation, my sense of futility in making contact with the patient's observing capacity in the face of transference conflict. My use of humor stated my acceptance of the limitation of my power to impose observation on his attention, and it did so without anger or accusation aimed at him. It also credited his power to frustrate me. Issues of his power or impotence later proved central in his analytic work. What is noteworthy is that it was with my expression of humor that his passing brief reflectiveness could be extended to a broader reflection of himself in the analytic context. I am not saying that the humor was what made the shift possible for the patient. It certainly exposed my style of coming to grips with my own impotence, whether that sense of impotence arose from my identification with the patient or from my own eccentric difficulties.

My own use of humor was in no way consciously planned or contrived. It happened to be my style of dealing with an inner conflict

within the constraints of the analytic situation. Perhaps the work would
have proceeded better had I been able to analyze the personal roots of my
frustration so that I could have more steadily interpreted the patient
directly. The humor revealed to the patient the fact that I had felt
frustrated. Since that exposure was, I believe, substantially devoid of
retaliation, it permitted and may even have facilitated the continuation of
the work.

There is no perfect, ideal technique. Rather a tension is always
present involving the multiple advantages of any intervention, silence, too,
being an active intervention. An analysis is the patient's show, not the
analyst's. While the analyst's narcissism and drives must be tamed, it seems
unrealistic and even destructive to think an analysis could pass with no
sense of the analyst's humanity ever revealed. Yet, it *is* the patient's show.
The manifest analysis of the patient's mind takes place in a matrix of
reciprocal self-inquiries (Gardner 1983), but analysis is not a two-person
group therapy. Like a very powerful spice, the analyst's humor contributes
most when used in exceedingly sparing doses.

More is at stake than the technical principle of abstinence. The
principle of the analyst's neutrality is of a broader range than mere
technical maneuvers. While the analyst's mind must be open to that of the
patient, its clinical use must always be in the service of the patient or else
the price is high for both.

Furthermore, we may be experienced by the patient as expressing
humor even when we neither intended to do so nor were aware of doing
so. Not only the analyst, but the patient, too, listens for multiple meanings.
There is more to the patient's mind than merely neurotic distortion, and
the patient is able to hear what the analyst says not only with distortion but
also with incisive empathic accuracy. Indeed, as an analysis proceeds, that
skill is sharpened.

At times an analyst makes a comment, anything from a simple
observation to an interpretation, and the patient will laugh, hearing more
levels than simply that of which the analyst had been consciously aware.
Very often the patient will ascribe conscious intent to the analyst, laughing
and asking, "How did you mean that?" Whether noted as such or not, the
patient often ascribes humor to the analyst.

The analyst's processing of what goes on takes place unconsciously as
well as consciously. The words we use to address the patient, therefore,
often carry messages beyond the narrow one immediately intended. The
patient, in this instance, is the one to hear the unwitting messages and to
move onward as a result. Analytic progress, understanding, mastery, and
the growing capacity for humor are contributed to by both parties in the
analytic venture.

CLOSING

As analysts we know more of pain and live more with pain than we do with humor. Humor merits recognition, respect, and study. As we respect its development in the patient, we must also be alert to its soothing siren call away from attention to psychic horrors, loss of love and esteem, castration anxiety,death and nonbeing.

Mature humor offers an opportunity for sustenance and consolation throughout life. Insightful humor not only has its "given" aspects but is itself a gift, a gift the ego gives to itself. It offers self comfort without denial. Indeed, its mark is precisely its capacity to soothe while at the same time respecting the power of inner conflicts and outer hurts. The facilitating of the development of the patient's capacity for mature humor is one of the happiest and proudest effects of clinical analysis.

REFERENCES

Chasseguet-Smirgel, J. (1988). The triumph of humor. In *Fantasy Myth, and Reality: Essays in Honor of Jacob A. Arlow, M.D.*, ed. H. P. Blum, Y. Kramer, A. K. Richards, and A. D. Richards, pp. 197–213. Madison, CT: International Universities Press.

Freud, S. (1905). Jokes and their relation to the unconscious. *Standard Edition* 8.

_____ (1927). Humour. *Standard Edition* 21.

Gardner, M. R. (1983). *Self Inquiry*. Hillsdale, NJ: Analytic Press, 1989.

Greenson, R. (1960). Empathy and its vicissitudes. *International Journal of Psycho-Analysis* 41:418–424.

_____ (1973). Personal communication.

Kris, E. (1938). Ego development and the comic. In *Psychoanalytic Explorations in Art*, pp. 204–216. New York: International Universities Press.

Kubie, L. S. (1971). The destructive potential of humor in psychotherapy. *American Journal of Psychiatry* 127:861–866.

Loewald, H. W. (1960). On the therapeutic action of psychoanalysis. *International Journal of Psyco-Analysis* 41:16–33.

Olinick, S. L., Poland, W. S., Grigg, K. A., and Granatir, W. L. (1973). The psychoanalytic work ego: process and interpretation. *International Journal of Psycho-Analysis* 54:143–151.

Poland, W. S. (1971). The place of humor in psychotherapy. *American Journal of Psychiatry* 128:635–637.

_____ (1975). Tact as a psychoanalytic function. *International Journal of Psycho-Analysis* 56:155–162.

_____ (1986). The analyst's words. *Psychoanalytic Quarterly* 55:244–272.

_____ (1988). Insight and the analytic dyad. *Psychoanalytic Quarterly* 55:341–369.

Rose, G. J. (1969). *King Lear* and the use of humor in treatment. *Journal of the American Psychoanalytic Association* 17:927–940.

Roustang, F. (1987). How do you make a paranoiac laugh? *Modern Language Notes* 102:707–718.

Sabatini, R. (1921). *Scaramouche: A Romance of the French Revolution.* New York: Houghton Mifflin.

Sharpe, E. F. (1940). Psycho-physical problems revealed in language: an examination of metaphor. In *Collected Papers on Psycho-Analysis*, pp. 155–169. London: Hogarth, 1950.

Shengold, L. (1981). Insight as metaphor. *Psychoanalytic Study of the Child* 36:289–306.

Sterba, R. (1934). The fate of the ego in analytic therapy. *International Journal of Psycho-Analysis* 15:117–126.

Weber, S. (1982). The shaggy dog. In *The Legend of Freud*, pp. 100–117. Minneapolis: University of Minnesota Press.

The Analyst's Use of Humor

Michael J. Bader

Among the fondest memories many people have of their analyses are of those moments when their analysts made a joke or expressed their sense of humor. Moments of humor are often important among those experiences of one's analyst's "humanness" and can become markers for the patient of the alliance and sense of partnership that were enjoyed. These expressions of humor from the analyst have multilayered meanings for the patient. They can screen out painful affects in both parties and thus reinforce resistances, or they can help deepen the analytic process and promote healthy growth in the patient. My purpose here is to attempt to understand the instances in which the analyst's expression of humor has efficacious results in the analytic work.

Many psychoanalysts view humor with suspicion. As Freud (1905) established, jokes often are a disguised expression of hostile and sexual impulses. Therefore, a patient's humor will always have a defensive and resistive aspect, and an analyst is usually alert to the risk of collusion if he or she reciprocally responds rather than analyzes this behavior. More important for my purpose here, analyst-initiated expressions of humor are especially suspect insofar as they are usually viewed as a countertransference enactment that wards off negative affects in both analyst and patient and/or covertly express countertransference hostility or seductiveness (Kubie 1971). The analyst must therefore engage in scrupulous self-analysis, either when the impulse to say something humorous first arises, or, retrospectively, after it has been enacted. At its best, the self-analysis reveals something important about the patient and, at its worst, some unanalyzed unconscious conflict in the analyst.

This stance toward humor is consistent with the more general rule of abstinence and the well-founded concern that the analyst not narcissisti-cally discharge his or her conflicts onto the patient. The analyst's mind must be open to the play of feelings engendered by the clinical interaction, but ultimately the use to which this "play" is put should always be to help the patient. The twin dangers, then, in an analyst's direct use of humor are that it defensively colludes with the patient in warding off problematic feelings and fantasies and that it needlessly imposes elements of the analyst's psychology on the patient, usually to the latter's detriment.

On the other hand, there is a growing recognition in modern psycho-analytic thinking that a wide range of emotional responses in the analyst is inevitably evoked, perceived, and misperceived by the patient, and can be used in the analytic process (Boesky 1990, Jacobs 1991, Renik 1991). In addition, attempts to understand the role of the affective responsiveness of the analyst as directly mutative (Kohut 1984) or as the background condition of safety (Weiss and Sampson 1986) that permits the growth of analytic insight are increasingly prominent in psychoanalysis today. Such research into the mutative role of the relationship and of the analyst's empathy has contributed to a more general critique of rigid forms of abstinence and of the popular caricature of neutrality in which the analyst must remain emotionally expressionless.

A sense of humor is one instance of the analyst's emotional respon-siveness that inevitably comes into play in analytic work. Although humor is a capacity that lies within the analyst, its expression is both cause and effect of the interactive field between patient and analyst. Several authors have attempted to understand humor in this spirit. Rose (1969), comparing the analyst's use of humor with the role of the Fool in *King Lear*, describes patients whose egos are so weak that the only way to reach them is through absurdity, caricature, or a "humor that, like some love, touches the truth lightly to avert madness" (p. 928). Chasseguet-Smirgel (1988), focusing mainly on the relationship between humor and depression, prefigures some of the ideas here when she describes the humorist as functioning as a "good enough mother to himself," reassuring the disconsolate child within by pretending "it's nothing, you'll be better soon" (p. 205). Rosen (1963) argues that in patients with extreme obsessive-compulsive disorder, laughter may further the work of interpretation by producing "a more optimal distance on the part of the patient from the subject matter or the transference" (p. 717). This is useful because of the extreme ways that these patients separate affects and objects, a process that humor tends to temporarily reverse. And in an interesting exchange with Kubie, Poland

(1971) argues that his own spontaneous use of humor and wit both reflected and strengthened the therapeutic alliance and promoted the analytic work, rather than derailed it as Kubie argued it always did.

In a more recent paper, Poland (1990) makes an especially important contribution when he stakes out the boundaries of a mature and healthy sense of humor that is acquired *by the patient* as an ego capacity with successful psychological development. He shows how patients' ability to laugh at themselves, appreciate irony, and humorously reflect on themselves and their analyst can sometimes arise only after various neurotic conflicts have been analyzed. Since the mature humor of Poland's patients is the same capacity that I will be discussing in the analyst, it would be helpful to quote at length from Poland's definition of this kind of humor. It is

> a capacity for sympathetic laughter at oneself and one's place in the world. Humor of this sort does not imply pleasure in pain but reflects a regard for oneself and one's limits despite pain. With such humor there is an acceptance of oneself for what one is, an ease in being amused even if bemused. This humor exposes a mature capacity to acknowledge inner conflict and yet accept oneself with that knowledge, even when it is the knowledge of one's narcissistic limits. Such humor, often linked to an appreciation of irony, requires a self-respecting modesty based on underlying self strength and simultaneous recognition of and regard for others. [p. 198]

Poland is describing a capacity to simultaneously deny the pain of reality through laughter while accepting the deflation of omnipotence that accompanies growing up. Thus, he situates humor in the context of the development of a mature sense of reality and a capacity for relationships *not* grounded in narcissistic or omnipotent denial.

As those who caution us about the pathogenic effect of humor repeatedly point out, the analyst's humor conveys more than humor. In the cases that I will discuss, the analyst's expressions of humor communicated meanings to the patient that facilitated the analytic process and the growth-promoting effects of treatment. Most important among these meanings were: (1) that the analyst was capable of tolerating and mastering certain affects and roles that were induced by the patient via projective mechanisms and the turning of passive into active; (2) that the analyst was not psychologically inclined to traumatize the patient through depressive withdrawal or a defensive one-upmanship; and, related to this, (3) that the analyst could pleasurably appreciate the patient's aggression and nonconflictually recognize the patient's attempts, however neurotic, to establish mutuality. It should be underlined that one of the threads running through these factors was the analyst's ability to sublimate, modulate, or otherwise adaptively channel his or her reactive aggression toward the patient.

Various dimensions of these patients' psychopathologies made them refractory to interpretation and insight and thus became the soil within which therapeutic impasses could grow. In highly idiosyncratic ways, these patients seemed to require a more visceral and affectively undeniable demonstration from the analyst that the relationship was safe enough to risk real analytic exploration, more than could be provided by an "average expectable" technique relying on interpretation alone. These patients' very sense of reality was based on certain pathogenic fantasies and expectations, particularly ones involving the analyst's psychology. These fantasy-based expectations made the patient exquisitely sensitive to the affective tone of the therapist's interventions, which usually led to the inadvertent confirmation of these pathogenic fantasies rather than to an increased capacity for perspective on them. In these cases, the patients responded better when the analyst's tone and style conveyed humor, playfulness, irony, and a readiness to openly express genuine pleasure in the patient.

Any discussion of the mutative effects of the noninterpretive aspects of the analyst's behavior will raise the issue of the relative curative weight of interpretation-driven insight and those relationship factors that often become labeled as "corrective emotional experiences." The focus of this paper, however, is not to review or take a position in this debate. My intent is not to argue that one or the other factor is primary, but rather to suggest that actual clinical experience challenges us to account in our theory for those instances in which spontaneous and deliberate *actions* of the analyst, such as using humor, have the effect of deepening the analytic process and outcome.

CASE EXAMPLE 1

John was a 30-year-old Asian-American who worked as a contractor at the time he entered treatment. He consulted me because he felt stuck in an unsatisfactory relationship with a woman of whom he was tremendously critical, but toward whom he felt too guilty to leave. This constituted a pattern for him: he would get involved in relationships, become increasingly dissatisfied, almost to the point of feeling "allergic" to the woman, but feel helpless either to assert himself with her or else to separate.

John was witty and articulate, quick to anticipate my interpretations, and ostensibly eager to please. We initially focused on his extratransference conflicts involving his tendency to become guiltily enmeshed with others to whom he then ceded power, his anxieties about separation, and his worries that he hurt women with his feelings of superiority, narcissistic demands for control, and impulses to reject them. He felt enraged and then guilty about his sense that he could not control or even have an effective impact on the people close to him, but instead felt pressured to adapt to and comply with them. He tended to deny that these themes were operative between us. This denial was at first conveyed by means of an ostensibly reasonable "exploration" of the possible veracity of my trans-ference references, inquiries that always ended up yielding little in the way of confirmation. In spite of this obvious resistance, he was able to make use of some of this work to free himself from a relationship with a very troubled woman and to overcome some of the inhibitions that impeded his competitive ambition at work.

This initial interpretive paradigm and constellation of presenting problems made good sense in the context of an understanding of John's childhood and familial environment. The second of five children, he described his mother as driven toward success in her role as the owner of a sewing factory, and anxiously driving her children toward academic success in her role as mother. Although he understood that his mother was partly driven by a culturally reinforced need in the Chinese community to "make it" in America, he felt it had more to do with her character than her culture. He saw her as a woman who felt she had to drive herself and everyone around her to make up for an inner sense of being damaged and cheated. John perceived her as continually dissatisfied with his perfor-mance in school and with the numerous household chores he was assigned; he felt trapped under her critical control and burdened by the weight of her chronic feelings of inadequacy and victimization. He recalled, for instance, that when the family took Sunday drives, his mother would insist that the children not sit idly; instead, she would quiz them on vocabulary, arith-metic, and their knowledge of the specifications of the other cars on the road. Mother worked six days a week and would always be doing more than one task at a time. His father had died soon after he was born, and his mother had quickly remarried a man who worked for her in her factory, a rather maternal man who doted on the children, but who John felt could not appreciate or respect his stepson's competence and autonomy. He viewed his stepfather as weak in relation to his mother and disappointing as a father figure.

John's ambivalence about women was seen as a repetition of his extremely conflictual relationship with his mother. He was full of rage at his mother's efforts to control him and despaired of ever being able to please her. He felt his masculinity and his sense of self-worth to be endangered by his mother's relentless criticism, and yet he was helpless to oppose her will. This was worsened by his sense of her internal depression and self-criticism, which he was impotent to ameliorate. Instead, he internalized her accusatory and punitive aspects. He was able to maintain his loyalty and attachment to her through this kind of identification and compliance. He thus became harsh with himself and perfectionistic with others. He warded off his desire to separate from or condemn her too severely because of his conviction that she could not tolerate his criticism and rejection.

In his adult relationships with women, John could neither stay nor leave. Staying meant feeling increasingly controlled and angry, but leaving meant destroying the woman and feeling guilty. The relationships gradually became sadomasochistic, with increasing covert and overt battles for control and a growing sense of despair. He could not get the woman to do what he wanted, and he could not freely give her what she wanted. He felt tremendously dependent on the woman and thus vulnerable to pressures to bend to her will, but also extremely guilty about his subtle but relentless critical attitude toward her. He felt his needs for control, for admiration, and so forth, were repugnant to others, inappropriate, and destined to be frustrated.

As our work progressed and John felt closer to me, he could no longer deny that some of these issues were surfacing in our relationship. The form they took usually involved his insistence that I tell him what to do to solve a problem, setting the stage for a struggle between us as to the nature of our work together. He would demand to know, for instance, what practical steps to take when he felt that a sibling was being overly critical, so as not to internalize the criticism. I would attempt to understand this insistence, more or less empathically, and he would accuse me of trying to blame or"one-up" him. Or, if I pointed out that his demand for advice might protect him from thinking, feeling, or understanding, he would experience my comments as evidence of my inability to empathize with him, "pulling rank" to protect my embattled authority, and an attempt to blame him and tell him he was doing things wrong. If I empathically articulated a specific subjective experience of his, he would retort, "Well, what should I *do* about it?!" He was exquisitely sensitive to feeling blamed and accused. And when I was silent, he would excoriate me for hiding my inadequacies behind a ridiculous technique.

In the countertransference, I felt myself intermittently demoralized by his fierce dissatisfaction and the brilliant way he often expressed it. I felt repeatedly drawn into struggles with him. At these times, I would indeed be tempted to enact my hostility and frustration by playing my "abstinence card"—by, for instance, simply remaining silent or continuing to interpret when he had warned me that he experienced this as aversive. Mostly, though, I tried to talk to him about various aspects of our interaction and to find ways to make this understanding useful to him. I would talk about how his relationships eventually turned into struggles of dominance versus submission, and how he had a great many anxieties about mutuality and collaboration. We reconstructed family history that seemed to relate to this problem. We talked about his worries about his being too close to me and about his guilt over separation, but while he agreed, he did not find these ideas helpful. I pointed out to him that he was showing me, by turning passive into active, what it was like for him to be the object of his mother's chronic dissatisfaction and pressure for perfection, unable to bring pleasure to her eyes. He agreed, but felt this insight to be sterile and unhelpful. I explored with him his fantasies of magical rescue and his wish that we collude in denying our respective limitations. He felt criticized, but it did not change his basic stance toward me. He was aware that he was acting in a provocative manner that was unfair to me, and he felt guilty about it, but was trapped in his own reflexive need to defensively denigrate my attempts to help him. This guilt and the worry that I would retaliate sometimes led to reparative impulses to comply with my interpretations, but eventually the dissatisfaction would surface again. In spite of some symptomatic improvement, the analytic work began to feel like it was at an impasse.

My frustration and growing sense of despair led me to seek outside consultation and to engage in a determined self-analysis. The introspection revealed that my experience of John's "assaulting" me with his dissatisfaction contained elements of my relationship with my mother, who had often burdened me as a child with her complaints of being cheated and dissatisfied as a mother and a wife. These infantile echoes could be felt in my resentment of John's intense critical scrutiny and complaints about my effectiveness. Understanding this association helped modulate my feelings of helplessness and reactive aggression that had led me into power struggles and a withholding affective style that I rationalized as neutrality. Consultation helped me use this self-analytic insight to more compassionately understand how John's need to frustrate and torment me expressed his identification with the aggressor, turning passive into active, and various projective-introjective solutions to anxiety. All in all, I felt less trapped by the situation, more empathically appreciative of his struggles, and internally freer to respond *in violation of* the "rules of engagement" by which John had coerced us to play.

In this context, I found myself beginning to respond to John in a more playful way. This meant responding to his sarcastic jibes with humor rather than with either silence or proffered insight. Sometimes my humor would be self-mocking, and other times it would confirm his accusations in a caricatured way. For instance, John might make a comment like "Did they teach you in school to make interpretations that your patients can't understand or use?!" I would respond, "Do you think I went to school to learn how to do this?" Or else I might retort, "Yes—it was in the same course where they taught me to blame the patient for my mistakes!'' John ended one session, during which he was complaining that he was getting worse and that my neurotic need to do the *wrong* thing rendered the therapy useless, with the comment, ''Perhaps you could work through your conflicts about this with a consultant or your own therapist before our next session,'' to which I responded, ''If I do, can I raise my fee?''

One instance of banter was when John, as he was wont to do, was imperiously and coolly instructing me in exactly how a comment of mine had been worded poorly and had implied that he was bad; it could have been worded differently so as to make him feel appreciated. He ended it all with the question, ''Are you able to follow this?'' I responded, ''Wait . . . could you speak more slowly?'' He replied that he was trying his best but that I was a poor student. I sensed that he was now ''playing'' with me more than before, and I responded: ''But I thought this was just a Sunday drive!'' This allusion to his account of the pressure-filled Sunday drives with his mother made him laugh, and he then began to talk about how one of his clients had been ''picky'' about some remodeling that he had done for her. He realized that this kind of criticism could spoil his whole day, but imagined that *I* might think of this as an overreaction. I commented that perhaps we had just gotten a glimpse of where part of his conflict might have originated, and John responded, ''Sunday was supposed to be a day of rest—but I don't even get that.'' After a pause, he demanded, ''O.K., so now what?!'' I replied that he didn't want me to get lulled into the delusion that we were actually working together! He then went on to ridicule my apparent hopefulness, although his tone seemed to remain ambiguously playful.

These interchanges became common and were usually brief. I understood them as reflecting a gradual deepening of John's ability to be self-reflective in my presence and to begin to collaborate. John gradually made explicit both his awareness that I had changed my style and his reactions to it. In our discussions about this shift, John seemed mainly to feel that I had ''heard'' him, that his complaints and needs had indeed had some effect on me, and he seemed able to see more clearly how his persistent expectation of criticism from me had more to do with an internal object than an external one. He continued to be dissatisfied and critical, but both of us recognized that this felt increasingly like a hollow accusation. John had a dream in which a physician he knew was arrested for illegally cashing his patients' welfare checks, and John knew in the dream that somehow the physician was being framed. In his associations, John was struck with the absurdity of the image, since the physician was one of his most honest and generous friends. John's associations led him to the fact that he had been accusing me these many months of exploiting him and that he realized that these charges were, in fact, bogus and that I was his ally. In general, he seemed to be increasingly able to think about how burdensome it was to be expected to be perfect in order to please someone else, and his punitive conscience began to soften, as did his insatiable demands for perfection from me.

When I first began joking with John, it was partly a result of my reflections on the meanings of the intense pushes and pulls he was exerting on me, reflections that took place in the context of self-analysis and outside consultation. Through this process I was able to gain enough perspective on my countertransference reactions, and enough of an understanding of the meanings and developmental etiology of the transference impasse, to allow me to be more affectively and technically flexible. This meant opening myself up to my own capacities for irony, humor, and playfulness—all of which included aggression, but an aggression somehow harnessed to my empathy for the patient. By this I mean that I was able to moderate and gain perspective on my aggression and express it in a way that reflected a healthy mastery and a sensitivity to the patient's welfare. The fact that I allowed myself to make particular use of *humor* was a function of my sense that John's capacity for wit and banter was an adaptive strength and one that I shared. The banter with John was never forced; it was consistent with my own form of humor. Sometimes it was elicited by him, but other times it was initiated by me and reflected the outcome of my own internal analytic work on the feelings he was stirring up in me, together with my deeper understanding of what he needed.

My use of humor was therefore both reactive and deliberate. After it became clear that it was efficacious, I consciously decided, on the basis of my understanding of the patient's dynamics and the meanings of my humor to him, to let myself respond to him with humor even *more* freely. I believed that John felt reassured by my humor in ways that enabled him to analyze himself more confidently. He was, for instance, able to spontaneously talk about his terrible fears of being cut off and alone only after he reassured himself through our joking repartee that I would not leave him "alone" in the session. Of primary importance was that my humor showed him a way to deal with the unreasonable expectations of perfection that he had felt from his mother, which were enacted with me in the transference. The humor conveyed my acceptance of my limitations and an ability to defend myself against any expectations to be otherwise. Further, it showed that I was not hurt by his attacks, something he greatly feared, nor was I discouraged and demoralized as he had been as a child and in his adult relationships. Finally, I believe that my ability to laugh and joust with him reassured him that I could appreciate and enjoy him on his terms. This vital narcissistic experience was missing from his childhood, and his experience of it with me was crucial in his acquiring a greater feeling of self-acceptance.

John's capacity for self-reflection slowly increased and he became able to reflect more on how often he put others in impossible binds and how dissatisfied he had been with himself for most of his life. This seemed to help him *not* have to externalize so much, and I felt the beginnings of a spirit of collaboration. As he felt himself to be less embattled in his relationships—including the one with me—he began to recover memories of his deep sense of hopelessness as a child and of his mother's depression.

CASE EXAMPLE 2

Fred was a 41-year-old single man when he sought treatment for chronic asthma and other stress-related somatic problems. He worked as a lawyer in a firm known for its advocacy of liberal political causes. Fred reported feeling tense much of the time. He generally linked the tension to his preoccupation with pleasing others—his sense that he often felt under great pressure to suppress his feelings in order to avoid rejection as well as to avoid guilt over potentially hurting others. He felt angry about this and punished himself when he noticed himself being self-sacrificial. He worked in a field in which he was often in conflict with others; his guilt and inhibition resulted in a constant state of tension.

In his romantic liaisons, Fred tended to choose women who were critical and withholding, partners by whom he repeatedly felt castrated and for whom he repeatedly surrendered his phallic strength and autonomy. He saw these women as both rejecting and weak, and he alternately experienced himself as their whipping boy and their caretaker. Fred complained about feeling sexually inhibited with women, in part because of a fantasy that they did not really enjoy sex or at least that they felt threatened by being aggressively pursued. This led to a sense of sexual passivity and an ultrasensitivity to any cue—real or imagined—that his partner did not want to be sexually approached. All of this led him to feel bottled up and angry, which led to further guilt, inhibition, and despair.

Fred had recently finished a five-year analysis with an analyst whom he initially described in glowing terms, but who he later felt had traumatically misunderstood him. He portrayed the former analyst as using what one could call a caricature of classical technique. He told me that his analyst rarely spoke except to comment on transference material and these interpretations were very spare and relatively infrequent. He never answered questions or showed much affect. To Fred's recollection, he never acknowledged a mistake, accepted a gift, or gave advice of any kind. The patient felt that he quickly learned the "rules" and, in fact, soon became a caricature of a patient. He never asked for or demanded anything; instead, he explicitly reduced his own needs, desires, or criticisms to the status of neurotic transference distortions that he invited his analyst to analyze.

Fred's reported experience of his previous analysis was a narrative that emerged over time. According to Fred, the analyst seemed bent on interpreting his problems along several lines. First, he confronted Fred repeatedly with the *gratification* he was getting from his self-castration at work and with women, and he emphasized that Fred's inability to stand up to women was due to his experiencing them as powerful preoedipal mothers whom he was terrified of defying or leaving. Fred felt that his analyst saw him in fact as weak, and was implying that he ought to stand up to these women (and their surrogates) who actually were trying to dominate and castrate him. He experienced his analyst as trying to get him to "buck up" and act tougher with people. Unfortunately, the "people" never included the analyst. Fred would frequently be overwhelmed with feelings of helplessness, self-loathing, and rage in the sessions, which the analyst interpreted as a transference enactment of a fantasy that Fred was a little boy unwilling to grow up because of fears of castration and separation, fixated in the painful throes of preoedipal gratifications. Fred felt he got little help with his relationship or work problems during his analysis.

It gradually emerged that Fred had experienced his previous analyst as blaming him for his tendency to be masochistic, particularly with women. He inferred that this stance was due to the analyst's intolerance of dependency and weakness of any kind in himself and because of a defensive need to denigrate women. He saw the analyst as subtly promoting and hiding behind Fred's transference idealization because of a rigid fear of closeness, exposure, and competition. Whether or not the analyst, in fact, had any or all of these problems, Fred experienced the analyst as having a personal difficulty that interfered with his analyzing Fred's perceptions and fantasies about the analyst's psychology. Fred repeatedly castrated himself by enacting the role of a compliant, tortured patient who turned all his critical and phallic impulses inward so as not to challenge his analyst. He felt that he never got help on his intense conflicts over his phallic exhibitionism, aggression, and sexuality because he believed that his therapist had a similar impairment that neither of them wanted to admit. Fred's neurotic conflict was thus enacted and confirmed. Most important, these fantasies and perceptions were never analyzed. The analysis functioned as a kind of trauma, deepening his conviction that significant others require compliance, denial of shortcomings, and suppression of phallic strength.

These convictions and fantasies were first generated in Fred's family, where Fred felt as if neither parent enjoyed his masculinity. Fred perceived his mother as being threatened by masculinity insofar as it symbolized abandonment and inferiority for her. She used her son's dependency to keep him close to her and seemed to view his willful phallic behavior as a betrayal. His father was intensely competitive with his son, who reported that his father had to win every argument they had and every game they played. Fred felt put down but also sensed that his father's power was belied by great insecurity over his own masculinity.

Thus, Fred entered treatment with a deeply entrenched characterological inhibition arising from pathogenic family relationships. He had been retraumatized by an analyst who Fred felt had encouraged a regressive form of compliance in his patient because of psychological problems hidden behind his "classical" technique. Fred was therefore exquisitely sensitive to those moments in which he construed that I was defensively hiding behind my analytic "role." For instance, if I was too silent or did not answer a question, he would become gradually more masochistic, feeling like a needy neurotic "worm" who was not as self-sufficient as I was. He took my silence as rejecting and as a defensive attempt to "pull rank" because he expected too much or was some kind of threat to me. Over all, early in the treatment I came to see that his masochistic self-denigration was in part a compliance with what he sensed I needed, an inference he made from whatever possible countertransference enactments accompanied my interpretations and personal style, as well as simply from the various manifestations of normal analytic listening, neutrality, and abstinence.

I repeatedly pointed out that these inferences were highly meaningful constructions, and linked them to prior experiences in his life, including his previous analysis. Fred could not seem to make use of these insights. His responses were often intellectualized and compliant, but the insights did not seem to help him revise his expectations and fears. I felt that his compelling expectation was that I, like his previous analyst, could not enjoy him, his strength, his criticism, or his love because my own psychopathology was too strong; and the stakes were too high for him to risk analyzing this particular assessment of the danger. He had psychologically hobbled himself in response to a pathogenic family and had been further frozen in this state by a psychoanalysis that he experienced as pathologically confirmatory.

Relatively early on in our work, I discovered that when I used humor to interact with Fred, he was able to mitigate the intensity of his masochistic flailings. Two processes led to this discovery and my subsequent intentional use of it. First, and most important, I had developed a fairly clear picture of the traumatic effects of what he perceived as his previous analyst's rigidity and, in Fred's eyes, defensive self-control and humorlessness. I had witnessed his masochistic retreats from my attempts at resistance interpretation, including those aimed at the retreats themselves, particularly when communicated within a serious and sedate professional ambience. In other words, I developed a hypothesis that Fred required a different analytic ambience that would allow him to hear my words and think about them; I then proceeded to test this out by allowing myself to respond to him in a more humorous way. As was true with John, I sensed in Fred a capacity, albeit an inhibited one, to be quite witty and sardonic. As I have confessed earlier, this is a comfortable affective stance for me, so humor was a natural vehicle for conveying this analytic ambience.

The second process that led to this tack was that I began to think about how it felt to be emotionally restrained and abstinent with this particular patient, in contrast to how it felt when we shared some humorous observation. I discovered in myself a conflict about enjoying a playful, intimate father–son closeness with Fred. Instead, I recognized the temptation to identify with my own father's rejection of such a connection with his son. I became aware of a subtle inclination on my part to collude with Fred's shame over his wishes for paternal strength and protection, strength with which he could identify, and of my own tendency to keep him at arm's length with elements of an abstinent technique. Analyzing this issue helped me become less guilty about and therefore more open to a pleasurable interchange with Fred, marked at times by a kind of male teasing and repartee. Of course, both of these sources of my use of humor would have led elsewhere if Fred himself was not possessed of a witty and verbally creative intelligence that was ready and willing to enjoy and share such humor.

Fred began to become more assertive and confidently competitive with me, and to free up his capacity for self-observation. One form my use of humor took was to make fun of my own mistakes or foibles, or of the image he had of me as needing to be an oracular authority, wrapped in somber analytic technique. I might tell him, for instance, that I was certainly relieved that he blamed himself rather than me for his frustration with his progress in a session, but didn't he think, therefore, that I should be paying *him*? Or I might joke that the only reason I had been silent so long was to carefully craft the perfect interpretation that the "books" said had to be less than twenty-five words! He responded with great pleasure to this self-effacing humor and seemed to feel an increased safety in noticing my errors. He heard my jokes as an invitation to be a strong man, an invitation based on what he perceived as a nondefensive self-confidence on my part and an appreciative openness to *his* perspective. We explored his experience of embarrassed excitement in response to my humor. He was able to explicitly analyze how these conflicted but pleasurable interactions with me highlighted his childhood shame about male camaraderie, and how his interpretation of his former analyst's seriousness reflected an externalization of these internal conflicts and guilt. Fred seemed to develop a deeper awareness of the ways he had experienced his previous analyst as unable to tolerate his aggression or critical scrutiny and how this stimulated him to diminish himself and implode with feelings of helplessness.

Another use of humor involved Fred's inhibition of his phallic narcissism and exhibitionism with women. He was talking, for instance, of his guilt-ridden negotiations with a very critical girlfriend, and her demands about how he divided his time on the weekend between watching sports, doing housework, and talking to her. Fred was frantic and guilty about provoking and hurting her feelings and determinedly presented the issues from her point of view. At one point, I said, "The next time you negotiate with her, try floating this proposal: that *she* clean your apartment while *you* watch sports and then the two of you can talk during the commercials!" Fred roared with laughter at this comic articulation and caricature of his phallic narcissistic desire. He couldn't get over how this joke captured some of the essence of what he felt was forbidden to him. He was forcefully struck with how abhorrent yet pleasurable this scenario was; and how it brought into sharp relief the images of "bad" masculinity that he spent so much time warding off with extreme shows of compliance and self-abnegation. He went on to talk about how much her anger frightened him, but how he knew at the same time that this anger came from her deep insecurity. He wondered if the latter somehow scared him and made him "cave in." He then dryly wondered if he could negotiate with her on how many of the commercial breaks had to be used for talking versus eating! We both laughed, and the patient was again aware of his embarrassment and worry that he could betray her even with such thoughts.

On another occasion, Fred seemed to be struggling against acknowledging profound feelings of disappointment and hurt that his girlfriend had said she was "too busy" to come and stand at the finish line to cheer for him when he competed in his first bicycle race, a charged accomplishment for him. He compliantly agreed with her that it wasn't such a big deal and that it should be enough for him that she was willing to attend a champagne brunch he was hosting later in the day. He was working his way into a tirade against his "infantile" feelings about this when I suggested that while he would probably ride faster in the race, knowing that he had to get home to prepare a good brunch for her, the other alternative was to tell her that in order to be invited to the brunch, *she* had to prepare it in his honor and, in addition, welcome him at the finish line with it! Fred's pleasure in this kind of ostensibly misogynist repartee led to his recognizing how rejected and castrated he had felt in this situation and how a proud wish to display himself to her so often came to feel like a mean-spirited demand. He was able to see that this was a result not just of her pathogenic responses, but of an internal readiness to condemn himself on "trumped-up" charges of selfishness and sexism.

My putting this into comic words made it palatable for him to become aware of these dynamics because it signified my acceptance of certain derogated and dangerous phallic desires. It was as if through an identification with a longed-for paternal strength, conveyed via my joking interpretations, Fred could overcome his shame and anxiety about his masculinity enough to begin to confront this conflict. By using humor, I conveyed not only that I was *not* threatened by his phallic aggressive wishes, but that I could take pleasure in them. My jocular style with him emboldened him, not to deny or cover-up his shame over his "dirty" masculine impulses and fantasies, but to face some of these feelings from a more secure base in our alliance. We also became able to reflect explicitly on my use of humor and to gain further insight into how he used his interpretations about his previous analyst's "humorless" mental state in order to confirm his own neurotic expectations and determine his behavior. He felt freer to analyze his expectations of my disapproval in the face of a more visceral sense of my empathic availability and appreciation, a sense that he derived from my expression of humor.

DISCUSSION

The treatments of John and Fred can be viewed as "experiments-in-nature." In each case, the style of the analyst changed, resulting in the patient's increased psychological growth and an increased capacity to tolerate and analyze feelings and fantasies that had been warded off or compulsively enacted. One dimension of the change in the analyst's style was his willingness to respond to the patient with humor, and eventually to do so intentionally. Of course, while John had a single therapist who altered his stance in the middle of the treatment, the change for Fred mainly involved a change in therapists. I am therefore not making a scientific claim by describing these cases as "experiments." Obviously, there are multiple meanings and competing interpretations possible in discussing what occurred and why; these clinical vignettes as such prove nothing. However, I think that cases in which an analyst decides to alter his or her approach with a patient and observes different results, or a patient works on identical issues with two different analysts and achieves vastly different outcomes, provide us with an interesting opportunity to analyze which factors in the analyst's temperament or technique seem to facilitate or inhibit the analytic process and therapeutic change.

I believe that the most important reason my willingness to express humor in these treatments produced a beneficial result was that it functioned as a metacommunication to the patient about my internal psychological state and that this information and new experience increased the patient's sense of safety and confidence in ways that enhanced the treatment. For some patients, a serious, emotionally restrained analytic ambience with a therapist who modulates his or her affective expressiveness in order to convey analytic neutrality can reinforce certain pathogenic expectations and fantasies rather than help the patient face and work through them. In the treatment of these patients, a therapist whose emotional range in the sessions goes only from flat to matter-of-fact, and whom the patient does not perceive as enjoying the work, unwittingly enables the patient to repeat maladaptive patterns because the latter's worst fears are covertly being realized. Attempts to analyze these transference-based resistances to insight and change are made more difficult if done in an atmosphere that the patient can construe as somber and humorless, because the therapist's accurate insights get drowned out by the meanings that the patient attributes to the affective tone of the interpretation.

As the cases presented here suggest, aspects of so-called classical technique that promote emotional restraint can be tenaciously used in the service of resistance because of specific traumatic experiences that a particular patient may both seek and yet fear repeating. In John's experience, for instance, the fact that he felt helpless to please and satisfy his mother, thus internalizing her critical and accusatory attitude, made his experience with me inevitably fraught with blame, accusation, dissatisfaction, and despair. He interpreted my neutral analytic stance as accusatory and as intended to make him feel responsible for everything that happened to him, including everything frustrating that happened in his therapy. His mother, who blamed him for everything, could not enjoy him, and neither could I. As my self-analysis revealed, I not infrequently got caught up in this cycle of blaming. He turned the guns of his harsh superego on me both as his best defense against this imagined attack and as a wish to get some kind of relief. I found that any interpretation of the fact that John experienced analytic technique itself as a (not unexpected) retraumatization was simply incorporated into our ongoing struggle.

My discovery of the efficacious use of humor and its subsequent deliberate incorporation into my interactive style was crucial in the resolution of this impasse because it reassured John on a number of psychological fronts. First, it reassured him that he had not hurt me with his attacks of dissatisfaction, that I was psychologically sturdy enough to maintain my balance in a storm, a state of mind that had always been beyond his reach as a child but with which he could now begin to make a tentative identification. I did not have to be perfect, and now perhaps he

could envision that possibility for himself. Second, my humor communicated that I liked him and could maintain an appreciative connection with
him in spite of his provocativeness, that I did not mistake the part for the
whole and thus was not blind to the longing and appreciation he felt for me
even while we were dueling. If I could tolerate ambivalence and relational
complexity, and adaptively sublimate hostility, perhaps he could as well.
Humor thus facilitated the beginning of an identificatory process that was
necessary to counter his sadistic superego and its projected representations
in various impaired relationships.

For Fred, in a previous analysis a caricature of abstinence had
retraumatized him, confirming over and over that in order to avoid guilt,
he had to debase and castrate himself. He reflexively turned the "eminently
reasonable" attitude of seriousness with which I approached our work into
a dangerous (but not unexpected) symptom of an underlying need to
maintain my authority in the face of the threat of his phallic exhibitionism
and critical scrutiny, exactly like his previous analyst. He was unable to
hear my interpretations of these issues except through this sadomasochistic
lens.

My use of humor seemed to free up Fred's ability to use his critical
faculties with me and others, and to begin to express and enjoy his phallic
capacities with women and with me. I gently made fun of my own foibles
and thus communicated to Fred that I would not retaliate if he also did so.
He became aware of and could think about his conflicts over criticizing me
only after he was reassured by my humor that it was safe to do so. Further,
I playfully expressed, with wit and caricature, Fred's forbidden phallic/
sadistic fantasies and wishes toward women. The patient's pleasure in this
kind of male "solidarity" enabled him to feel freer with his phallicness and
therefore to see in clearer relief how dangerous and conflictual these
behaviors, feelings, and fantasies actually were.

In both cases, the patients got better. They were more able to reflect
on, analyze, and master certain transference expectations, inhibitions, and
characterological reflexes after I began using humor than before. Further,
both patients were able, to some degree, to reflect on the relationship
between the analytic ambience established by my use of humor and the
resulting benefits for our work. In both cases, it appeared that particular
expectations, based on accurate perception as well as on unconscious
fantasy, about my internal psychological state were motivating the patients
to repeat their maladaptive patterns with me, much as these expectations
and fantasies were doing similar damage to their other relationships.
Humor disconfirmed these expectations and functioned to counter and
correct these fantasies enough so that the patient could (1) examine the
fantasies that now stood out in sharp relief, and (2) experience a new form
of relatedness in which certain painful and debilitating affects did not have

to control the participants. The gratifications of the new kind of relatedness, modeled by my use of humor, was a spur to further analytic progress.

I suspect that one of the distinguishing features of patients with
whom humor has these effects might be the extent to which their core
traumas involved humorless parents who burdened their child with expectations that were impossible to meet, with the result that the child felt
enraged and helpless but was ultimately compliant. The parents' humorlessness may have reflected an underlying depression or narcissistic injury
that the patient felt prevented real connection. Instead, the patient, as a
child, had to resort to identification with the aggressor and masochistic
submission, which became models for future relatedness. These models
for relatedness are maintained and defended by these patients because
they are felt to be the only ones possible and are somehow built into the
texture of the patients' sense of reality. The experience of trauma, the
expectation of its repetition attendant on self-analysis, and the actual lack
of experience of alternative realities make a powerful distorting lens
through which the analyst's technique is read as an expression of the
latter's underlying psychopathology.

I would like now to consider the issue of the deliberateness of my use
of humor and the processes that led to its use. The capacity for humor is,
first of all, a character trait of the therapist, one that varies among
therapists in type and quantity like any other trait. And, like any character
trait, it is inevitably expressed in one's work. In this sense, one does not
exactly choose to respond in a humorous or witty way if one is a humorous
person; one's technique with a patient always expresses one's being. The
texture and ambience of a psychotherapy or a psychoanalysis bear the
stamp of the idiosyncrasies of both participants whether they like it or not.
In addition, it does not seem quite right to say that the therapist chooses to
be humorous when such humor seems to be a reaction to the complex
invitations and undertows of the patient's communications. Instead, one
might understand this phenomenon as the therapist using his or her
psychological reactions (Jacobs 1991), in order to retrospectively understand both of the meanings of these interactions and their mutative effects
on the patient (Renik 1991). Or, finally, one might think of humor as part
of analytic "tact" (Poland 1975) in the sense that therapists always aim to
convey an empathic respect for the difficulties of analytic work in the
form, style, tone, and timing of their interpretations. Tact, when successful, is really not deliberate but serves as the empathic background for
interpretive work.

While all of these issues were operative in my use of humor, it was
also quite deliberate. I chose to give myself permission to openly enjoy
certain interactions in which I had previously exercised a certain emotional
caution. When I describe my prior stance as one of caution, I am referring
to the ordinary restraint that an analyst feels about temptations to engage

the patient in playful interactions that might collude with the patient's desire to avoid thinking about difficult issues. A stance of caution also involves how one feels about openly expressing the pleasure one privately enjoys in working with a patient for fear of being seductive or of imposing an obligation on the patient. However, in these cases I *decided* in effect not to restrain these playful and humorous tendencies in my own personality as much as I do with other patients. I was neither hurling myself into the relationship with abandon, nor calculating each witticism with surgical precision. I was instead modifying or overriding my own analytic superego with the intention of helping the patient lessen the sadistic impact of his own superego. The concept of a "neutral" stance should not only accommodate the wide range of personality styles among analysts, some of whom rely on humor and some of whom do not, but should also subsume those ways that an analyst deliberately shapes his or her affective style and posture in accord with the patient's needs. By this I mean that as analysts we are always expressing aspects of our personalities in response to the various transference gambits of the patient, but we are also always *choosing* which instruments in our emotional orchestra we will consistently allow the patient to play. Those aspects of ourselves that we determine will be analytically efficacious are made more available for use. Others are kept in stricter abeyance. In the cases I presented, I believe that I chose to make my humor available to the patient with the belief that it would help the patient feel safer, provide an alternative model of mature relatedness with which he could identify, and expand his capacities for self-analysis. I was alert to his reactions to this humor, including distorted ones, and I believe that I was open to changing my style if the evidence warranted it.

The process of freeing my capacities for a certain kind of playful responsiveness involved, particularly in John's case where an impasse existed, a self-analytic process that revealed how the patient's projections, his turning passive into active, and the particular content of his suffering were pressing on related conflicts of my own. These dynamics contributed to the impasse, insofar as I came to share the patient's sense of helplessness in an exaggerated way and temporarily lost my analytic perspective. After I became aware of the reasons for my countertransference hypersensitivity and came to a deeper understanding of the patient's transference enactments, I regained my analytic balance and felt freer to choose to communicate that balance via humor.

THE HUMORLESS ANALYST

Analysts are often pilloried by the popular media for their reputation as humorless, rigid, and withdrawn characters who sit behind their patients muttering "uh-huh" in response to their patients' pleas for help. This caricature of analytic abstinence and neutrality has been thoroughly debunked in modern analytic theory; it usually does not conform to the day-to-day ambience created by most analysts. However, it is also true that a certain percentage of people drawn to doing analytic work tend to have inhibitions about the spontaneous expression of feeling, including passion and humor, as well as a certain propensity for depression. There is no evidence that the incidence of these problems is any greater among analysts than in the general population, but it is my impression that these depressive and inhibitory tendencies are often not significantly eliminated by a training analysis. The unique feature of depression and affective rigidity among analysts is that we have a theory of technique that can be misread as justifying our neuroses, and we can enact them under the guise of abstinence and neutrality. This can create multiple problems in our thera- peutic work. Our patients are only too quick to comply with what they think we want. Often, they infer that we want them to be like us, emotionally abstinent and neutral. These patients may have had depressed parents with whom they had great difficulty connecting or to whom they had to submit and comply. Our "classical" analytic stance, however "tactful," can repeat this same traumatic relationship. Patients cannot see it because they expect it, and we cannot see it because we see ourselves as neutral. Our neutrality is their emotional absence. Our abstinence is their rejection. Our resistance interpretation becomes their compliance with authority. Misalliances or impasses can be the end result of what, to us, looks like a treatment based on good technique.

In this regard, I would argue that a willingness to look at the potentially salutary effects of humor can open up our own emotional range and that of the patient. Humor can have a particularly efficacious impact because it can simultaneously convey multiple meanings about the analyst and the patient, thus deepening the experience for both.

SUMMARY

Although there is a tendency for analysts to frown on the use of humor as a technique, moments of humor can often be precious to the patient. The appropriate cautions about using the patient or enacting various conflicts around aggression, sexuality, narcissism, and so forth, can sometimes be taken to mean that humor in the analyst is always counter- productive. Recently, there has been an increased interest in examining all of the analyst's emotional reactions and noninterpretive behaviors in his or her work to try to find a place for such phenomena in our theory of technique.

Two clinical vignettes were presented. In the first case, analytic work was at an impasse because of deeply entrenched superego resistances that took the form of the patient's relentless dissatisfaction with the analysis and constant accusatory and self-accusatory recriminations. The analyst, after various introspective and consultative experiences, changed his style and began actively using humor in the treatment. The patient responded with an increased ability to analyze himself and the interaction with the analyst, primarily because of identificatory processes and because the analyst's humor disconfirmed traumatic expectations. In the second case, the patient felt that neurotic fantasies had been traumatically confirmed in a previous analysis. The author's use of humor enabled the patient to feel stronger, both in his relationships and in the analysis, where he was increasingly able to face difficult material.

The analyst's technique is often taken by the patient as an expression of the former's internal mental state and, as such, can confirm or disconfirm certain pathological expectations, fantasies, and beliefs. In some patients who have been traumatically affected by parents who consistently blamed their children for their own narcissistic injuries and depression, the experience of an analytic technique that is emotionally restrained, flat, or too affectively "neutral" can reinforce symptoms and can be refractory to interpretation. In these cases, there can be some advantages in the analyst's deliberately allowing himself or herself to interact humorously with the patient.

REFERENCES

Boesky, D. (1990). The psychoanalytic process and its components. *Psychoanalytic Quarterly* 59:550–584.

Chasseguet-Smirgel, J. (1988). The triumph of humor. In *Fantasy, Myth and Reality. Essay in Honor of Jacob A. Arlow, M.D.*, ed. H. P. Blum, Y. Kramer, A. K. Richards and A. D. Richards, pp. 197–213. Madison, CT: International Universities Press.

Freud, S. (1905). Jokes and their relation to the unconscious. *Standard Edition* 8.

Jacobs, T. J. (1991). *The Use of the Self: Countertransference and Communication in the Analytic Situation*. Madison, CT: International Universities Press.

Kohut, H. (1984). *How Does Analysis Cure?* Ed. A. Goldberg with the collaboration of P. E. Stepansky. Chicago: University of Chicago Press.

Kubie, L. S. (1971). The destructive potential of humor in psychotherapy. *American Journal of Psychiatry* 127:861–866.

Poland, W. S. (1971). The place of humor in psychotherapy. *American Journal of Psychiatry* 128:635–637.

———— (1975). Tact as a psychoanalytic function. *International Journal of Psycho-Analysis* 56:155–162.

———— (1990). The gift of laughter: on the development of a sense of humor in clinical analysis. *Psychoanalytic Quarterly* 59:197–225.

Renik, O. (1991). Countertransference enactment and the psychoanalytic process. Presented to the San Francisco Psychoanalytic Society, October 14.

Rose, G. J. (1969). *King Lear* and the use of humor in treatment. *Journal of the American Psychoanalytic Association* 17:927–940.

Rosen, V. H. (1963). Variants of comic caricature and their relationship to obsessive-compulsive phenomena. *Journal of the American Psychoanalytic Association* 11:704–724.

Weiss, J. and Sampson, H. (1986). *The Psychoanalytic Process: Theory, Clinical Observation, and Empirical Research*. New York: Guilford.

Using Humor to Resolve Intellectual Resistances

Richard Friedman

Interpretations sometimes have the paradoxical effect of helping patients feel understood by the analyst while doing nothing to alter their inner lives. These emotionally ineffectual interpretations often serve to encourage intellectual resistances. Fenichel (1945) described the intellectual resistances as the mechanism where " . . . patients become enthusiastic supporters of psychoanalysis in order to avoid applying it to themselves" (pp. 28–29). One way to reach feelings in obsessive patients is with humor.

Stanley, a patient in late middle age, was a highly intelligent and well-educated obsessive who had been through a previous seven-year analysis with another analyst. Stanley described his earlier analysis as "interesting" and helpful in that it had given him a great deal to think about. From the beginning of his work with me, Stanley interpreted his own thoughts using the vocabulary and metaphors of traditional psychoanalysis: a dream was "oedipal"; a symptom was a "compromise formation"; an idea was "obsessive." He applied these labels accurately and often with sophistication. The difficulty was that Stanley's intellectual understanding had not had any ameliorating influence on his neurosis.

Stanley, who had been married for many years, also had a mistress. When he came to see me one of his complaints was that his married life had soured and his life with his mistress was shallow. (I will not speculate in this chapter about either his wife's or his mistress's motivation for sticking with this arrangement.) After about a year of work with me, Stanley decided that he would be happy only if he chose between his wife and his mistress and concentrated his affection on one woman. Because he genuinely liked his wife, respected her, and enjoyed her company (every place except in bed), he thought he would choose her over the girlfriend whose only attraction for him was sexual. Stanley became fascinated by this notion and over a period of many months played in his analysis with ideas about splits, displacements, whore–madonna complexes, oedipal implications of loss of sexual interest in his wife, and so forth. He sounded as if he were writing a psychoanalytically informed textbook on dysfunctional marriage.

While Stanley's insight grew, so did the pain of indecision. He began to talk about his fears in his characteristically intellectualized way. His marriage has been virtually sexless for many years. Sex with his wife had never been very satisfying, and he was convinced that he and his wife would never have good sex. He was also convinced (without any evidence) that his wife would leave him unless he became faithful. However, in these months of obsession about his wife, girlfriend, and marriage he did nothing to change his life; nor did his talk in analysis seem to offer any means for him to change. Stanley's discourse during this time was acknowledged quotation from his former analyst—from whom, I believe, Stanley had a fairly accurate interpretation of his ambivalence. I added a further interpretation of a split between the first analyst and me as parallel to the split between his wife and girlfriend. This was a mistake. Stanley wasted several weeks exploring (not for the first time) every avenue of similarity and difference between me and the first analyst and the transferential implications of each point. He then returned to obsessing about his wife and mistress.

Finally I told him that he reminded me of St. Augustine, whose growing awareness of a religious vocation challenged him to give up his mistress and an active sex life. Augustine prayed: "Oh, Lord! Grant me chastity. But not yet." Stanley laughed.

Stanley had laughed before with me. He had a rich, if somewhat sadistic, sense of humor. However, his laughter before had been either at something he had said himself that struck him as ironic or at something I had said that appealed to his syntonic defenses, as, for example, when I was trying to make his endless discussions of oedipal complexes more emotionally real and would comment about his identification with someone he was discussing from the day's newspaper.

Stanley's laughter after my comment on Augustine was different. Instead of an ironic chuckle, Stanley belly-laughed. And then he was suddenly sad. In the sessions that followed he talked, with feeling, about his fear of growing old, his sense of loss of sexual potency, and his antagonistic relationship with his son who was also his business partner. I was struck by the freshness of Stanley's language. He no longer used psychoanalytic jargon. Instead he talked, with strong affect, about how he felt. For the first time I felt that Stanley had achieved *emotional* insight. Neither of us articulated the tension that Augustine's prayer expressed and—understood humorously—released. Actually Augustine's words in the translation I am familiar with were, "Give me chastity and continency, only not yet" (Augustine 1961, p. 125). I do not believe that Augustine had any humorous intent. I did.

Throughout his writings, Freud suggested that there are only a limited number of ways of understanding the unconscious: dreams, free associations, parapraxes and other enactments, transference, and humor. Most of these roads from the unconscious are one-way streets; humor is an exception. People reveal their unconscious both by the jokes they tell and by what they find funny. It occurs to me that emotional communication can be made *to* someone's unconscious by a well-timed and appropriate joke. I believe that is what happened to Stanley with my comment about Augustine. I spoke directly to his unconscious and bypassed his intellectualized defenses. It is interesting to me that Stanley did not try to analyze the joke. He neither told me why he thought it was funny nor how he thought it applied to him. In fact, he did not even refer to Augustine for months and then only as a kind of short hand for his own ambivalence. To use an appropriately anal image, the Augustine joke seemed to have acted for Stanley as a kind of laxative. He was relieved that the purge worked and, as is often the case for someone who is relieved from intense discomfort, had no interest in how.

This is not the first time I have used humor with a patient. Over the years I have told many jokes to many patients. After eight years of analysis, one sexually inhibited patient described an elaborate fantasy about Tahiti and Tahitian women. My only comment was, "When is the next flight?" Through identification with my relaxed response to his sensuality, this particular patient was helped to relax his superego and experience his sexuality more freely.

When I discuss these experiences, some colleagues criticize me. They comment that humor can be misunderstood as sarcasm or it can be used as a socially acceptable way to create distance between patient and analyst. If both the patient and the analyst enjoy humor together, humor becomes an easily rationalized avoidance of serious emotional work. These colleagues raise points that deserve respect.

I use humor because I like it. I like to laugh and I enjoy helping other people laugh. This makes it easy for me to think of appropriate jokes. But it is also a danger. I have to discipline myself not to use humor indiscriminately. Humor, however, is no different in this regard than any other technique. To use humor effectively one needs the same safeguards against countertransference resistances that one needs with any other intervention: a good personal analysis, continuing self-analysis, and continuous consultation with colleagues. Used responsibly, I find humor to be an effective intervention where interpretation fails.

I would like to conclude this short chapter with a large question: namely, what is cure? A patient is not so much cured as helped, through a cognitive process akin to learning a foreign language, to know himself. It is a process in which the question about completion is not "Do you know?" but "Do you now know enough?" That is, cure is not absolute but relative; not healing but emotional learning; not a product but a process; not a completion but a way to continue. The ancient academic euphemism of "commencement" for the ceremony marking students' expulsion from the comforts and pleasures of the university is a more appropriate term for the end of formal psychoanalytic treatment than the bizarre and totally misleading "termination." I believe that psychoanalysis is a cognitive process. And one tool of education is having fun. If we ignore the fun and the funny aspects of psychoanalysis, we deprive ourselves of some of the pleasure inherent in our work, and we deprive the people who come to us for help of an important tool in their struggle for emotional change.

REFERENCES

Augustine. (1961). *The Confessions of Saint Augustine*. Trans. Edward B. Pusey. New York: Collier.
Fenichel, O. (1945). *The Psychoanalytic Theory of Neurosis*. New York: W. W. Norton.

The Oral Side of Humor

Jule Eisenbud

In a footnote that seems to be almost in the nature of an afterthought in *Jokes and Their Relation to the Unconscious*, Freud (1905) touches upon the highly specific physiological nature of laughter. He points out that the grimace characteristic of smiling appears first in an infant at the breast when it is satisfied and satiated and lets go of the breast as it falls asleep. Freud further suggests that this original meaning of pleasurable satiety may have brought the smile, which is the forerunner of laughter. According to later investigators, Freud was somewhat in error in supposing the feeding part of the infant nursing situation to be per se the earliest provoking stimulus of the smiling response. But he was certainly justified in drawing attention to the possible connection between this very early reaction to the numerous situations of expectancy and need gratification connected with the mother and nursing and a response that, as we experience it in later life, is (at least in one of its forms—let us say the "hearty" laugh) one of the only two—the other being complete orgastic discharge—bringing us the kind of tension release that introspectively we can link to the pleasurable feelings we presume the satiated nursling experiences. Insofar as there is a connection, moreover, between nursing and smiling at all—and I will leave to the nursery investigators just what finer *gestalten* or releasers come into play at different stages of neonatal life—we can hardly fail to suspect some significance in the fact that the physiological mechanism triggered off by what we call humor—that subtle and sudden psychological magic that so

wondrously, if only momentarily, takes the edge off difficult and unbear-
able situations—has come to be the one connected with smiling (the
learned aspect of laughter notwithstanding) and not, let us say, with
sneezing, or yawning, or any of several other mechanisms that simply have
to do with discharge of tension as such, or with the removal of noxious
stimuli. It is a curious fact, nevertheless, that the instance cited is the first
and last we hear from Freud about the relation between the nursing
situation and humor. Later authors, with the exception of one or two
allusions made in passing faithfully follow suit in their almost total neglect
of this side of things (Brody 1950, Partridge 1954).

It is not difficult to find in dreams and jokes and in life itself situations
that reflect the presumptive connection between laughter, and laughter-
provoking stimuli, and the nursing situation (which includes, of course, all
components of the union of the child with the mother and the breast).
Several years ago the keynote speaker of a Western Divisional Meeting of
the American Psychiatric Association began his talk by apologizing for not
having worked up a formal lecture. He then told the story of an earlier talk
he was slated to give on a scientific paper presented at the New York
Academy of Medicine. A couple of months before the talk he had started to
dictate the extended critical discussion he had in mind in connection with
this paper but somehow he was interrupted before he had got through the
first introductory paragraph and, what with one thing and another, he
never managed to get back to it. The first thing he knew, his secretary one
day handed him a slip of paper, saying, as she pushed him toward the door,
"Here, you've just got time to make your talk at the academy if you hurry."
He looked at the slip in the cab and saw that it contained the incomplete
first paragraph he had started to dictate a couple of months earlier, but
before he could gather his thoughts and get any further he was at his
destination, had paid the cabby and was on his way upstairs two at a time
and into the auditorium just as the lecture he was to discuss was ending.
Before he knew what was happening he was being introduced on the
platform by the chairman and suddenly he was on his own. He started off
with one or two general remarks about the paper that had just been given
and then launched boldly into his introductory and, in fact, only paragraph.
His gaze kept wandering agonizingly down to the vast empty spaces below
the few lines he had on his paper, and his mouth went dry. All of a sudden
his voice disappeared. Unable to get a sound out, all he could think of was,
"Nothing there! Nothing there!" Only empty space on his paper, emptiness
in his mind, emptiness in his throat. In nightmarish panic he frantically
signaled the chairman for a glass of water, but when the chairman got up to
pour him one, not a drop came out of the upended carafe. *It* was empty. At
this the audience howled with laughter and the speaker, miraculously saved,
went on to deliver, as he put it (pointing to himself and mugging to

indicate that of course this was only his own opinion) a brilliant talk. Here the audience to which he was telling this story broke into loud laughter and the charming speaker did then go on to deliver a brilliant talk.

If we ask what was so funny in this situation, especially for the second audience, which was in on the frightful predicament of the speaker *before* the ultimate debacle of the empty water bottle, it is a safe bet that by the time the speaker was telling about himself on the platform with not a thought coming, every person in the audience, to a man, must have been identified with him in his anxiety, more than one factor, of course, being presumably involved in this. The thing, however, that pointedly focalized the situation was the empty pitcher compounding the empty page and the empty mind. What brought release was precisely the fact that this was not the real prototypal disaster situation—no mother, no breast, no milk, extinction—but only a symbolically attenuated version of it, and one, moreover, that could be immediately put to rights by the speaker making up the deficiency by sucking, so to speak, from the rich reservoir of his own mind. He is not helpless, bereft, dry and empty after all. The feeding can go on. He can do it himself.

This denial and reversal, and the replacement of passively endured helplessness by activity, is incidentally not generically specific to the comic situation since it is allied to one of the most important "restitution" mechanisms in the creative process in general. It is to be seen repeatedly in the case of writers, poets and playwrights, particularly in those—and this appears to be a fairly large class—who have suffered separation from their mothers, through death or otherwise, early in infancy or childhood. It does not, thus, by any means account specifically and exclusively for the mechanics of humor or the laughing response as over against the anxiety-relieving aspects of other reparative, restitutive means of dealing with this basic anxiety. But the transformation of a passively endured oral helplessness into some active form of denial or reversal is nevertheless one of the more frequent latent situations to be found in humor and, if not sufficient or necessary in such situations (and I am sure that the search for the factor that *is* will not soon be ended), the kind that sets off the response of laughter does at least satisfy the requirement of economy of defense in the broadest sense.

A nice example of this was provided by a depressed patient who, from certain indications in the analytic reconstructive process, had been a severely orally deprived infant long before he lost his mother when he was three. In later life the patient reenacted in many ways the initial oral- and tactile-deprivation situation, and many of his symptoms amounted to magical protection against or denial of this, as well as of object loss. One night, after being stood up in a restaurant by a woman who, he confided sourly, had disappointingly small breasts anyway, he dreamed of reading certain items in a newspaper that struck him as ridiculous and improbable. He then went on to ad lib for someone present, as if he were reading from the paper, an item of his own invention, that his childhood nurse (into whose charge he had largely been given at his birth and who had remained with the family until his twelfth year) was going to model a bathing suit. This struck him as so absurd that he burst out laughing in the dream. When I asked him what was so funny about this, he replied that this nurse, because of her anatomical deficiencies, was the last person he could imagine modeling a bathing suit (he had just seen in a magazine some beauty contest winners of heroic mammary proportions). As to making this up as if it were an item in the paper, he revealed that one of his humorous stunts—he was considered to have a very "dry" sense of humor—was to do just what he had been doing in the dream, to read to someone out loud from a newspaper and to insert some absurdity of his own invention, usually involving the listener. The point of this, which usually elicited delighted laughter, was apparently the manipulation of reality, including the listener, to his own taste. It proved that he was not dependent on the meager and dreary fare he was given daily or twice daily, that he could, as it were, make his own. The overdetermined laugh in the dream—one might say a laugh of triumph as well as of release—was a denial of emptiness, the replacement of a dreaded abandonment (he had been stood up in a restaurant) by an active, creative mastery of the situation.

This connection between laughter and a symbolic threat to certain of the later derivatives of the infantile nursing situation can also be seen in the following dream of an alcoholic patient who had definitely, as a matter of actual record, been a marasmic infant. He dreamed one night that he was watching a dowdy, dried-up woman (whom he likened to the stock caricature of the old-time Women's Christian Temperance Union worker) giving a demonstration in a chemistry laboratory. She was standing along-side a huge glass tank of colored fluid and saying that the alcoholic percentage of a given solution could be detected by the changes in color of this solution under certain conditions. She used a phrase like, "If the solution turns red . . ." Suddenly, the tank burst; the gushing fluid swept away everyone, including the demonstrator, except the dreamer, who found this very comical. He awoke at this point and was rather startled to find himself laughing out loud. His wife, who was already awake and sitting up in bed, asked him what he could have been dreaming to have made him laugh out loud in his sleep; and now, although the patient was able to recount his dream, he couldn't quite see what was so funny about it.

The analysis of this highly condensed and overdetermined dream was actually somewhat more intricate than what I shall give here, but the key to the main latent thoughts was in any case contained in the demonstrator and what she said. She reminded the patient of a cartoon he had seen several days earlier in which eight of these sour looking killjoys were lined up at a bar and scowling at a harassed looking, but quite well tanked-up customer. The caption had him saying to the bartender, "Bring me one glass of water and eight Mickey Finns." The patient immediately thought of his wife, who had lately been on the warpath against his drinking, which he had started again in secret and which he was trying desperately to hide from both of his wife and me. The words, "If the solution turns red . . ." reminded the patient of the fact that his wife had become such an expert colorimetric diagnostician in almost thirty years of hard experience with the patient's drinking problem that she could tell if he had sneaked even one nip by the minutest changes in his facial and scleral coloring. Lately she had taken to peering at him in the most suspicious manner, and he could hardly turn around without finding himself under scrutiny. To hide the fact that he had been drinking on the sly he had taken to rubbing his face with the leaf of a plant to which his skin was sensitive, producing thereby a blotchy dermatitis that he could claim to be such but that would at the same time serve to obscure the secret source of his color change. A possible residue for the explosion in the dream was a newspaper account of one that had just occurred in a chemical laboratory.

Here the latent point of the dream lay in the removal of those agencies—the patient's wife and, via associations we need not go into here, me, his analyst—who were trying to take the patient's bottle from him. In the explosion, which got rid of the demonstrator who could detect alcohol colorimetrically, and in the association whereby the temperance workers were "Mickey Finned" out of commission, the patient achieves, in his regressive, magical fantasy, a clear road ahead to the gratification he so devoutly wishes, which may be construed to have been one of the meanings behind the highly condensed representation of laughter itself. Certainly the aggressive component, which has been so often focused upon, is present, but whether it alone would have been either sufficient or even necessary for the laughter is open to some doubt, in view of the fact that it, in itself (as it so frequently is), is presumably a derivative of the prototypal situation of early oral deprivation.

Laughter in dreams, incidentally, has been held to be comparatively rare. However, in checking over a collection I made for another purpose some years back of 200 dreams from as many individuals well distributed geographically, occupationally, and by age and sex, I found seven examples. (This does not represent comparative rarity; of almost 1000 different items—things, actions, attributes—only twelve, among which were food and mother, appeared with greater frequency.[1]) Interestingly enough, in

---

[1]The frequencies of a group of items selected more or less randomly from this catalogue by Professor Calvin S. Hall, then of Western Reserve University, agreed surprisingly well with those of comparable items, including "laughter," in a catalogue of 10,000 dreams (not from 10,000 individuals, however) made by him.

none of these dreams (for which, unfortunately, I have only manifest content) is there much suggesting frank aggression, whereas in four the oral content was not hard to find. For what this is worth (and I for one feel that there is a certain value in manifest content in a survey of this sort) in one dream, the dreamer's girlfriend was naked above the waist, and they were both laughing. In another, the dreamer felt nauseated when he realized he was supposed to marry a Japanese or Asian girl (a figure I intend to show elsewhere frequently to represent the mother specifically in the nursing situation). The girl was laughing. "I asked if she cooked. She laughed and said, 'A little.'" In a third, the scene took place in the mother's kitchen, and some evil-looking characters, "who were laughing like they would split," were about to rob the mother. In the fourth, a happy occasion with a lot of laughter all around was spoiled when a young girl (presumably the dreamer) who was present with her mother got sick from drinking too much wine.

In these dreams, which are about as transparent as the dreams of those just beginning therapy, we see various aspects of the prototypal nursing situation represented, presumably touched off (if we can press our psychoanalytic insight into service at all in such a connection) by some current threat or disappointment in the dreamer's life. A beautiful example of just such a transparent dream where we are fortunate in being given a little more background material is provided by Nathaniel Benchley (1955) in his biography of his late father, the well-known and beloved humorist Robert Benchley. Benchley, senior, a teetotaler in his early adult life, and an ardent prohibitionist, became a very heavy drinker later on when, as a conscience-ridden, depressed character, he could no longer successfully reconcile his strong drives toward utter bourgeois conformity with his equally strong needs to bust loose. In his early days he never quite knew whether his vocation was writing or social work, and he gradually swung to writing against strong inner resistances. His son writes:

> Whether he liked it or not, Benchley was tagged as a funny man, and in order to maintain his output he had to be constantly searching for material . . . and at times the search was a dismal and frustrating one. It was epitomized by a dream he had one night, from which he awoke in a warm glow of laughter. He had, in his dream, said something so excruciatingly funny that as he lay there, chuckling to himself, he was undecided whether he should write it in an article or save it and say it at just the right time, when he could relish the appreciation of the audience. It was the perfect quip, the bon mot of the century, and he knew that he had better write it down while it was still fresh in his mind, or it might fade with the other half-remembered dreams. He got up, found a piece of paper, and was just about to write the line when he became fully awake and realized what it was. He had dreamed that he and some friends were sitting in a restaurant, and that the glasses in front of them were empty. By way of asking whether they should have

another round of drinks, he had said brightly, "Well, should we refuel?" Sadly he put the pencil down and went back to bed.

We can hardly fail here again to see the shadow of the infantile nursing situation in the total experience of the dream and the events leading up to it. Benchley was in a spot quite frequent with writers and artists, whose terrible dread of the "material" not coming, of emptiness, of being left high and dry by a creative block, is often matched only by their intense ambivalence toward the stuff that does come. On the day of his dream, things were not coming; he was reduced to grubbing in the papers for items to be funny about, and "the search was a dismal and frustrating one." In his dream that night, Benchley's laughter patently signifies the triumph of the magical fantasy of never-ending, inexhaustible supplies over the latent fear of "nothing there," and in connection with this we can also glimpse his specific fear of breast-object loss—his fear that his wonderful line, actually his dream-breast itself, might fade away and be unrecapturable. Apropos of this glimpsed fear of object loss, we see in Nathaniel Benchley's account a factor that, as Freud (1905) pointed out, is so much part of the basic setting of joke humor as to be virtually an essential—namely, the use of the joke to hold an audience, and presumably to make it love the teller by putting its members into the primal situation of "glowing" satisfaction. (Benchley wanted to save the line and "relish the appreciation of his audience.")

A close counterpart of Benchley's dream situation, but one that reveals the underlying dynamic picture with a clarity that can be matched perhaps only in the dreams of children, occurs in a "dream within a dream" of the most famous comedian of modern times. The movie of that name—for it is in this "dream" that the dream I am referring to occurs—opens with perhaps the most hilarious treatment of the coldly mechanical feeding situation that exists on film or elsewhere: Charlie Chaplin, in agony, is a prisoner of a mechanical feeding machine that goes out of kilter and knocks him about, cramming nuts and bolts into his mouth, banging his lips with a mechanical wiper and in general committing oral mayhem. Somewhere further along in the picture the little tramp, cold, hungry and tired, falls asleep at a curbstone. (I don't remember the exact sequence, but at one point even his efforts to get into a snug jail by eating a sumptuous dinner in an elegant restaurant and then calmly turning his penniless self over to the manager, while he picks his teeth, as I remember it, with lofty nonchalance, are outflanked by fate.) He has a dream. He is sitting at a magnificent table piled high with viands, fruits, wines—the works—and is, in his Louis-the-XIVth fantasy, absolute monarch of all he surveys. Liveried flunkies move in and out at his almost unspoken bidding. Finally, when he is just about stuffed to the tonsils withsampling everything before him, he sits back in a gesture of complete satiety, holding his stomach with fondness. (I may conceivably be retrospectively embellishing somewhat, but the main facts I will vouch for.) But then comes an afterthought. He snaps his fingers, and in from the wings lazily ambles a cow. At a second signal, the cow squirts its milk into a vessel, after which it is casually waved away ("I can take you or leave you") in the lordly manner that Chaplin could make into high art and high comedy. I forget whether he wakes up at this point or not, but what more could there be to dream?

Much of Chaplin's humor, while we are discussing him, and perhaps his most hilarious but at the same time most poignant bits—his humor sometimes strikes so close to home that we cannot always be sure whether we are snorting or sniffling—have to do with various aspects of eating. When he snitches a chicken leg from a kitchen maid and surreptitiously nibbles on it behind her back in the kitchen, or manages to snare someone else's drink at a very posh party, we laugh. (No one can resist succumbing to the way he does these things.) When he betrays the fact of just having gulped something down by a guilty burp, we laugh. We even laugh—how can we help it?—when he himself, in a paranoid inversion of the regressive fantasy, becomes the breast-object (the chicken) hallucinated by his starving partner in the Gold Rush (which ends, however, with Mother Earth finally supplying his partner and him with inexhaustible riches from her bounteous bosom). But our laughter is almost too anxious to be wholly pleasurable, in the archaic sense, when he is stood up and left to "dine" alone in the unforgettable Christmas Eve scene.

Almost every picture of this great comedian deals in one way or another with the nuclear mother-breast-child situation, even his semiserious pictures, as for instance, where he plays the part of Bluebeard in *Monsieur Verdoux*. And Chaplin's life itself seemed to be (how could it be otherwise?) a part of this never successfully worked through complex. His son writes in a biography (Chaplin 1960),

> He had a way of eating that made me feel like stuffing myself all over again just to watch him. Even seeing Dad chew on that old shoe in *The Gold Rush* sequence makes me hungry. It's the way he cuts his meat so fastidiously, holding his knife English style, a tender, absorbed expression on his face. He lifts the morsel of meat to his mouth and slips it carefully in. He chews it slowly, savoring it with every taste bud—as if it were the most precious thing in the world. . . . He could never bring himself to part with anything he owned. . . . My father kept himself well supplied in everything, as if he were always afflicted by a vague fear of running out.[2]

---

[2]Wherever possible, Chaplin kept two of everything on hand, always had a spare ready if something—like toothpaste—gave out. Similar hoarding behavior, reminiscent of Hunt's orally deprived rats, was typical of the great and comically

There seems to be no dearth of jokes (except, as I have indicated, for some reason in books and papers on the subject of humor) whose entire point would seem to hinge economically on some mechanism for dealing magically with situations deriving their threatening qualities symbolically from one or another aspect of the multifaceted primal nursing relationship. Reversal of situations or roles, denial of "hard" reality, or of what might be termed the "marasmic" affect associated with the life-threatening significance of certain events, magical restitution or transformation of emptiness or separation into plenitude and togetherness—these can be seen as often in jokes as in dreams, the mechanisms of which, as well as the concealed regressive purposes, are, as Freud brilliantly and conclusively showed, similar. "Oral" jokes range on a wide spectrum. At perhaps the most archaic level, we see the ubiquitous and recurring jokes and cartoons about missionaries or explorers being cooked and eaten by cannibals, to the accompaniment of some crazy caption like, "Throw this one back, he's too bony." One up-to-the-minute variant of this showed up recently in a cartoon of this sort with the cannibal chief pointing to a rotund sailor and saying, "Don't take him—he's too high in polyunsaturated fats"; and on a 1960s television show of a well-known comedian came another: The United Nations getting a telegram from the Congo saying, "Send more troops—they're delicious." In all these the infant's primitive fears of being eaten by the witch-mother—a projection of its own frustrated devouring aggression that we see represented and dealt with in many ways in art and culture—is treated as ridiculous and trivial. The story in this category that most neatly points to the underlying significance of laughter as a defense against this one of the terrifying fantasies deriving from the nursing situation is the classic about the explorer who, on being rescued from this infantile nightmare at the last second and asked by his horrified rescuers if his impalement on a spit didn't hurt terribly, replied, "Only when I laugh."

At the other end of the "oral-joke" spectrum we see those finely attenuated derivatives of the original situation where primal rejection by the mother is represented by social rejection, and where crude forms of devouring oral aggression or satisfaction are replaced by the highly subtilized expressions of humor known as wit, as in the one about the Jew who said deprecatingly to the Gentile, "When your ancestors, my friend, were grubbing around in forests for acorns, mine already had diabetes." Many of the well-known Baron Rothschild stories, one or two of which were included in *Jokes and Their Relation to the Unconscious*, are basically of this genre.

---

bibulous W. C. Fields, who is said to have died, as a matter of fact, leaving in banks throughout the country perhaps hundreds of savings accounts under assumed names, which he never revealed to anyone. Children, however, he did not hoard; when asked once how he liked them, he replied, "Parboiled."

In the broad middle range of oral humor are numerous jokes about alcoholics in thinly veiled oral situations, some of which, indeed, still incorporate references to the ambiguous pleasure–pain aspects of the original nursing situation, as in the "How'd you like a bust in the mouth," crack of the hard blond who is accosted by a leering drunk. In this range, too, we find one of the stable items on the menu of the cartoon-offering magazines, not to mention cartoons of the type cited by Almansi (1960) in his revealing paper on the face-breast equation where, incidentally, the face as the releaser of the supposedly earliest and most dependable smiles of infancy can be seen in its connection with nursing. In the broad middle range, finally, are the many comic plays and movies—the "laugh riots" of the press agents—whose highly oral latent content seems unconsciously calculated to trigger off a certain amount of regressive drooling. One of the most successful plays of the 1940s, in fact, was one in which the chief gimmick was a six-foot-one-inch rabbit that (or maybe who) is the constant companion, confidant, and drinking pal of an appealing guy whose family, not quite going along with his somewhat alcoholically blurred rejection of the workaday values of the rest of the world, is trying to sequester him in a mental hospital. It is really the rest of the world, we are given to understand, that is crazy. As for Harvey (the rabbit—presumably straight in the tradition of the blanket tags, pillow ends, fur bits, and other mother-breast substitutes of infancy and later childhood), only those who have or manage to achieve "grace" can experience his reality; and grace, we gather, is largely a state of regressive alcoholic semistuporousness that enables one to escape the reality principle and enthrone the pleasure principle. People who can't do this are slobs, while people who spend all their time in Charlie's Bar are the salt of the earth who love and are beloved of everyone. Women spontaneously rush up to kiss the hero, Elwood P. Dowd. This "laugh riot" ran for four years on Broadway.

Perhaps the greatest fund of jokes which, like *Harvey*, make nonsense out of the reality principle in their very manifest content is provided by the so-called shaggy-dog story. In Partridge's (1954) collection of these stories about half take place in a pub, as Partridge himself notes, though others turn out to be basically oral nonetheless. The story Partridge cites as the original shaggy-dog is not about a dog at all, but about a shark who stole some sausages and found that they were merely empty skins (or sausage "sarcophagi," as the story, which I won't retell here, is given).[3] Undoubt-

___

[3]Immanuel Kant, in his *Critique of Pure Reason*, considers the comic "an expectation that has come to nothing." In the section of *Jokes and Their Relation to the Unconscious* in which this theory is cited, Freud (1905) gives an example of his own:

I have let myself be enticed by my expectation into an exaggerated expenditure of movement . . . if, for example, I lift a fruit which I have judged to be heavy out of

edly predating this, however, is the beloved nursery rhyme that makes a lilting joke of separation, weaning and, in the very way in which it is staged, hard reality, which is essentially the acceptance of the necessity of renunciation. Can we not glimpse these things behind "Hi diddle diddle, the cat and the fiddle/the cow [these *cows!*] jumped over the moon/the little dog laughed/to see such sport/and the plate ran away with the spoon"? At all events, the "shaggy-dog" story reflects in many ways one of the stages on the hard road to the development of a sense of reality where the thing that appeals to us is precisely the controlled, well-structured, and anything but frightening *un*reality of the situations and characters represented. Children in the fluid reality-learning and testing stage almost invariably squeal with delight at some of the situations represented in the shaggy-dog story ("That's funny—a dog can't talk !") and one wonders if the adult doesn't get some part of his secret pleasure from these stories in their throwback to this stage of childhood. Undoubtedly, however, the greater part of the economic gain involved comes from the way the deadly serious underlying business is manipulated.

Just about all basic aspects, derivatives, and transformations of the latent nursing situation with its primal anxieties are beautifully represented in the following classic shaggy-dog story cited by Partridge. (This is one, incidentally, that turns up repeatedly in various guises.) I would suggest that particular attention be paid to the incidental detail in the manner of the telling. "Like the preceding tale, this one also takes place in a public-house, as so many of the best 'shaggy dogs' tend to do, perhaps because the 'public' is the ordinary man's club . . . [and] one of the most fertile nurseries of this type of story)."

---

a basket, but which, to my disappointment, turns out to be a sham one, hollow and made of wax . . . I am laughed at for it. There is at least one case in which the expenditure on expectation can be directly demonstrated measurably by physiological experiments on animals. In Pavlov's experiments on salivary secretions . . . the amounts of saliva secreted . . . vary according to whether the experimental conditions confirm or disappoint the dogs' expectations of being fed with the food set before them.

A fine example of a dog providing a comic situation through "an expectation coming to nothing" is given in another context by Grotjahn (1957):

A group of American fliers was stationed in England and succeeded in "liberating" a refrigerator that produced highly valued ice cubes. A little dog that served as a mascot developed a fierce passion for ice cubes. He played with them, and they seemed to come to life when he worked on them. If he got several at the same time, he went out of his mind. He buried some of them in the ground hoping to return to them later. It was irresistibly ridiculous to see the poor thing return to the burial place later, looking and sniffing and digging in the ground for ice cubes that were no longer there.

A man had two dogs. He was very fond of them and took them with him whenever he went to his "local" in the evening. Well-behaved, they did him credit and never caused him the slightest embarrassment. . . . At the pub he would seat himself always on the same stool. On his right, Fido would sit; on his left, Lassie. He would order a mild-and-bitter for himself and a small gin for each of the dogs. Although he never dawdled, the man would drink in a leisurely way. The two dogs genteelly sipped their gins and usually finished level with their master; and over their masks a beatific grin would slowly creep, without, however, the slightest loss of decorum. As soon as they had finished their drinks—they never took more than one—they went out quietly and quietly walked home in perfect companionship.

The barman soon came to recognize them as regular and orderly customers and perhaps to regard them as an asset, so that when, one evening, the two dogs arrived without their master and hopped up on to their customary stools, he served them with the customary gin apiece and, when Fido gallantly offered to pay, waved the offer aside with an easy and courteous gesture.

The next night, the two dogs returned, their master with them, and sat down as usual. To the barman, their master said, "I owe you for two gins. Take the price out of this note. And, by the way, I'd like to thank you for being so good to these two. They've got so used to their nightly tot that they miss it—miss it very much, I fear. To show you that they and I appreciate your kindness, I want you to accept this small lobster."

"Thank you very much, sir. I'll take it home for supper." "Oh no, don't do that, barman—er, I mean, I'd rather you didn't. You see, he's had his supper. Just put him to bed."

This story, if viewed as we would any dream-style secondary elaboration from a presumptive primary content, has in it almost the entire complex of pleasures, pains, and anxieties in the original nursing situation, along with the whole gamut of mechanisms for denying and transforming the painful and anxiety-charged components in it and reinstituting the postnursing "beatific grin," the satisfied sleep, the "perfect companionship." Here time, in the sense of the regularity and orderliness that can be a defense against unexpected absence and drought, plays a safeguarding role in the latent content of the story. In the very next story given by Partridge, however, we begin to detect an ambivalent mocking attitude toward time as already the disturbing wedge of reality that must sooner or later, but inevitably, change the early blissful and beatific state of drinking in the harmony of perfect companionship into a life where things are expected of one and one is lonely. "A dog goes into a saloon and asks the bartender for a gin, which he drinks without fuss or delay. The dog leaves quietly. The bystanders have been gaping at this civilized performance, and after the dog's departure one of them says to the bartender, 'That's *quite* a dog! Does he always do that?'

'Oh no. He usually comes in at seven o'clock.' '' But in the following story, one that, according to Partridge, "must, by any criterion, rank very high," we have almost the ultimate in denial of time and every other anxiety-provoking parameter of reality, and of any however faintly en-grammed primal horror. The oral humor here is so subtle that if it provokes a smile at all it would be the merest glimmer, the merest trace of one, as we would perhaps fight off a need to fall peacefully asleep. "One hot summer afternoon," runs this idyl, "a couple of hippopotamuses were basking in the turbid waters of the Nile with their nostrils showing just above the surface. They appeared to be very contented and even a little drowsy. Finally one of them raised his snout and said dreamily, 'Somehow, you know, I can't help thinking that this is Thursday'.''

And now our time is up. It *is* Thursday, and we must all get back to reality. We have not solved the problem that was by implication posed at the beginning of this talk—how it is that there has been what almost appears to be a systematic avoidance and neglect in the literature, analytic as well as other, of the oral side of humor, an avoidance that, in other situations, would probably be held to spell out some deep-lying resistance. But perhaps it is just as well we wind things up at this point, mindful of the proverbial caution against looking a gift horse in the mouth. For humor and the seemingly gratuitous laughter it provokes is not only the perfect gift from someone else (and this may, after all, approximate a necessary ingredient, one easily overlooked when we take the social setting of a great deal of humor so much for granted) but also, and along the same line, it is a situation par excellence where an important feature of the economic gain always is the passive listener (or spectator) effortlessly getting something for nothing. This alone, for many of us, has it all over what we went through at the breast.

REFERENCES

Almansi, R. J. (1960) The face-breast equation. *Journal of the American Psychoanalytic Association* 8:43–70.

Benchley, N. (1955) *Robert Benchley*. New York: McGraw-Hill.

Brody, M. (1950) The meaning of laughter. *Psychoanalytic Quarterly* 19:192–201.

Chaplin, Jr., with Rau, N., and Rau, M. (1960) *My Father, Charlie Chaplin*. New York: Random House.

Freud, S. (1905) Jokes and their relation to the unconscious. *Standard Edition* 8.

Grotjahn, M. (1957) *Beyond Laughter*. New York: McGraw-Hill.

Partridge, E. (1954). *The Shaggy Dog Story*. New York: Philosophical Library.

5

Recognizing Unconscious Humor in Psychoanalysis

Robert R. Barry

Examination of the communications of psychoanalytic patients reveals that with surprising frequency, the communications are unconscious jokes. What I mean by this is that the statements have the structure and content of jokes except that the humorous affect is missing. These communications are almost never perceived as jokes by the patient and are rarely interpreted as such by the analyst. Indeed, when these communications proliferate in the analysis of certain patients, they may be interpreted as signs of thought disorder. If they are accurately analyzed the apparent thought disorder is resolved.

My interest in this issue was generated by an episode in the analysis of Mr. A. There was nothing obviously humorous about this gentleman. Tall, handsome, and exquisitely dressed, he was often worried or distracted, but always deadly serious. He was quite as serious as usual, when, in describing to me what an independent thinker he was, he remarked, "I'm not one of the herd. . . . That's h-e-r-d." I was irresistibly reminded of a joke from an old movie. George Burns and Gracie Allen are viewing an English country estate. George asks the host, "Do you herd sheep?" The ever-helpful Gracie interrupts, "No dear! One says, 'Have you heard sheep?' or, 'Do you hear sheep?' One never says, 'Do you heard sheep!' "

I did not respond to the implicit joke in Mr. A.'s comment for several reasons. First, he did not consciously intend it as a joke, and I wondered if my association was idiosyncratic to me. Second, he was extremely vulnerable to ridicule and if I said something was funny he might have felt ridiculed. Third, I was interested in another aspect of his thinking, which had to do with issues of independence and separation.

Despite these considerations, the sense of the joke stayed with me and I began to notice that there were indeed comical aspects to Mr. A.'s persona. Despite his good looks and careful tailoring, there was something ludicrous about his exquisite appearance. Indeed, as someone had remarked of him, he looked like a magazine ad come to life. His obsession with clothes was emphasized by a remark he made while temporarily separated from his wife: "You don't know what loneliness is until you hang your clothes in a strange closet." Although one is aware of the pathos behind the statement, it is nonetheless comical.

Mr. A.'s speech was rife with malapropisms, many of which actually reversed his conscious intention. He would say, "recant" instead of "recount," or "excise" instead of "exercise" (e.g., "I excised my right of free speech"). Other malapropisms created irresistibly funny images, such as substituting "demured" for "demurred" (e.g., "They wanted me to give the presentation, but I demured."). Before I had given any thought to the unconscious humor, I had noted Mr. A.'s obsession with his appearance, his fanatical neatness, and his pedantic, frequently inapt verbalizations. These characteristics were noted by me as expressions of his narcissistic and obsessional personality traits, but I had the feeling that there was some communication I was not understanding.

After the comment I associated with the Burns and Allen routine, I thought more freely about the comical way he presented himself. It is obviously simpler to say that one "told" a story than that one "recounted" it. It is more difficult, however, to find an "accidental" substitute for the word "told" that as thoroughly undermines its meaning as does substituting "recant" for "recount." Significantly, the malapropisms continued even after they had been repeatedly recognized.

Eventually it occurred to me that Mr. A. had identified himself with someone whom he was now presenting for ridicule. The mechanism was identical with the one that Freud had described as basic to melancholic depression. Noting that the depressed person, although savagely self-critical, did not conceal his supposed faults from others, Freud (1917) concluded that the person was really talking about someone else, someone with whom the person had identified.

The most obvious source of identification was Mr. A.'s father, an immigrant whose command of English was limited and who therefore made many mistakes. Father was also pretentious in his clothing. A carpenter, he nevertheless wore a suit and tie to work. He dressed in imitation of his idol, the movie actor George Raft. Mr. A. consciously saw nothing at all absurd about his father. He readily admitted being terrified of him but became anxious and resistant only when his father's power came into question. I made a mistake that was almost fatal to the analysis when I suggested that the actor George Raft was a rather comical character. After a very strained and difficult period, Mr. A. allowed that George Raft had, in later years, caricatured his non-movie persona.

What eventually emerged was that the powerful father image represented a defense against a maternal introject of terrifying malevolence. The maternal superego introject could be seen occasionally behind the paternal image. Mother, who was American-born, ridiculed Father's speech behind his back. Her own pretensions and her sensitiveness about her lack of education were gradually revealed. For example, when he asked her the meaning of a word, she might say, "Go ask your aunt, she's the one who swallowed the dictionary."

The frightening maternal introject was analyzed at first indirectly through associations whose manifest content related to the father. There were also numerous derivatives of the patient's early relationship with his mother expressed in the fear of women that was barely concealed behind his masculine bravado. The unconscious joke quoted at the beginning of this paper represented, among other things, his fear of merging with the maternal image. He did not hear the joke in his remark; what he did perceive was an ambiguous statement that he had to correct. Ambiguity was perceived by Mr. A. as "feminine."

Despite recognition of the importance of the paternal idealization in Mr. A.'s defensive structure, this idealization still had to be analyzed. In this analysis the dangerous subversive power of humor and the need to suppress its recognition was clearly manifested. It is this material that is most germane to the concerns of the present discussion. Mr. A. for a long time stubbornly defended the virile image of his father against a string of contradictory memories. He acknowledged that his father was selfish, violent, and sadistic, but the question of his father's strength remained.

One day Mr. A. revealed that, as a child, he had been terrified of Charlie Chaplin movies. Despite this inexplicable fear, he went to every Chaplin film that he could. I recalled that he had recently told me that during World War II his father affected a Hitler mustache. When I reminded him of this and pointed out that Chaplin's mustache resembled Hitler's, he agreed, but speculated that it was Chaplin's resemblance to Mr. A.'s terrifying father that made him fear Chaplin. He denied having seen *The Great Dictator* in which Chaplin impersonated and thoroughly ridiculed Hitler. Despite this denial, however, he subsequently recalled having seen the film. Mr. A.'s knowledge that he had repressed the memory of this film was significant in the process of recognizing his need to repress his perception of his father as a comical character.

I will close my description of my work with Mr. A. with an account of his first breakthrough of genuine humor in the transference. I had been given a picture of Freud that I was in the process of hanging in my office, when the doorbell rang announcing Mr. A. I left the picture standing at the base of the wall and shortly thereafter, ushered Mr. A. into the office. Mr. A. glanced at the picture on the floor and wisecracked, "How the mighty have fallen." He had dared to make a joke about my presumed idol and by implication about me. I chuckled in appreciation.

In contrast to the work with Mr. A., during most of which humorous affect had to be avoided, was my experience with Ms. B. in which my spontaneous laughter led to an emotional breakthrough and a deepening of the therapeutic relationship. Ms. B.'s feelings seemed almost totally inaccessible. Her facial expression was dull and masklike and her voice was flat and colorless. I had managed to make some emotional contact with her by analyzing my countertransference reactions, but the incident I will relate constituted the most dramatic emotional breakthrough in her treatment.

Ms. B. had begun telephoning me between sessions to ask me if she should discontinue smoking. The question was not trivial since her mother and sister had both died of lung cancer. Mother had been a heavy smoker and there were numerous indications that Ms. B. had repressed the idea that Mother had caused her own death. This warded-off idea was further defended against by a conscious denial of the connection between smoking and lung cancer. Her own smoking simultaneously reinforced the denial and served as a self-punishment for death wishes toward her mother. I felt therefore that I understood the significance of her question, but not why she was telephoning me to ask it.

The breakthrough occurred during a session in which she had been talking about her mother's death. For the first time she revealed that her mother had telephoned her from the hospital on the night before she died. Ms. B.'s calls to me were inevitably in the late evening. Reacting to this new information, I exclaimed, "She *called* you!" Ms. B. responded in her blandest tone, with perhaps the slightest of hints that she was talking to a backward child, "Yes, she was in the hospital and I was at home so she had to call [telephone] me."

Ms. B. was very surprised when I began to laugh. I explained how I understood her remark, that is, as a sarcastic comment on what I had said. It was as if she had said, "Of course she telephoned me, Dummy, what was she supposed to do, call out the window?" Now Ms. B. began to laugh. The mask cracked and splintered. She laughed for several minutes gasping and choking, with tears streaming down her face. Finally she managed to say, "Why do I do that?" (that is, make these unconsciously sarcastic remarks). I explained what I thought was the case, that she thought my blurted-out remark about the telephone call was ridiculous. She was talking about something very serious, and I was playing some silly game about phone calls. I made the additional interpretation that, if she were being sarcastic, she would have to conceal that fact even from herself, since she was sure that I would be unable to tolerate being ridiculed.

This analytic interchange proved very helpful in the following work with Ms. B. The memory of her affective state at the time remained with her and proved useful in the analysis of subsequent instances of unconscious jokes and sarcasms. Also jokes and sly humor began to be part of her conscious communication.

It appears that in the case of neither Mr. A. nor Ms. B. was there a developmental deficit in sense of humor. The sense of humor existed but its recognition was somehow repressed. This proved to be true in every other patient I have worked with who seemed to lack a sense of humor.

A brief review of psychoanalytic literature on humor may prove helpful in understanding the apparent lack of humor in such patients and its apparent recovery in analysis. Freud (1905, 1927) wrote two papers on humor. The first (1905) considered humor from the economic and topographical point of view. Freud demonstrated the structure of jokes and showed how they were created by the same mechanisms employed in dream formation. Nevertheless there is not much one can glean from this paper with respect to the role of humor within the personality.

In the second paper (1927), however, we find a dramatic new formulation. Now humor is described in the light of Freud's new structural theory of id, ego, and superego proposed in 1923. Humor is explained by an extraordinary new formulation: in the face of calamity the superego may behave toward the ego in a benign and protective fashion. The discussion is based on a joke made by a man about to be hanged on a Monday to the effect that this is a fine way to start the week. Here, the powerful superego takes the man's side enabling him to dismiss his fear of death.

After Freud, Ernst Kris (1952) wrote a number of papers on the subject of humor. This writer focused primarily on issues of ego development and control in creating the capacity for humor. With respect to the question of development or recovery of the capacity for humor, Kris had this to say:

> One is reminded of persons to whom the comic in general is unknown; they fear the regression in all comic pleasure, they lack the faculty of letting themselves go. One finds in analysis that this is due to a lack of strength in the ego. If patients of this type acquire or reacquire the faculty of humor in analysis, it is only after the dominating power of the ego has been restored, and thus regression to comic pleasure has lost its threatening aspect. [p. 203]

A problem with Kris's analysis of the inability to enjoy the comic experience is that it neglects the significance of the child's interactions with the parental figures. One thinks of the function of the child's identification with the parental attitudes in the process of mastering developmental vicissitudes, especially in those attitudes related to superego formation. These superego identifications are particularly significant in view of the intimate connection between the superego and humor described by Freud (1927), who wrote that in humor we observe the superego functioning in an unexpected way. In a moment of difficulty, the ego may be exempted from criticism by a superego that is acting in a benign and protective fashion. Acting in this way, the superego may even permit a humorous expression that defends the ego against a catastrophic reality.

If it is true that in some individuals the superego may function at times in this benign and protective fashion, it seems reasonable to consider this function in the light of identifications that constitute the superego. In the backgrounds of both Mr. A. and Ms. B. were potentially terrifying parental figures who were not to be trifled with. Analysis of these introjections led to the recovery of the humor. Indeed there were times when a significant step toward independence of these introjects was marked by the analysis of an unconscious joke.

I will cite just one example of such an analysis from the work with Ms. B. Ms. B., whose hair was dyed a vibrant red, told me that she was thinking of returning it to her natural color. A friend said to her that she would look old with her gray hair. Ms. B. said that she did not know whether her natural color would be gray or brown. Since she had begun dying her hair 25 years earlier because it was graying, it seemed highly unlikely that it would now be brown.

Ms. B.'s puzzling attitude about her hair color was clarified by a remark that her mother's hair had never turned gray. Her associations indicated that she really believed that mother dyed her hair although mother denied it and Ms. B. consciously accepted the denial. The meaning of Ms. B.'s idea about her own hair became clear. It was as if she were saying sarcastically, "If I'm going to believe that my mother didn't dye her hair, I might as well believe that my own hair is still brown."

Analysts have taken different positions with respect to the structural problems in patients who lacked a sense of humor. Kris (1952) emphasized the role of the ego; Kramer (1958) emphasized the role of the superego. Poland (1990) implicated both ego and superego. These investigators differ from the present writer in that they did not give serious consideration to the role of unconscious jokes. They also maintained the position, unlike the present writer, that humor may be "developed" in the analytic process. These are related issues. My position is that, in the patients described, the unconscious jokes and the absence of conscious humor are two ways of viewing the same phenomenon. The unconscious joking *is* the patient's sense of humor.

I believe that humor is too vital a function to be entirely absent and that analysis of patients who seem to lack a sense of humor will reveal the humorous activity to be taking place on an unconscious basis. We are always dealing with the repressed humor rather than with an absence of humor. Both Kris (1952) and Kramer (1958) took the position that a sense of humor might be developed in analysis for the first time, Kris through strengthening the ego, and Kramer through superego analysis.

Poland (1990), addressing both of these positions, found there were two categories of patients who seemed to lack a sense of humor. One category was composed of obsessional patients who, because of rigid character defenses, had never developed a sense of humor. Such patients, through the analysis of their rigid character defenses, became able to identify with the analyst's psychic flexibility and therefore became capable of humor. The second category was comprised of depressives, who because of intolerant superegos had to repress any sense of humor. Superego analysis permitted the release of the repressed humor.

I disagree with this separation of ego and superego issues. Ego defenses are employed at the behest of the superego. If it is true that humor depends on the strength of the ego, then ego strength is dependent on the relative severity of the superego. Schafer (1990) had this to say on the subject: "What we ordinarily call ego strength is seen . . . as a matter of the natural relations between ego and superego; the availability . . . of energies in the ego to be used in adaptation seems to depend in large part on a faithful and benevolent superego" (p. 175).

My position is that regardless of diagnosis or defensive structure, a deficiency in humor results from a harsh and punitive superego. The two patients described above exemplify Poland's (1990) two categories. Mr. A. presented as a compulsive personality, and Ms. B. was fundamentally depressive. In each case the lack of humor resulted from a harsh and punitive superego. Mr. A., the compulsive personality, could hardly be said to be devoid of humor, however much repressed. Additional evidence against the idea that individuals with obsessive-compulsive defensive structure do not develop a sense of humor is provided by the most celebrated case of this disorder in the psychoanalytic literature. Freud's famous Rat-Man (1909) demonstrated in his obsessive and compulsive symptoms a number of examples of unconscious humor. Freud wrote,

One day while he was away on his summer holidays, the idea suddenly occurred to him that he was too fat (German *dick*) and that he must make himself slimmer. So he began getting up from the table before the pudding came round and tearing along the road without a hat in the blazing heat of an August sun. Then he would dash up a mountain at the double, till, dripping with perspiration, he was forced to come to a stop. . . . Our

patient could think of no explanation of this senseless obsessional behavior until it suddenly occurred to him that at the time his lady had also
been stopping at the same resort; but she had been in the company of an
English cousin, who was very attractive to her and of whom the patient
had been very jealous. This cousin's name was Richard, and according to
the usual practice in England, he was known as Dick. [p. 188]

I will not elaborate here on Freud's explanation of this phenomenon.
I will merely state what appears to me to be a sarcastic pun: "You want
Dick, I'll give you Dick."

The fact that previous writers have not recognized the significance of
unconscious humor may be related to how they define humor. For
example, Kris (1952) and Poland (1990) are uncomfortable with Freud's
idea of humor. Both of these writers are critical of the joke that centers
Freud's 1927 paper on humor. Kris calls it an example of "grim humor"
and Poland calls it "extreme." Both of these writers have a concept of
"true humor," which is described as having a gentle self-deprecating
quality.

Certainly, unconscious humor is rarely gentle and is not self-
deprecating. If the humor does seem to be self-disparaging, it is because it
is actually an unconscious disparagement of the internalized object. However, I would dispute the idea that grim humor or contentious humor is not
"true" humor. Humor is subversive. It is not devoid of aggression. Indeed,
it might be argued that humor provides the most sublimated and constructive way of dealing with aggression. It might even be that there is a certain
appropriateness to specific expressions of humor. It seems to me, for
example, that sarcasm is a precise response to hypocrisy.

Perhaps the basic disagreements about humor are philosophical.
Writers like Kris and, to a lesser extent, Poland seem to favor a respectful,
it not reverential attitude toward the vicissitudes of life, especially the
ultimate catastrophes, the exemplar of which is death. Kris (1952) has this
to say on the subject:

Freud's criminal as he is led to the gallows on a Monday morning remarks:
"Dear me, this week's beginning well!" This is called "grim humor" and
I think we are justified here in recognizing a particular form of rebellion
against fate; self-irony, a form of the comic which is related to cynicism
and sarcasm and bears the stamp of aggression. This difficulty in drawing
the boundary between humor and self-irony reminds us again of how
imperfect is any happiness which the comic can offer us. *We see a man as
an eternal pleasure seeker walking on a narrow ledge above an abyss of
fear.* [p. 216, emphasis supplied]

The point of view expressed by Kris could be considered pessimistic
rather than objective. Certainly the entire Freudian canon tells us that there

is no direct correlation between experiences and internal consequences. Death, for example, would have to be understood in terms of earlier experiences. This would seem to open up some room for coping, even a kind of mastery of seemingly most catastrophic of experiences.

Since philosophical questions can only be answered philosophically, I will conclude by alluding to another attitude toward death, the great catastrophe of life. In Shakespeare's *Henry IV, Part II* the character Feeble, when asked about fear of dying in a war replies, "We owe God a death . . . he that dies this year is quit for the next." It may be matter of philosophical bent as to whether this is considered fatalism or mature wisdom.

It may be that the question of humor in analysis reflects more about attitudes toward structure and authority than it does about a strict concern with effective technique. In my experience the only jokes that further the analysis are those that poke fun at the analyst. This, of course, reflects the reenactment of the ridiculing of the parental figures. Examples of this in the literature are very hard to find.

A humorous appreciation of jokes at the analyst's expense does not violate neutrality and clearly furthers the analysis. Not acknowledging the humor replicates the terrifying parent's inability to tolerate ridicule. Space does not permit an exhaustive discussion of the degree and quality of analytic responses. However, the rule that governed the analysis of the patients discussed here was, "If the joke is funny, laugh."

REFERENCES

Freud, S. (1905). Jokes and their relation to the unconscious. *Standard Edition* 7:3–245.

_____ (1909). Notes upon a case of obsessional neurosis. *Standard Edition* 10:153–249.

_____ (1917). Mourning and melancholia. *Standard Edition* 14:237–261.

_____ (1927). Humor. *Standard Edition* 21:159–167.

Kramer, P. (1958). Note on one of the preoedipal roots of the superego. *Journal of the American Psychoanalytic Association* 6:39–46.

Kris, E. (1952). *Psychoanalytic Explorations in Art*. New York: International Universities Press.

Poland, W. (1990). The gift of laughter: on the development of a sense of humor in clinical psychoanalysis. *Psychoanalytic Quarterly* 59:197–225.

Schafer, R. (1990). The loving and beloved superego in Freud's structural theory. *Psychoanalytic Study of the Child* 15:163–188. New York: International Universities Press.

6

Anxiety and the Mask of Humor

Norman Shelly

Freud informs us that psychic reality enters into every aspect of human communication from body language to verbal expressions of feeling and thought. Derivatives of unconscious conflict and intentions are expressed, for example, through creativity, mythology, religion, group dynamics, and behavior.

In the psychoanalytic situation psychic reality is examined in particular in the way the patient communicates with specific symptomatology, free association, slips of speech, daydreams, and dreams. In his book on jokes, Freud (1905) applied his understanding of "dream-work" to the pleasurable effect of jokes by examining a special technique and the tendency of the joke, that is, the joke-work. His paper on humor (1927) assigns some of the pleasure to the alleviation of the superego. In this paper Freud wrote, "It is not everyone who is capable of the humorous attitude: it is a rare and precious gift, and there are many people who have not even the capacity for deriving pleasure from humor when it is presented to them by others." Fine (1979) makes the point of seeing the "mitigation of the severity of the superego" as allowing the teller of the joke to engage the listener in a kind of collusion to bypass the superego, therefore making it an "exercise in communication." This engagement illuminates the fact that both parties are involved in a psychic conflict and are mocking the superego. This process is unconscious in nature and allows for some gratification of the participants' needs. This is somewhat similar to a performance in the theater where a sharing of unconscious dynamics are experienced (Freud 1905). In the theater the actor is in the spotlight and the audience is literally and figuratively in the dark, allowing for participation and the discharge of unconscious fantasies. However, if at that moment these fantasies were to become conscious all would be lost, the superego would establish its superiority, and the performers would be made to feel impotent. In this chapter I will give some brief examples of how a patient handled his unconscious anxiety with humor. To be sure, this was not the whole of the analysis.

Raymond, a clever patient given to theatrics and with an active sense of humor, exclaimed on taking the couch for the first time, "Ah! Here is wherein I'll couch the conscience of the king!" At the time I did not understand how overdetermined this statement was with all its implications of castration anxiety, rebelliousness, and homosexual submission. This brief communication was a preamble to the many phases of the developing transference and the unfolding of his oedipal conflict.

Raymond had come into analysis hoping to discover more about himself. His love life had gone "sour" and he had recently ended a relationship that had lasted for several years. He was in a creative field and though his work was gratifying he felt that he should be more successful. He described himself as not being aggressive enough.

During the time Raymond was sitting up I found myself smiling at his humorous renditions of his experiences. I felt he expressed a creative playfulness that under other circumstances I would have laughed at openly with sheer enjoyment. This capacity for humor is what Freud referred to as the lifting of inhibition in the person who expressed a sense of humor and in the listener who shares in the "joyful acts of recognition." As time went on I became much more aware of the multicolored levels of meaning in his use of humor and I became selective with my responses.

It was much later that Raymond told me how frightened he had been on using the couch. He had not wanted to lose sight of me and the wish to experience me as a loving audience, that is, as the mother who returned his efforts at being bright and entertaining. To lie on the couch meant that he would lose me as the mother he wanted to possess. He felt secure when he could see me smiling.

These wishes became much clearer as we worked through the various phases of the transference. What he really wanted was for mother to confirm his omnipotent wishes and the potency of his penis. When asked to describe how he felt about his penis, he laughed and said it was a joke. This demeaning comment reflected his intense ambitious fantasies and his inability to honor his competitive wishes. He would say that his penis was too small. By contrast, when he was in the early stages of a relationship with a woman, he would elevate his penis by referring to it as the "Bishop."

At this point he was in a honeymoon stage somewhat similar to the initial phase of the analysis. In his efforts to amuse me he paid particular attention to what he perceived to be acceptance or rejection. If he felt I was forthcoming he would feel elevated; otherwise he would feel deflated. Upon exploration, these reactions were connected to his wish to be special and omnipotent and his fears of separation and loss. The terror of castration surfaced when his wish to reduce father to laughter became a prominent theme. As he had wanted to have mother adore him, he wanted to bring father to his knees with laughter. The use of condensation in the *Hamlet* quotation (couch–catch) underscored his wish to be potent and covered up his fear–wish to submit and be penetrated. As the transference intensified and his longings for father surfaced he began defending against his homosexual wishes for closeness. His sense of humor went underground and he became suspicious that I was gay. At another time, and being unaware consciously of what he was saying, he argued that "Gays have it all backwards. First they have sex and then they have a relationship."

He then began a brief period of coming late and missing sessions. One time he called and left a message that his feet fell asleep and he didn't want to wake them up. I inquired into this obvious expression of his passive-aggressive behavior and his wish to weaken me. He defended himself by accusing me of not having a sense of humor. He held on, like a bulldog with a precious bone, to the need to diminish me. I was like his father, who he claimed was mostly very serious, even though there were times when he had sat on his father's lap and played games. One game he remembered playing was to slide his finger down his father's nose toward the mouth and his father would pretend to bite his finger off. Raymond would scream with glee and play the game over and over again.

He was struggling with the move from mother to father and the transference reflected this conflict. As he narrated more of his relationship with his father, which had been one of closeness at times and unavailability at other times because father was often away on business trips, he began to acknowledge how much he felt he had missed out on. The transference shifted to a wish for me to be the father he never had. He wanted me to give him advice on many issues that he obviously knew more about than I did. He said, "My father never reared me." As he began to express his deeper longings for father and he attempted to dilute the feelings with a humorous quip, I began taking up his need to avoid and make light of these meaningful feelings. As Raymond became more aware of his use of humor as a defense, he was able to identify and acknowledge what was formerly an intolerable idea or feeling.

The use of humor attempts to modulate unconscious anxiety and transforms the content of unconscious conflict into a different shape. This is much the same as other acts of creativity. Humor is a communication that bypasses the superego of the narrator and the listener. In addition humor is exhibitionistic and is accompanied by feelings of pleasure, which intensifies its value as a positive attribute. However, when used extensively as a resistance in the therapeutic situation it becomes apparent, as it did in the treatment with Raymond, that if this defense is not analyzed the therapy runs a real risk of floundering. "The ability to live creatively rather than in repetitive stereotyped situations is one of the major hallmarks of mental health. This creativity relates to inner growth, not to outer achievements" (Fine 1986). Raymond, as do many creative people, thought that if he submitted to what he experienced as penetration and castration he would lose his "creative thrust" (Schneider 1950). He also coveted his sense of humor and felt it to be one of his more valuable assets. Eventually he was able to tolerate more conscious anxiety and to understand that he would not suffer an irreparable narcissistic injury, but rather he would gain a greater understanding of the dynamics of his unconscious conflicts.

REFERENCES

Fine, R. (1979). *A History of Psychoanalysis*. New York: Columbia University Press.

_____ (1986). *Narcissism, The Self, And Society*. New York: Columbia University Press.

Freud, S. (1905). Jokes and their relation to the unconscious. *Standard Edition* 8.

_____ (1927). Humor. *Standard Edition* 21:161–166.

Schneider, D. (1950). *The Psychoanalyst and the Artist*. New York: Farrar, Strauss.

7

Humor and the Joke of Psychoanalysis

Louis Birner

> Dr. Spielvogel, this is my life, my only life, and I am living it in the middle
> of a Jewish joke! I am the son of a Jewish joke—only it ain't no joke!
> Philip Roth, *Portnoy's Complaint*

If Alexander Portnoy was caught in the middle of a Jewish joke, it is worth noting that psychoanalysis itself is a very close cousin to the joke. Humor and psychoanalysis both share as their goal relieving others of their psychic burdens. Humor provides the listener or the patient with a pleasant change of emotional affect. A good laugh is an event that removes some superego pressure from the ego and helps the listener to feel better. A valid analytic interpretation also has a similar psychological effect of making the patient feel better by reducing the pressures of psychic conflict.

Much of what we know today about jokes and humor from a psychoanalytic point of view originated with the exploratory works of Freud. As early as 1897, Freud wrote to Fliess (Masson 1985) that he was collecting source material in two areas: (1) deeply significant Jewish stories, and (2) Jewish jokes. It was also known that Freud spent a great deal of time collecting dreams and studying them in preparation for his great work, *The Interpretation of Dreams* (1900). So, before the turn of the century, Freud was vitally interested in the study of dreams, and Jewish jokes and stories.

Freud (1905) relates that his own personal reason for exploring the

79

subject of jokes came from his reaction to a comment made by Fliess after his reading the proofs of his *The Interpretation of Dreams* (1900). The dreams cited in the book were too full of jokes, protested Fliess. Freud indicated that he was provoked by this comment to study the subject of jokes and humor in much greater depth and detail. Indeed, Freud's writing contains a rich abundance of wit and humor. He was very fond of telling jokes and stories and had a keen mastery of the use of irony and the different elements and forms of comedy. His own personal Jewish tradition was more of enjoying Yiddish jokes and stories than practicing religious faith and observance. He had that rare ability of being able to spontaneously inject some form of humor into any situation. Any man who under mortal threat "could recommend the Gestapo to anyone" has a powerful and a novel sense of irony, wit, and sarcasm.

In his seminal work *Jokes and Their Relation to the Unconscious*, Freud (1905) notes that certain elements of the dream work are present in jokes. For example, jokes may employ the mechanisms of condensation, displacement, and indirect representation. Like the dream, jokes can be brief, symbolic, have multiple meanings, and touch on many different psychic levels at the same time. There is present in humor an economic factor, a dynamic factor, and a compression of psychic conflicts and issues. The pun is seen as an ideal example of compression. (Puns usually consist of one or two words.) Freud concurred with the traditional consideration of puns as the lowest form of humor, as they are primarily plays on words and lack many of the intricate psychic mechanisms that are to be found in the structures of other forms of humor. More intricate styles of humor make use of the representation of the opposite, condensation, substitute formation, and symbols.

Jokes of repartee can provide psychic pleasure to people witnessing such a style of exchange. Repartee is an act of verbal defense against an act of verbal aggression. The attacker is paid back through repartee. A psychological unity is established between both parties. The aggression of one party is countered and nullified through the defense of repartee by the other party. Verbal dueling, of course, is the most pleasant form of combat. This is true for the observing audience as well as the combatants. Joy is to be found in observing the act of paying back an insult with an insult.

Some people can make those special observations that create humor for themselves, for the other person, or for both. Humor can also have value as a way of socializing group members when they share and enjoy the common ground of laughter. A good joke tranquilizes and soothes individuals and groups and may serve as a positive addition to the general social atmosphere.

One of the marks and measures of culture is its level of wit and humor, or the lack of it. Sexist humor, styles of sarcasm, and jokes of prejudice reveal a lot about the level of psychic problems and conflicts of a particular culture. A person's jokes are often quite diagnostic of his or her deeper conflicts and strengths. Handling or overcoming the hostility of others can for some be achieved through the timely and apt use of a joke. Freud (1905) states: "By making our enemy small, inferior, despicable, or comic we achieve in a roundabout way the enjoyment of overcoming him . . . to which the third person who had made no effort bears witness by his laughter" (p. 103).

Freud theorized that jokes are formed as a type of preconscious thought. This preconscious thought can experience another revision in the unconscious. The outcome of this interaction between the preconscious and the unconscious thought can be seen in the formation of a new conscious perception, which can produce a feeling of humor or a humorous verbal response. Freud (1900) thought that the psychological processes necessary to produce a joke often involve the same psychic mechanisms found in dream formation. Like the dream, the joke gives us pleasure in and from a savings in the psychic expenditure of affect. A good joke produces in the listener an immediate and soothing psychological reaction and touches one on many emotional levels.

Jokes, like dreams, serve to avoid pain and can give us a certain sense of pleasure. In his paper on humor, Freud (1927) considers that humor is a triumph of narcissism and has that quality of the ego's victorious assertion as to its own invulnerability. The use of humor is seen as a triumph of the ego. Humor is also a victory for the pleasure principle. In humor, the pleasure principle asserts itself through and over the varied difficulties of everyday existence. Freud indicated that there was a great value in humor because it can to some degree positively alter our emotional states when we are faced with the prospect of dealing with cruel reality. Humor is the emotionally healthy way of dealing with the problems and dilemmas of life, as opposed to unhealthy ways such as drug addiction, depression, neurosis, and psychosis. The ability to use humor easily is a wonderful psychological aid to both staying in reality and upholding the use of the pleasure principle.

It is noteworthy that Freud readily used humor to deal with the vicissitudes of his own life, and he came from a social tradition that used humor to fight everyday unhappiness as well as the abuses of discrimination and anti-Semitism. His Jewishness, background, and talents were in a sense antithetical to the anti-Semitic culture of his time. He constantly had to confront the sad fact that Jewishness was not embraced or welcomed in the Vienna of his time. At best, being Jewish was tolerated; at worst, the Viennese warmly welcomed Hitler's virulent anti-Semitism.

At that time every creative Jewish writer faced the dilemma of giving up or not giving up the identity of "Jewishness." One possible hope was for the Jewish writer to develop a very close symbiosis with German culture and to lose all trace of anything Hebraic, Yiddish, or Jewish. Even then the "purified" Jewish writer would probably face one of the old and classic anti-Semitic charges—that Jews had a secret language! So even if a Jewish writer changed his religion and wrote the *purest* of German prose, his work could still be labeled "Jewish."

Anti-Semites do not use humor to solve life's problems. In effect, they think on different levels. They use hatred and belittlement as a way of gaining a feeling of superiority; hence, they can never give up their bigotry. Indeed, they gain narcissistic gratification through the process of the devaluation of the work and creative efforts of "inferior people."

On some level, Freud knew early on in his life that he was to be a great writer, but becoming a writer was not a possibility for him in the Vienna of 1873. His family could not support him as a writer, and the Austrians had no great love for Jewish writers or journalists. Thus, he never actively considered the possibility of becoming an author when he was a young man. There were, according to Jones (1953) only four professions open to him: business, industry, the law, or medicine.

Jones (1953) notes that in school one of Freud's teachers recognized that he had a unique literary style and in a letter to a friend Freud joked that he might someday be a man of letters. That Freud never expressed an early wish to become a writer is indeed a paradox and a contradiction, since he became one of the most widely read, original, and creative writers of this century. What was even more an irony was that the anti-Semitic Germans gave him the Goethe prize for literature toward the end of his life!

Mahoney (1982) has done extensive research on Freud as a writer and has made some important observations about his outstanding literary abilities. Freud is psychoanalysis' greatest, clearest, and most prolific writer, and its most original and brilliant theoretician. To this day his writing style remains unsurpassed. His speaking style was simple and beautiful.

Mahoney (1982) observes that Freud was probably like Goethe, who felt that he did not fully assimilate an experience until he had written about it. Freud's genius centered on the use of language and took many literary directions, as he could write in diverse genres such as history, biography, autobiography, letters, lectures, dialogues, scientific treatises, and the language of dreams. It is of significance that he personally identified himself with the great Viennese playwright, Arthur Schnitzler, whom he considered his double (Mason 1985). He once told Stekel (Gutheil 1950): "In my mind I am always constructing novels, using my experience as a psychoanalyst; my wish is to become a novelist—but not yet; perhaps later in my life" (p. 66).

As a young man, Freud was a potential literary genius with no place to go and nothing to write about. He was to become a physician and a neurologist with little chance to demonstrate his literary or scientific genius. He was like a powerful genie, caught and bottled by his historic time and his own emotional conflicts.

All artistic and creative German Jews must have experienced the grim reality of living in a society that would not accept and recognize them. Jews often would joke that they were not fully accepted, even after they converted. Consider, then, the immense creative dilemma of having one's work degraded and scorned because of its "Jewishness." The Jewish artist, and in many cases the scientist, in the German state had the problem of individuating against a cultural background that constantly worked to make the Jew feel ugly, inferior, and hated. Full integration and artistic recognition was, therefore, impossible. Developing a unique, creative individuality and self leading to artistic satisfaction was most difficult in that historic frame. Yet, Freud attained considerable artistic satisfaction by producing a vast body of creative work that expressed his own personal sense of individuality and creativity. Freud's artistry helped him craft and create a new type of language and joke, and its name was psychoanalysis. He gave up his Viennese psychiatry with its magnets, rest cures, hypnotism, and water treatments, and found something quite new.

Humor was used by Freud as an additional way of understanding the deeper levels of the mental processes. Indeed, he created the talking cure and could see certain clinical problems in terms of the dynamics of jokes. In his writing he quotes a cure suggested by a colleague for an hysterical problem (Freud, 1914):

> Rx. Penis normalis
>   dosim
>   repetatur
>   [pp. 13–15]

Indeed, with such a humorous prescription he recognized the sexual problem of the patient's marital situation. Of course, one of the brilliant, great ironic quotations of Freud (1895) is to be found in *The Studies on Hysteria*, where he wrote:

> When I have promised my patients help or improvement by a means of cathartic treatment, I have often been faced with this objection: "Why, you tell me yourself that my illness is probably connected with my circumstances and the events of my life. You cannot alter these in any way. How do you propose to help me then?" And I have been able to make this reply: "No doubt fate would find it easier than I do to remove you of your illness. But you will be able to convince yourself that much would be

gained if we succeed in transforming your hysterical misery into common
unhappiness. With a mental life restored to health, you will be better
armed against that unhappiness." [p. 305]

Serious students of Freud's life and thought can cite dozens of stories
highlighting his wit and his sense of irony as he endured the fated events of
the genesis of the psychoanalytic movement. To look at psychoanalysis
itself as a creation of humor, one is immediately struck by many similarities
between humor and psychoanalysis, including the following:

1. using story form and speech
2. using dream mechanisms
3. releasing emotion by discharging affect
4. using emotional contrasts
5. dealing with conflicting emotions and wishes
6. meeting resistance
7. sharing paradoxes
8. working toward reducing pressures on the ego
9. increasing the level of psychic awareness

Freud discovered a new language when he revealed the dynamics of
the unconscious. He also created the analytic process for the expression of
the unconscious, conscious emotional conflicts, the tragic and the comic,
and the event of the dream. He founded a new language and a new universe
within the parameters of the patient's transference and resistance. Comedy
and psychoanalysis are forces that liberate patients by revealing those
truths that neurosis or psychosis works to hide from conscious awareness.
In revealing truth, be it in humor, transference, or dream interpretation,
one moves the patient toward a less troubled emotional state and a stronger
ego. Psychoanalysis may be the only healing profession that is able to use
jokes as a part of its process of diagnosis, growth, and cure.

One colleague and disciple of Freud who used wit and humor
frequently in his therapeutic work and writing was Theodor Reik (1960). In
his effort to understand the unconscious process of his patients, he studied
the various psychic mechanisms of the joke. Reik attached to the joke the
elements of unconscious shock when the joke brings a repressed feeling or
tendency to conscious awareness. Humor for Reik lives in the emotional
realm between fear and laughter and can be enjoyed both consciously and
unconsciously.

In discussing the similarity between the dream and the joke, Reik
(1964) states: "Dreams—a major source of data in analytic work—often
sound like bad jokes" (p. 246).

Like Freud, he sees a similarity between dreams and jokes and feels that the analyst can also employ the joke to clarify and explain psychological data. Psychotherapy and wit are considered by Reik as being psychocathectic and involving the liberation of affect. In the patient's laughter there is the element of surprise and also an acknowledgment that something once hidden can now be revealed. In revealing hidden truth, the patient is in a position to work through some aspect of repressed emotional material and to illuminate some dark area of conflict. The patient's laughter can often signify that the analyst said the right thing at the right time and that the patient now has gained new emotional knowledge.

Reik makes the unhappy observation that many present-day psychologists have a contempt for wit and humor. He asserts that the topic deserves much greater attention and investigation by members of the analytic community. On one level, the study of the effect of wit and humor is the study of the unconscious, preconscious, and conscious in operation. Both wit and psychoanalysis counter the mechanisms of isolation, repression, and denial and strive to clarify psychological conflicts and issues in a new and creative way. The analyst's own humorous feelings and sense of wit in communicating with a patient are important factors in treatment because the therapist's use of humorous feelings can dramatically and forcefully point to a psychological truth and lead to the clarification of unconscious communication. Reik mentions a rather interesting paradox: jokes hide problems, and problems make jokes. This paradox reveals the intimate relationship between humor and human conflict.

In more recent times, different dimensions and positions have been explored in the technique of psychoanalytic treatment. The present-day paradigmatic form of psychotherapy is a style of treatment that tries to show to the patient exactly what it is that the patient presents and communicates to the analyst. At times, when the therapist, through a form of mirroring, will side with the resistance of the patient, a reaction of laughter will follow.

For example, a patient may say, "I'm pretty bad." The analyst may respond, "You are the absolute worst." "That's not true," the patient will protest in joyful disagreement, thus countering the former neurotic posture.

Quite often, as the patient laughs at this form of therapeutic intervention, the analyst will also share in the pleasure. On some level, they mutually enjoy weakening the power of the patient's superego and strengthening the position of the ego. Part of the process of this form of treatment is the creation of change by interventions of repeating back to the patient his or her own neurotic communication. As the patient goes through change, he or she may laugh and react in the session with humor because in the act of laughter and wit one can often sense the emergence of psychic change and emotional growth.

When a patient enjoys something ironic, he enjoys considering a psychic play between two meanings. Jokes of irony can lead one to a greater awareness and enlarge the scope of emotional meaning and understanding. Words of moral judgment always have at least a double meaning, since they are understood from objective and subjective points of view. The greater the level of psychic pathology, the greater the level of the subjective distortion of objective words.

Severe judgment of the self when confronted with a joke may yield to humor and better self-regard. It is all right to shout "shit" to one's M-O-T-H-E-R. Even if Mother never makes mistakes. Humor is one of the finest tools a therapist can employ to help the patient gain an appropriate reality sense and give up the gross indignity of the neurotic posture. Humor is vitally sought after by many people who are not in treatment; a good theatrical comedy or a very funny book enjoys an immense popularity in our time and culture. The world has an insatiable craving for humor, especially the type that provides one with insight and lightens the emotional burdens of everyday life.

The analyst's humor and the patient's humor, if well used, can lead to a greater understanding of the patient's problems and serve to confirm the worth and values of the analytic situation. For humor to work for the betterment of the patient, it must lead the patient to gain at least a greater degree of comfort and at best provide greater ego strength and a lessening of emotional conflict. The joke must help the patient to mediate between both id impulses and superego demands. The ego, through humor, must find new solutions to old problems. A joke is worthwhile in the treatment situation when it can be employed as a new way of looking at, clarifying, and understanding an old emotional problem. A joke also has great value when it affirms the patient.

Consider the following joke brought into treatment by a borderline patient suffering from an abandonment depression. He had idealized his former girlfriend and felt that she was the very best person, woman, and sexual object in the entire world, and that there was absolutely no replacement for her at all. Now that she was gone from his life, he was depressed and felt hopeless. She was his one and only unique and perfect woman. He was most unhappy.

One day, the patient came and said, "I made a fascinating discovery today!"

"Yes," said the analyst.

"Did you know that there are a lot of beautiful women in New York City?" he proclaimed in a theatrical way.

The irony of that remark can only be appreciated if one were, as a therapist, to have heard months of the patient's depression and splitting off of his true feelings for the woman and his denial of reality in order to construct and maintain a series of false idealizations about his one perfect woman. Now the patient was trying to relieve himself of his feeling of abandonment and depression, through his jokes. He was working to give up the very negative influence of his maternal introject who wanted him to cling to the image of his former "perfect" girlfriend. His joke, in effect, was a call for his much-needed psychological separation and individuation from her. The joke for him symbolized a new psychic point of view that there are no perfect women and certainly no need for morbid attachments. Now he was able to start to work on emotionally separating from a toxic type of symbolic mother figure. His realization of this needed separation process was first revealed in his joke. Yes, there are more beautiful women in New York City. The recognition of this truth started with a revelation made through a humorous remark.

Sands (1984) makes the point that humor should only be used by the therapist in the ethical sense of being helpful to the patient. Just telling a joke without any therapeutic motive on the part of the analyst is a counterproductive procedure and can be hurtful to the treatment process. The most important humor in the therapeutic situation is the humor that is expressed by the patient. Humor, he feels, must be used to add to the self-esteem of the patient.

Grotjahn (1971) makes the observation that it is good for the therapist to laugh appropriately at the patient's humor because it is the only acceptable affect that can be readily shared in the treatment situation. The laughter is also an appropriate way for the therapist to express his own humanity to the patient.

Although it is easy to talk about good jokes and pleasant types of humor, little has been said or written about the psychology of the bad joke and the presentation of bad humor. One obvious characteristic of the bad joke is that it very quickly disappoints and does not communicate or produce a positive feeling or sense of laughter. The reason for this non-event is a lack of true connectedness between one range of ideas or emotions and another. It may well be that if a patient tells the therapist a bad joke, he is speaking of his lack of inner connectedness and his ego conflict. The inappropriate joke can reflect feelings of personal inappropriateness. The bad joke can be a communication of conflict in a particular area.

The issues of countertransference and transference are sometimes more fully clarified if we suddenly try to make jokes out of those feelings that we do not fully understand. Mr. C. had a past life history of being addicted to sleeping pills. He came from a very abusive alcoholic family where both parents drank and physically hit and verbally abused him. He was emotionally and physically safest as a child when his parents were asleep or in the trance state of deep intoxication. He would talk in the treatment situation in a very soft, mellow, and soothing tone. Irrespective of the level of analytic material, it was very hard for me to stay awake, as his voice was so soporific. One day, as Mr. C. was unwittingly trying to lull me to sleep, I saw the humor in the situation; namely if the therapist falls asleep, he, the patient, is then emotionally and physically safe. He was, on an unconscious level, not interested in treatment; he was, however, interested in putting the analyst to sleep. The resistance to treatment was that he felt that the analyst should not be permitted to stay awake.

In the middle of one of his sonorous deliveries, he was told, "I like you. You don't have to put me to sleep."

The patient comically responded with, "I like you too. You can sleep."

After joking about sleeping back and forth from both sides of the couch, the patient was then ready to communicate more on an emotional level, and his soporific sleep-inducing tone was now easily interpreted as a resistance to expressing his true feelings.

The biggest joke in town for the longest time has probably been the psychoanalytic situation. Never before was there a human process with the potential for so many ironies, contradictions, and opportunities for the emotional discharge of humor, laughter, criticism, and a host of other assorted feelings. Even one's mistakes can be laughed at, if they are wearing a good Freudian slip. Plays and books have frequently used the theme of analyst and patient to produce a variety comedy. Movies have centered on the ridiculous plight of either analyst, patient, or both, to produce laughter. Often one encounters the plot line of a confused hero seeking out the counsel of an analyst so that he may become even more confused. Of course, certain mystery novels and movies now no longer use the butler—it is the analyst who did it! No cocktail party is ever truly complete without a reference to one's analyst or some analytic joke.

If Freud had accomplished nothing else, he created for the world a new type of theater and literature, a new type of dynamic process and comedy. We can speculate on the question of why Freud created psycho-analysis. Vocationally, his life was a marked contradiction. He was a brilliant medical student without any real interest in medicine! He saw himself as a psychologist and considered his practice of medicine as being a long detour away from his study of psychology. Why did he take that long, hard, isolated road of ostracism and abuse for the publication of his sexual theories? Why did he continue his work, even if he was the number one butt and joke of the medical societies, in and out of Vienna? Why did he endure the consequent isolation, insult, and poverty?

While it is true that Freud benefited greatly from the effects of his own self-analysis and that he helped himself, another motivation is also possible. Freud became the first psychoanalyst and psychoanalytic writer because there was no other place for his genius to flower and grow at that point in time and history. The sad fact was that Freud was born a poor Jew in a very anti-Semitic part of the world. He was at an early age made aware of being Jewish and of all the sorrowful limitations that came with this fate, along with cruel and insulting consequences. Jones (1953) states:

> A gentile would have said that Freud had few overt Jewish characteristics, a fondness for relating Jewish jokes and anecdotes being perhaps the most prominent one. But he felt himself to be Jewish to the core, and evidently it meant a great deal to him. He had the common Jewish sensitivity to the slightest hint of anti-Semitism and he made very few friends that were not Jews. He objected strongly to the idea of their being unpopular or in any way inferior and had evidently suffered much from school days onward, and especially at the university from the anti-Semitism that pervaded Vienna. It put an end to the phase of German nationalist enthusiasm through which he passed in earlier years. [p. 22]

The traumatic observation of the humiliation of Freud's own father by an anti-Semite probably scarred his sensitive soul. This sad event took place when Freud was 12 years of age. It must have then become very clear to Freud that whatever vocational road he traveled, he would always be seen as a second-rate Jew among the first-rate Viennese. An ordinary man would probably bow his head and accept his unhappy fate. There has never been a cure for the practice of any form of bigotry and social discrimination. Most Jews in Vienna had accepted a life of second place and second fiddle. This was not to be the case with Freud, however.

In any traditional vocational or professional area, he would have been regarded as a "Jewish" second rate. His genius violently rebelled at this grim possibility and took him to a totally new frontier where he was first to be alone and isolated from his Austrian culture and then to finally become internationally accepted by Jews and non-Jews alike. Freud used his own hatred for his anti-Semitic environment to gain international recognition by forging the joke of psychoanalysis and becoming its first and most original writer! He discovered the unconscious is never baptized or Bar Mitzvahed, is never Jewish or Christian, but is a unique force of instinctual power that can give us humor and emotional understanding. The true analyst sees patients not as ethnic religious types, but only as human beings. The unconscious does not react to labels. It is a unique and common entity shared by all. When it comes to treating human beings, analysis is hate-free and religion-free. This is probably one of the reasons that Freud encouraged non-Jews to study psychoanalysis and did not wish to make the art of psychoanalytic treatment a "Jewish business." In his book *Totem and Taboo*, he asserts that modern man and primitive man share similar conflicts. Everyone possesses the same psychic mechanisms and apparatus. Mankind as a group must deal with its guilt and oedipal conflicts. We are all fairly similar, according to Freud.

When Freud discovered the mechanisms of the dream and the presence of the unconscious, he had to forge a language then that was totally new. He became the first writer who wrote of that new language and in that new language. He deeply enjoyed this work and its fruit of psychological insights. In effect, he took himself out of the censure of his hostile anti-Semitic Vienna and developed for himself a special form of joke and paradox—psychoanalysis. Psychoanalysis is the one joke and paradox that can cure. Psychoanalysis by its nature is neutral and certainly without any ethnic or moral bias, and it is indeed very un-Viennese. It is no wonder that during his lifetime, no one in Vienna could truly understand him or his dirty Jewish obsession with childhood sex! It is not really shocking that his books were finally confiscated and burned during the Nazi period. Neither the Viennese nor Freud could live in comfort with the other.

In looking for the ironies, jokes, and paradoxes in our everyday life, we can only learn something new. Consider the case of a particular Germanic analyst who studied both Freud and the tragedy of the Holocaust survivors, and yet he will only take students into his seminars who are on a "high enough level" in thinking and scholarship! Those who are on a "different level" are naturally excluded. The analyst decries horror of the Nazis, but maybe this person uses their "high-level" superior standards. In this life there is always the possibility of encountering a paradox. In understanding the range of different meanings in the paradox, one better understands the joke of human existence. No one knew the vagaries of human existence more clearly than Freud, who always looked for a joke or paradox to lighten his day. As he once wrote to Lou Andreas Salome, he "cannot get used to the idea of a life under sentence." Yet, he truly understood how to ease his "life sentence" through humor. The world's first analyst knew that a good joke is worth looking for on a daily basis.

REFERENCES

Freud, S. (1893–1895). Studies on hypsteria. *Standard Edition* 2:1–306.

_____ (1900). The interpretation of dreams. *Standard Edition* 5:583.

_____ (1905). Jokes and Their Relation to the Unconscious. *Standard Edition* 8.

_____ (1914). On the history of the psychoanalytic movement. *Standard Edition*. 14.

_____ (1927). Humor. *Standard Edition* 21:159.

Grotjahn, M. (1971). Laughter in group psychotherapy. *International Journal of Group Psychotherapy* 21:234–238.

Gutheil, E. (1950) *The Autobiography of Wilhelm Stekel*. New York: Liverwright.

Jones, E. (1953). *The Life and Work of Sigmund Freud*, 3 vols. New York: Basic Books.

Mahoney, P. (1982). *Freud as a Writer*. New York: International Universities Press.

Masson, J. M. (1985). *The Complete Letters of Sigmund Freud to Wilhelm Fliess, 1887–1904*. Cambridge, MA: Belknap Press of Harvard University Press.

Reik, T. (1960). *The Secret Self*. New York: Grove Press.

_____ (1964) *Listening with the Third Ear*. New York: Pyramid.

Roth, P. (1969). *Portnoy's Complaint*. New York: Random House.

Sands, S. (1984). The use of humor. *Psychotherapy: The Psychoanalytic Review* 71(3).

II

PRACTICE
CONSIDERATIONS

The Destructive Potential of Humor in Psychotherapy

Lawrence S. Kubie

The late John M. T. Finney, Professor of Surgery at the Johns Hopkins School of Medicine, would often say to his classes: "There is only one 'never' in medicine; never say 'never.' " Then he would sometimes pause reflectively for a moment and add, "No, that is not quite right. There are two. The other is never say 'always.' " With this precept in mind I want it clearly understood that this paper is not designed to persuade anyone *never* to use humor or that humor is *always* destructive. Its purpose is to make it clear that humor has a high potential destructiveness, that it is a dangerous weapon, and that the mere fact that it amuses and entertains the therapist and gives him a pleasant feeling is not evidence that it is a valuable experience for the patient or that it exerts on the patient an influence toward healing changes.

The interactions between patient and therapist have been studied most intensively in relation to the treatment of one individual at a time. Therefore I will limit my discussion to the influence of humor on the exploratory and therapeutic aspects of individual psychotherapy. This one-to-one model will serve as a point of departure and of comparison for later consideration of the influence of humor on group therapy and child therapy. Although these problems are important, I will not attempt to deal with them here.

As we consider the uses and abuses of humor in psychotherapy, we naturally carry over into our thinking some of our experiences with and observations about humor in ordinary social situations. We know that in spite of all that can justly be said about the role of secret malice (i.e., *schadenfreude*) in the social scene, humor can also exert a humanizing influence. It can sometimes be a social lubricant, easing certain kinds of tension and shyness, and thus facilitating for some participants the opening gambits of conversation and communication. Yet others are sealed off and frightened into silence even by a general impersonal atmosphere of joviality.

Sometimes humor expresses true warmth and affection. At other times it is used to mask hostility behind a false facade of camaraderie or to blunt the sharpness of disagreement. Thus even in social situations humor is not always kind. And since both kinds of humor can occur simultaneously, it is not always easy to be sure which is dominant.

SIGNIFICANT DRAWBACKS OF HUMOR

If we examine the therapeutic situation more closely, we will find that only under special circumstances does humor facilitate the flow of free associations in a fashion that furthers the processes of therapeutic exploration. Too often the patient's stream of feeling and thought is diverted from spontaneous channels by the therapist's humor, and it may even be arrested and blocked by it.

It is clear that the patient may pay a high price for our use of this device. Usually the patient realizes how easy it is to use humor as a mask for hostility. He feels the hurtfulness of the true word spoken in jest. Belated efforts to soften such jibes by explaining "I was just kidding" mean to the patient only that the therapist is "kidding" himself and especially that he is kidding himself that he was not being nasty.

Moreover, the therapist's humor often confronts the patient with a confusing option: wondering whether the therapist is serious about what he is saying or "only joking."

One may bribe the patient into pretending to accept humor, but this does not release either his affective responses or his free associations. In fact, when an interpretation is presented to the patient in humorous terms, the humor tends to restrict the range of the patient's responses; for the patient to treat solemnly, by associating to it earnestly, that which the therapist has treated lightly is tantamount to correcting the therapist.

Humor often serves as a defense against our own anxieties as therapists and also against those of the patient, either of which may be hard to tolerate. Indeed, it may be used as a defense against all forms of psychological pain. The sad "gay" society of the homosexual is an example of this defensive use of humor. Of special importance is the fact that patients frequently use humor as a defense against accepting the importance of their own illnesses. They may mock even their own symptoms in their efforts to evade the acceptance of help. If the therapist steps into this trap by echoing the patient's humor about his symptoms or his ailment he will reinforce the patient's neurotic defenses.

Many additional considerations make me hesitate to use humor in therapy. I will cite a few more of the important drawbacks. Even when humor is at the patient's expense he usually feels constrained to join in, if only to prove to the therapist that he too has a sense of humor. Yet a later study of that patient, especially if it is made by another therapist, will often show that under the forced smile of his responses to the humor of the prior therapist he had boiled with hidden and persisting anger, although the therapist's mask of humor made it impossible for him to express his anger.

In fact, the therapist's humor tends to make it impossible for the patient to express any of the resentful components in his feelings. Such a bottling up of anger has a destructive effect on any form of psychotherapy; when this impasse is deliberately created not by the patient's neurosis but by ours, it is indefensible.

Moreover, as a similar expression of their neuroses, patients often undervalue their own best traits and capabilities by treating them with mocking humor. To join the patient in such humor at his own expense is another way of stepping into a trap set by the patient's neurosis. This will deepen his depression and stir up an intense but usually masked hostility.

This applies equally to many forms of humor that are not always intentional. For example, any imitation of a patient by his therapist seems to the patient like mockery no matter how serious, compassionate, and educational the intent may be. In contrast to this, when we make it possible for a patient to study his own visual and auditory image we avoid any hint of mockery. This is one of the many advantages of the use of what Cornelison has called the *self-image experience*, as described in detail in an article by this author (1969).

These misgivings about any deliberate imitation of a patient apply even to responding to a patient's silence by silence. This often drives the patient into deeper silence, just as does open mockery, sarcasm, or irony. Yet this response to silence has usually been overlooked by those who adhere too strictly to the analyst's preference to make the patient speak up first. Furthermore, this is one of the reasons why the echolalia technique of Carl Rogers is not always evocative, especially if it is not used with discerning discrimination.

The Patient's History

There are differences in the impact of humor between man and man, man and woman, woman and man, or woman and woman. Age differences influence the effects of humor both in social and therapeutic situations. Many special considerations arise about the use of humor in the psychotherapy of children. Of primary importance is the question of to what extent the patient was exposed to teasing and mockery in earlier childhood. This influences the later effects of humor on the therapy of the adult as well. The therapist must always remember that he is rarely the first person who has found something "amusing" in the patient's life, in his idiosyncratic patterns of speech and behavior, or in his symptoms. In none of this does the patient find much to smile about, especially because someone other than the therapist has usually smiled or commented mockingly about these thing long before.

The therapist inherits a patient's buried reactions to earlier humor. Only at the end of long analytic study will the therapist discover that some of the most destructive people in the story of a patient's life may have been those who always found something to smile about whenever the patient was in pain. This predecessor may have been a father or mother or an older or younger brother or sister, or it may have been a friend or even some relative of a friend or a teacher. All of this confronts us with complicated problems that have far-reaching importance and should be explored separately.

Consider, for instance, a woman patient who was the last of several children, all but the oldest of whom were brothers. At first she had been a happy and aggressive little tomboy, accepted as such by her older brothers and their friends with praise, pleasure, and indulgence. Inevitably, however, these older brothers and their friends moved on into adolescence, whereupon they did not want the little tomboy anymore but instead a little girl with frills, the very kind of girl whom they had previously looked upon as a "sissy." From that point on they made fun of her tomboy traits, teasing her about that for which they had previously praised her. She developed a rigid intolerance to humor and a serious, crippling defensive-mindedness.

No therapist could have known of this when he was launching her treatment. (When she came to me I had known that she had left two therapists, but I did not know that it was because they had tried unwisely to treat lightly and teasingly the symptoms and fantasies about which she felt so deeply.) She could not have told anyone that she had fled from these two previous efforts to find help because the two therapists had "bantered" in the dark, something, parenthetically, that no therapist has any right to do. Furthermore, these two painful experiences with humorous therapists had made it almost impossible for her to try again, causing her to postpone definitive treatment for years and to bring into her third attempt even greater resistances and defensiveness. This is only one obvious example of the dangers inherent in the use of humor and of how easy it is to misuse it.

Many argue that if humor is not aimed openly and directly at the patient, but rather at the patient's "opponents" in life, it communicates a human touch that can bridge gaps and bring patient and therapist closer together. There is some measure of truth in this, but this truth is limited by the fact that it is hard for any patient ever to feel sure that he is not in some unacknowledged way the butt of this humor. This may be only because he resents the fact that he is suffering while the therapist is taking things gaily and lightly. For it is never any fun to have a neurosis, nor is it ever fun to be in treatment. Consequently, no matter how consciously well intended the therapist's humor may be, the patient usually perceives it as heartless, cruel, and unfeeling.

Moreover, while we may be masking our own hostilities with this humor, we silently pressure the patient to accept it without manifesting the justifiable resentment that he feels toward us for treating his suffering in so cavalier a fashion. The problem reminds one of the court jester, that mocking figure who had a special license to poke fun at the monarch, but with the threat of the king's wrath always hanging over his head. Here, the patient is the monarch who may "lose his cool." Thus even to poke fun gently may endanger the therapist's leverage.

Two examples of mocking interpretations are reported in an article by Victor Rosen (1963, pp. 719, 720). In this account the disturbing intrusion of disguised hostility from both sides is evident, yet the immediate and remote consequences are not fully explored. This does not prove that the effects are either creative or destructive, but only that they are subtle, complex, and often unpredictably dangerous.

Impairment of the Therapist's Role

Humor also impairs the therapist's necessary incognito. The highly charged psychotherapeutic relationship is one of the most important relationships in the world, but also one of the most subtle and difficult. It puts demands on us as psychotherapists for which the human race is hardly ready. We have not reached a degree of maturity or a quality of wisdom and generosity that justifies our attempting to play this role at all. Yet the pressing needs of sick patients force us to attempt it.

As a result, most of the technical devices of analytic therapy (such as the effort to preserve the analytic incognito and the separation between social and professional relationships) have as one of their central goals the protection of the patient from the frailties of the therapist. Therefore these provide generous and important contributions to the patient's welfare. We can leave their protection only with many precautions. Yet humor is a subtle way of circumventing their protective restrictions.

For example, whether or not the therapist seeks it, he is placed automatically in a position of almost unquestioned authority to which he never is entitled, for the therapist's position vis- à-vis the patient enables the therapist to project secretly and by substitution many of his own unsolved problems. He transplants these unconsciously out of his own troubled past; in doing so he is likely to use the patient (and also the patient's family) as whipping boys, as surrogates for his own parents, siblings, spouse, old friends, and so forth. Against the therapist's authority, humor provides the patient with no protection but leaves him even more vulnerable and more exposed.

The price of internal freedom (i.e., freedom from the internal tyranny of one's own past) is that same vigilance that is required for the protection of our public liberties from external tyrannies. We can maintain this indispensable vigilance only if we remain emotionally objective and uninvolved. But humor blunts the vigilance of our self-observing mechanisms and our self-correcting efforts. Furthermore, the sharing of humor automatically creates a powerful secret emotional involvement, just as does the sharing of grief. It is all too easy to shut our eyes to the fact that our manifestations of humor can be a form of self-display, exhibitionism, or wooing. They say to a patient, "See how bright and witty and amusing and charming and delightful I can be."

Consequently, humor is especially tempting for the relatively constricted, sober, and humorless among therapists; it gives such a man an opportunity to parade himself as a wit before the eyes of his patients and, indirectly, his colleagues. Humor is also a way of letting down the bars against the manifestations of countertransference, as the therapist smuggles humor in as a gesture of enticement. Humor is perhaps the most seductive form of transference wooing.

Under a barrage of the therapist's self-gratifying and exhibitionistic humor, the patient suffers silently. Whether he admits it or not, every patient is in pain; to have somebody viewing the patient and his pain with charm and easy humor may gratify the self-admiring therapist, but never the patient. And when the patient feels constrained to laugh along politely, he is merely trapped in a "laugh-in," because he is afraid to anger the therapist by not joining in. The secret devastation that goes on inside comes to light only much later.

The patient has no escape hatch. He is the therapist's captive audience, if the therapist is callous enough to misuse him in this way. The patient does not dare to say "We are not amused," as did the good Queen Victoria when a court favorite attempted a lighthearted takeoff of some of her easily recognized mannerisms. In this respect humor in therapy is reminiscent of H. G. Wells's pithy comments on humor in the classroom: "Academic humor! Ugh!" Humor, then, is a way of taking advantage of the patient. Over the latter's desperation the therapist's humor runs a steam-roller. I have picked up traces of patients' delayed, bitter responses to the lighthearted or bantering approach of the therapist more often than I care to contemplate.

For the beginning therapist these dangers and reservations are doubly loaded. It is especially to the beginner that humor seems to be easier than any other way of introducing topics that are painful both to the patient and the therapist. In fact, it is during the learning period that humor is most alluring and its use most dangerous. Unless he is psychologically callous and unfit, the young psychiatrist, new to the therapeutic situation, takes up his responsibilities with a tense combination of masked terror and anger, from which humor is an escape and against which it is a defense.

Over long years of experience in supervising in private and hospital practice both analytically informed psychotherapy and young students of analysis, I have seen humor tried countless times. Yet I cannot point to a single patient in whose treatment humor proved to be a safe, valuable, and necessary aid.

That even the therapist who defends the use of humor and banter feels some secret guilt about being humorous is proven by the fact that he almost never reports his own humor in his accounts of therapeutic sessions. He forgets it, hides it, and reports seriously what he actually presented to the patient with humor. Consequently, the use of videotape recordings of therapeutic and supervisory sessions would be the only possible way to study a true sample of the use of humor in therapy.

Sometimes the joke is on the therapist, who cannot allow himself to appear angry when the tables are turned in this way. He cannot always laugh along, because if he does he will lose an invaluable opportunity to help the patient to gain more insight into the latter's use of humor as a weapon. The therapist walks a tightrope, or better, a whole network of crisscrossing tightropes. There can be no rigid or inclusive rules about how to handle this. Yet we hold always to the ultimate question of whether humor facilitates the patient's free associations. This is the ultimate test of humor's effects on the process of therapy.

Let me make it clear that much of this applies equally to that which the patient may smuggle past his own repressing mechanisms by using humor. Yet the effects on the patient of his own humor are not identical with the effects of the therapist's humor. I have seen patients speak the true word in jest quite freely, only to sit or lie in stunned silence as the realization slowly grew of the true implications of what they had just said.

The critical difference is between smiling or laughing *with* someone (which rarely does harm) or smiling and laughing *at* them. Therefore, there is nothing in what I have written here that suggests that it is inappropriate or damaging to respond with appropriate amusement to a patient's spontaneous humor, particularly if such an interchange of humor enters into the therapeutic interchange only as one of the signs of improvement after the process is well along. Yet even here there is a hidden danger. The patient who has a gift for humor may offer humor not only as a screening device but also as a way of seducing his therapist out of his therapeutic role into one of happy participation in fun.

APPROPRIATE USE OF HUMOR

Therefore I can qualify my reservations about the use of humor in therapy only to a limited extent and under special circumstances. It is never justifiable to make fun of patients or their symptoms, no matter how strange or grotesque these may seem, or of neurotogenic patterns of general behavior that are the symptomatic expressions of the underlying neurotic process. This serves only to increase the patient's pain, resentment, and defenses.

However, as a patient gradually achieves a progressively deeper self-understanding, gentle and sympathetic humor can sometimes help him to mobilize a determination to use his new insights so that he can limit, control, and guide the symptomatic expression of what remains of the neurotic process. In other words, as insight helps the patient to emerge from domination by his own unconscious processes, the incorporation of these new insights into new conscious controls can sometimes be assisted by the light touch, but only then.

In the hands of a senior therapist, humor certainly can at such times be a safe and effective tool. Yet I am not ready to accept even so limited a claim without at least one serious reservation. What the senior does the junior soon will imitate. In fact, every senior, whether or not he has formal status as a teacher, provides a pattern that younger men will try to imitate. Thus even if it could be demonstrated beyond question that the use of humor late in therapy is safe in the hands of the experienced, how can the inexperienced be dissuaded from imitating too early so easy, seductive, and self-gratifying a device?

A special warning is in order against the type of bitter banter that Harry Stack Sullivan used so destructively. Here the therapist indulges a fantasy that he has a license to attack under a thin disguise of humor. One is justified in making one generalization about this: Those who are most violent in their defense of humor in psychotherapy often have faces that are distorted with anger even when they think they are at peace and unobserved. Any lecturer on this topic, particularly if the group is not too large, can spot them in the audience by their chronic expressions of tense resentment. These men do not want to be deprived of their right to use and misuse something that they misterm "humor."

Conversely, a dour approach can also have its dangers. Some patients have had parents who were overserious and dour and who acted as though they were reluctant ever to feel or express humor with a child. If the therapist assumes a similar attitude toward a child or adult who comes from such a background, the patient will be forced to identify the therapist with that kind of parent. One cannot know this ahead of time about anyone; but when it occurs it creates special difficulties in launching treatment. Later, however, it may feed useful material into the therapeutic process. Consequently, it is more likely to create temporary obstacles at the start than lasting difficulties. This applies to all ages, but it means that in dealing with adolescents there is special danger in a dour rejection of the adolescent's humorous overtures.

Whenever the therapeutic process seems to be approaching a successful termination or interruption, a mutual interchange of humor can have some positive advantages and certainly few risks. Even here, however, one risk remains: the danger that with humor both patient and therapist can fool themselves that the end of treatment is approaching. In itself humor is so much more pleasant than the harsher and more self-denying rigors of formal therapy that it can be used to hide persisting symptoms and other residues of unresolved and still buried conflicts. It can be misused to fool ourselves with premature hopes that we are reaching the end of treatment. Against this the one safeguard is the eternal vigilance that one learns to maintain only out of long, painful, and repeated experiences of having been fooled before.

Humor has its place in life. Let us keep it there by acknowledging that one place where it has a very limited role, if any, is psychotherapy.[1]

REFERENCES

Grotjahn, M. (1957). *Beyond Laughter*. New York: Blakiston Division, McGraw-Hill.
Kubie, L. S. (1969). Some aspects of the significance to psychoanalysis of the exposure of a patient to the televised audiovisual reproduction of his activities. *Journal of Nervous and Mental Disease* 148:301–309.

---

[1]After reading this paper some experienced internists and general practitioners commented that similar cautious warnings and considerations are of equal importance in all forms of medical and surgical practice.

Mendel, W. M., ed. (1970). *A Celebration of Laughter*. Los Angeles: Maria
    Books.
Rosen, V. (1963). Varieties of comic caricature, and their relationship to
    obsessive compulsive phenomena. *Journal of the American Psycho-
    analytic Association* 11:704–724.

Use and Abuse of Laughter in Psychotherapy

Robert A. Pierce

Ideally in psychotherapy people are dealing with conflictual material and are trying to extend mastery to areas of their lives where they have had uncertain control. This is exactly what humor is about, achieving mastery, however briefly, over rules, impulses, or the limitations life imposes on us. If this is true, how come therapy is so often so sober an enterprise? I believe that for most of us our professional training is the main reason that there is so little laughter in our psychotherapy sessions. In an effort to teach fledgling psychotherapists to take their clients' problems seriously, I think we have too often taught them to take them soberly and humorlessly. I also think, by the way, that we may do better, livelier therapy than our students realize. When I tape sessions of my own, I find that the presence of the tape makes me tighten up. It makes me less easy and less humorous. Then when I do get some lively, humorous moments on tape it feels risky to share them with colleagues or students because it means sharing so much of myself. Many humorous interchanges are particularly lively and personal, probably among the most personal moments shared in therapy. So while I don't think most of us use enough humor in our therapy sessions I think we use more than we let other people know.

I would like to discuss different kinds of humor beginning with three I think *do not* belong in psychotherapy. The first is the easiest to define. It is that clearly psychonoxious humor in which the therapist is using humor to aggress against the client. In this kind of humor the therapist belittles, laughs at, or mimics the client. In his much quoted 1971 paper (Chapter 8, this volume), Lawrence Kubie is referring mostly to this kind of humor when he recommends that therapists not use humor at all in psychotherapy. While agreeing with his intention to shield clients who are already hurting from further iatrogenic harm, Kubie's proposed cure seems worse than the disease. What does make sense to me is that in instances where we are feeling angry with a client we either refrain from using humor or use it very sparingly. A humorous statement is one that is often made quickly, without planning, and one that involves our own unconscious to a significant degree. When we do not feel we can trust our unconscious with a particular client, or at an especially stressful time in our lives, it makes sense to limit the freedom we might otherwise give it. Demeaning humor is used frequently by a few therapists and probably some time or another by all of us, but it is without doubt harmful and to be avoided whenever possible.

There are two other types of humor to be avoided but they are not quite as obviously harmful as the first. One of these is humor that is used defensively, probably by the client but conceivably by a conspiring therapist as well, which directs attention away from emerging feelings to safer territory. At a recent therapy workshop, for example, a client was talking about how she will probably never have children. She began to get sad about that and then started making a frantic series of jokes about how she used to think about *Cheaper by the Dozen*, "Leave It to Beaver," and "The Waltons" and it looked like she would not have that kind of family. I said "Not having those dreams come true is not funny. It's sad." She stopped joking, let herself feel the loss, and cried. In this case humor was being used defensively and interrupting that defense allowed her to experience her underlying sadness. Humor is quite often used defensively in this way and represents more a loss of opportunity than a genuinely harmful event such as the first kind.

The third nonuseful kind of humor involves comments by the therapist or client that are irrelevant to the therapeutic purpose. They may not be specifically defensive but, in draining energy and attention away from the main thrust of the work, they are wasteful. All of us like to be noticed and the therapist's job can sometimes be a lonely one. At times we are pulled to tell a story or make a funny comment, not because there is any real point to be made or to move the client deeper into feelings, but simply as a way to garner a few seconds of narcissistic gratification. These, then, are the three types of humor that seem, to me, worth avoiding. There are several others that are worth pursuing.

Clients come to therapy to get help reaching certain goals. In order to help them, therapists have their own goals about what should happen in therapy. There are three goals, widely subscribed to by a broad spectrum of therapists from varying therapeutic schools, the pursuit of which can be aided by humor. One is that the client identifies and expresses feelings. A second is that the client insightfully grasps new relationships between various parts of his/her life. And the third is that the client has an important and healing relationship with the therapist. It is my contention that the use of humor in psychotherapy can significantly aid the achievement of each of these goals. Let's take these areas in turn.

First, there are a number of ways in which humor facilitates the recognition and expression of feeling. Let's take embarrassment and shame, for example. We all enjoy being looked at and admired. And we all dread being laughed at or feeling foolish. At times the line between these is vanishingly small. When we've done something or think we've done something that makes people look at us and think we're foolish, or that uncovers some feelings we'd like kept hidden, we feel embarrassed. One thing we can do with that is go into a closet for the rest of our lives and never again confront the people who know these dreadful secrets about us. Another possibility is to laugh. Let's take me, for example. At about 13 I was acutely aware of strange things growing and changing between my legs. I was swimming late one evening with a minister and a young attractive woman from our congregation. We were playing monster games and coming up out of the water in the semi-darkness and scaring each other. I came up out of the water, held my hands above my head, my fingers spread apart like an octopus, my shoulders hunched and said very loud and very clear, "Look at my testicles!" In that moment, as I realized I had said testicles instead of tentacles there was a dead silence. And the moment after I realized it, I sank beneath the water and wished for all the world that I could stay there and never come up. When I did come up, they were laughing and I laughed and every time since, when I tell that story, I continue to laugh. It is a story of my conflict between being seen and not being seen, between hiding and exhibiting my sexuality and there is nothing to do after you have said something like that but laugh. And laughing, I am convinced, is the curative agent, quite specifically, in the case of embarrassment and shame. When a client tells an embarrassing story it is often told softly, almost reverently, and we are expected to treat it respectfully. Laughing at him or her is the worst thing we can do. Yet we do not want to buy into the client's belief that what was revealed in the embarrassing episode was really as shameful as he or she experiences it. We need to let the client know that we fully understand how painful the experience is but that our own view of it is less catastrophic. In inviting the client to laugh about the embarrassing incident we invite him or her first to alternate rapidly between the catastrophic and noncatastrophic view of the incident and ultimately to adopt a position of mastery over it by taking the noncatastrophic view. In telling the story I just told I was in part continuing to work through an embarrassing moment by retelling it, laughing, inviting you to laugh with me, and adopting an attitude toward the story of mastery and noncatastrophe.

Humor can also be used as a way of helping people get to feelings of disappointment or anger. At the recent workshop I mentioned earlier, I decided to bring in an assistant to help me run it. A week or two before the workshop I sent out a letter telling what to bring, directions for getting there, and so forth, and I buried within it (or tried to) a two-sentence section saying that so-and-so would be co-leading the group and that he was a very good therapist. Not surprisingly the clients had feelings about this interloper and eventually got around to voicing them. The discussion was tentative and cautious until a woman with a keen sense of humor and timing began telling about how she reacted when she heard the news. "I got the mail and went to the bathroom and I'm sitting on the pot opening the mail and it's okay and I get to the letter about the workshop and I'm reading through it. No big deal and then there's this little section buried way down at the bottom of the page. I'm not sure but I think the type may have been smaller and it says this guy's gonna be my leader and he's a very good therapist. I guess I must have groaned because the next thing I know my roommate is asking me through the door if I'm alright." As she went on she made us all laugh hard as she skillfully used humor to voice the group's anger about the new leader that none of them knew and about my defensiveness in presenting him to them.

Here is what I think happened: Many members of the group were feeling angry and also frightened about the consequences if they were to voice their anger. The leaders were nervous about the mildly voiced criticism they had heard, knowing there was more where that came from but not knowing how much. In this context of high arousal, anger, and fear, this client, like a good politician, found the perfect compromise—a way of recasting the experience so that the anger is expressed and the message gets through but we are all relieved to laugh together. It is "just" a joke. This time the anger will not lead to either retribution or guilt. It is okay to be mad at the leader and to have been defensive about bringing in the co-leader, and it is okay to be the co-leader. The humor expressed the anger in an acceptable form and resulted in a more open and much less tense discussion than we had prior to her intervention.

Finally humor can be used in a paradoxical way to help people get to feelings of sadness and loss. We have all seen our children, our clients, or ourselves laugh until we cry. At a funeral, for example, people may be recalling the person who has died and begin telling funny stories about him or her. The sense of energy there is volatile and can be experienced as laughter or as tears. At certain times laughter is more accessible and as people laugh they may move directly into crying and begin sobbing about the person who is gone. At times like that you can feel how close hard laughter is to sobbing.

The other day a man was talking about his mother's impending death but having trouble feeling his loss. Rather he was complaining about how controlling she had always been. He told about a conversation he had with his sister and how they were joking about what their mother's will might say. "I told her 'I betcha it says I can't use any of the money for booze.' And then my sister said, 'It probably says you can't have the money till you get married.' " At this he laughed hard, briefly, and then suddenly started sobbing. Often the difference between a humorous perspective where that kind of hard laughter is involved and a keen sense of loss is nothing more than a particular word, phrase, or thought that comes to mind.

One further point about the relationship of humor to the expression of feelings is that humor can be used to lighten as well as deepen clients' involvement with their feelings. Most of the time we are probably going to be working to deepen a client's experience of feelings but at times, perhaps at the end of the session, or at a time when the client seems to be too immersed in the feeling, we may want to use humor to help the client lighten up. The right kind of humorous twist by ourselves or by the client (and clients often spontaneously make these kind of statements as they see the end of the hour approaching) gives perspective in a way that is a particular gift of humor. This type of humor is not the knee-slapper, fall-down-laughing sort but has a more philosophic tone that sets our pain in a larger perspective and suggests, however much it may hurt, that life will go on and will flourish despite these losses or angers or embarrassments.

At the most general level humor can be used to move clients to a particular level of feeling experience. It can be used to help clients contact their feelings more deeply or to move to a lighter or more distant perspective.

A second goal of therapy for most therapists is insight—the cognitive/emotional grasping of a personally relevant connection. It may be a connection between past and present, between feelings and behavior, or it may involve a transference connection between therapist and early caregivers. Humor can facilitate insight in a number of ways. First, humor can be used diagnostically. What a person finds funny often tells us, and sometimes the client, where the conflict is. If a client smiles when describing someone else's bad fortune we can easily guess that the client is mad at the person he/she is discussing. Similarly a client's favorite joke can tell us something about his/her conflict areas or defensive style.

Humor can also increase insight by helping nail down the truth of a half-known, feared, or suspected state of affairs. When my oldest daughter was 16 she had not yet found a boyfriend whom I found worthy of her.

They all seemed nice enough but lacking the intelligence, thoughtfulness, grace, and human sensitivity I thought she deserved. Suspecting that I might be a bit hard to please in this regard I invited her boyfriend over for dinner. When he arrived my children and our guest, Allen, sat down and I brought the food out and went around the table putting food on each plate. As I headed back into the kitchen Allen called after me: "Mr. Pierce, I hate to say anything but you didn't give me any food!"

What could I say? My unconscious was there for all to see. We all laughed for a long time and any doubt I had about my possessive feelings toward my daughter were removed. In an instant I knew what before I had only suspected. The increased insight was there as an intrinsic part of the humorous confrontation.

As a final example of how humor can increase insight, I was working with a middle-aged, fairly conservative woman who had begun dating after a long hiatus following the demise of her marriage. She told about petting with a man she dated and then felt cheap when he stopped seeing her and began seeing someone else. She said that what she had done was okay but became cheap when he took up with the other woman. She was very hard on herself during the session, called herself bad names, and cried as I held her. As she left she noticed the wet spot on my shirt from her tears. "You don't mind going around with a wet shoulder half the day?" "No" I said, "not as long as you don't cry with anybody else. If you did that I'd feel really cheap." She laughed hard and saw the connection.

A third objective of most therapists is to provide the client with a healing relationship. In the process of addressing the client's problems, two people are spending time together and developing a relationship. Most therapists see this as an important therapeutic ingredient, although there is considerable disagreement as to what aspects of the relationship are most helpful. My own sense is that however much of his/her personal self the therapist chooses to reveal, there is an irreducible essence of being people together in the world, the recognition of which can be useful. Humor can facilitate this recognition. This is a very difficult concept to illustrate because it is extremely subtle. Lily Tomlin said, "Let's remember! We're all in this alone." There's a moment in laughter when the laughers' eyes meet and for a moment they are not alone. There is a shared, sometimes very intimate, message, "I know exactly what you mean. I've been there too." Because it is not overtly stated or even consciously decided upon, but rather happens, it can be among the most spontaneous moments in therapy.

A client in group was complaining about women, and specifically how his wife used her pain, her beauty, and the waxing and waning of her warmth to control him. He wound up his peroration by saying "Sometimes I don't know why I put up with it!" As he said that, he looked at an attractive female group member who was looking at him in a very warm and open way. Without missing a beat he continued "and other times I do!" We all laughed with him and we shared a moment of eye contact that I know conveyed to him the certain knowledge that I was with him in his pain, and in his triumph over it through his joke.

Another client was complaining about a number of things and was on a roll. He began crying, reached for the Kleenex but the Kleenex ripped as he pulled it from the box and he came up with a thin ribbon of ripped tissue between thumb and forefinger. He looked at it, surprised, and went right into his best Alexander Portnoy tone and said "Look at this, Doctor! Even the goddamned Kleenex lets me down!" We laughed for a long time, alternately looking at each other and looking away. There was a lot of contact and intimacy as our glances met (which may be why we could not stay with each other very long at a time). There was, again, a kind of gallows humor in which we both recognized a common, human, painful situation and enjoyed mastery over it through humor.

To summarize briefly, in psychotherapy some humor is degrading and psychonoxious, some defensive, and some wasteful and distracting. Much, however, is helpful and liberating. Specifically it can be used to move clients to deeper (or lighter) levels of feeling-expression, to increase insight and make it more impactful, and to deepen the relationship between client and therapist by emphasizing their common humanity.

REFERENCE

Kubie, L. S. (1971). The destructive potential of humor in psychotherapy. *American Journal of Psychiatry* 127(7):861–866.

Treating Those Who Fail to Take Themselves Seriously: Pathological Aspects of Humor

Ned N. Marcus

Patients not infrequently use humor as a means of trivializing the serious import of material they bring to mind in the course of psychotherapy. Because finding things funny is by its very nature pleasurable and because its adaptive value is so often evident, not only patients, but researchers and clinicians have failed to focus sufficiently on the phenomena of being amused (Chapman and Foot 1976). Significant pathology associated with the employment of humor as a psychological defense has escaped the scrutiny it deserves.

Alluded to by Allport (1960) as the *tenderness taboo*, the professional reluctance to analyze good feelings and risk spoiling the patient's fun may occasionally bring progress in therapy to a halt. Such an impasse is not likely to occur, if therapists (1) regularly make use of patients' nonverbal expressive behavior during sessions and (2) adhere to the guiding principle that affect is intimately linked to and modified by specific cognitions that, when irrational, can be corrected.

"LINKAGE" OF THOUGHT AND FEELING

It is easy to demonstrate that beliefs or cognitions of a specific type are invariably linked to certain kinds of emotional experiences. For example, grief is sustained by the conviction that one has lost something of value; anxiety, by the idea that one is likely to be subject to an intolerable event. Hence, it does not seem overly speculative to assume that a specific belief system or network of cognitions might also be associated with being amused.

Beck and colleagues (1979) noted that the "automatic thoughts" associated with pathological feelings are often initially outside the patient's own awareness. Nonetheless, they can frequently be made conscious, most especially when patients undergo relatively intense emotional reactions.

DEALING WITH SALIENT SMILING AND LAUGHTER: A NEW COGNITIVE STRATEGY

During sessions it is not necessary for patients to tell therapists when an affective outburst is occurring. Affect is convincingly communicated nonverbally (Marcus 1985). Even if a patient denies any subjective awareness of his manifest affect, should he be laughing he will have a hard time convincing the therapist that nothing funny is going on. This is because in those instances when there is a discrepancy between what a person says he is feeling and how he "looks," the observer tends to discount the verbal communication (Mehrablan 1972). Hence, by making people aware of how they "seem to be emoting" and what its significance to others might be, therapists can guide patients to understand why others sometimes see them differently than they see themselves.

Should dysfunctional or nonadaptive thinking accessed in this manner be connected with or responsible for an individual's peculiar sense of humor, once determined, such thinking could be modified and made more reasonable. In so doing, feelings and, by extension, behavior would be altered therapeutically, as well.

The following vignettes are presented to clarify more precisely the technique suggested in the above discussion. In particular, they are meant to demonstrate how therapists can successfully intervene when dealing with patients who, whether intentionally or not, appear to be treating problems, pathology, and sometimes even the entire therapeutic process as if it were "all one big joke."

Case 1

Milton P. came regularly late to sessions. When questioned about his lack of punctuality, he first responded by saying he had no feelings or thoughts whatsoever about his repeated belated arrivals.

However, after the therapist mentioned that the patient had been chuckling to himself while answering the therapist, M.P. admitted that he had, indeed, been amused.

In this instance, in spite of himself, in spite of what he was saying, the patient could not stop himself from thinking that he was a "liar" and that he really "got a big kick out of making people wait."

M.P. was encouraged to consider whether having contradictory thoughts about oneself was all "that absurd." Having stopped smiling, he integrated the insight that it was not that unusual to be "of-two-completely-different-minds" about something. Also the "somewhat wild" implications of his "ego-alien" ideation were on second thought, more meaningful than he had originally believed.

Even though he "mostly wanted to do the right thing," a "little part of himself" really did enjoy his seeming incapacity to get anywhere at the appointed time. Perhaps he had been "jumping to conclusions" about how he had "no feelings" or "certainly no good feelings" about his general lack of success in doing what he was supposed to do. He could now see that his "failure" to come on time might represent the actualization of what had been an unconscious wish to be unconventional. Perhaps he had been proclaiming that he was free "to do any 'impolite' thing he wanted." He ended the session, remarking about his feeling less "pressured" than he had for a very long time.

Case 2

Frank M., an elderly retired executive, appeared to have become morbidly preoccupied with death and dying after having suffered a myocardial infarction. His internist referred him to a psychiatrist.

In the first couple of sessions the patient described how "silly" it was for him to keep thinking of "jumping out the window." He explained that he did not take himself very "seriously" and smiled as he repeatedly assured his psychiatrist that he had never done and never would do anything to hurt himself. It was his evident "love of life" that made this kind of "sick joke" so ridiculous.

F.M. had already revealed, however, that his heart attack had undermined his sense of control. Thus, in spite of his constant smiling, he had been left with a brooding sense of impotence which he "just couldn't get rid of." This was especially disturbing as he had always been a person "who had been in charge of everything."

The psychiatrist ultimately got F.M. to realize that what he saw as his black humor was not as silly as he imagined. Thinking the way he did had certain important advantages of which he was not yet aware. Also, "even though he might find this difficult to believe," his so-called pseudo-suicidal ideation, on some level, represented an internal scenario he very much wanted to entertain! This would explain the repetitive nature of his ideation.

The psychiatrist intimated that, when properly understood, F.M. could even take some genuine pride in "thinking the unthinkable!"

To begin with, the psychiatrist told F.M. that the repetitive thought of jumping out the window could be viewed as a manifestation of the importance F.M. had always placed on considering all options. Insofar as the suicidal ideation did represent an escape, albeit only in fantasy, it could be viewed as a "fantastic strategy" by means of which F.M. gained some control over when and how he would die—a dilemma associated with his life-threatening cardiac condition.

F.M. was finally able to formulate himself a more rational response; that thinking about jumping out of the window was not only a means whereby he was able to imagine he was in control of when he died; it was, more importantly, a strategy that allowed him to exercise more control over himself in order to live longer. Conjuring up the fantasy was precisely the way he clung to life. Others might carry out "unreflective crazy behavior" because they "didn't think before they acted." Thinking about jumping out the window naturally included a consideration of the consequences, and these consequences, insofar as they were irreversible were now recognized by F.M. as possible, but totally unacceptable.

F.M.'s smiling was now much diminished. The patient had stopped ruminating so much about the whole subject of life and death, having proved to himself that he could "handle it." He agreed that his sense of self-efficacy had been much enhanced.

FOCUSING ON SMILING AND LAUGHTER

Kris (1952) a classical analyst who wrote over forty years ago, felt that should patients fail to mention any thoughts connected with their smiling and laughter, it might be reasonable to altogether exclude consideration of such nonverbal expressive behavior (NEB). He argued that the analyst would otherwise be inadvertently encouraging the analysand to favor a regressive or primitive form of communication that would necessarily prove to be an impediment in achieving a more complete and definitive analysis of the analysand's psyche.

There are dangers connected with being excessively interested in or impressed by NEB. Overvaluing the nonverbal can lead to a mindless "therapy of the heart." In these instances patient and therapist may be reduced to merrily smiling and laughing at each other, but doing little real work. Although it cannot be denied that such an approach may be occasionally effective at certain junctures in the therapy, if the therapist cannot see his way beyond such an existential, phenomenological empathic exercise, his success in effecting a more complete cure is likely to be a good deal more modest than it needs to be.

By making any type of NEB explicit, the danger mentioned above can be greatly minimized. Admittedly, nonverbal affective presentations are less capable of being translated into words than thinking and, hence, are necessarily somewhat ambiguous. The therapist, therefore, does not tell the laughing or smiling patient "how he feels," but rather "how it *looks* to the therapist that the patient might be feeling." The spirit in which the inference is proffered may be most important.

Depicting affect representationally, that is, linking it not only with the correct words, but with any words at all, aids patients in fashioning a cognitive structure of that affect. This, in itself, transforms and further refines the entire affective experience, making it more mature and adaptive (Lane and Schwartz 1987).

Also, although both cases presented in this article evidenced some pathology connected with their NEB, laughing and smiling are not necessarily pathological. The very opposite is true. As Haig (1986) has indicated, humor always has both constructive and destructive features. It is just that the admixture of the two only becomes fully apparent after one examines the extent to which those thoughts most intimately linked to the NEB in question are reasonable or dysfunctional.

Before considering what the immediate thoughts linked with feeling amused are, let us consider the manner with which the therapist broaches the subject.

M.P., the first patient presented, had regularly denied experiencing any pleasure connected with his characteristic tardiness. F.M., in the light of his concern over his medical status, passed his smiling off as "just plain silliness." Although it is impermissible to deny that the patient is the final arbiter of what he is feeling, it is still reasonable for the therapist to assume that an incongruent affective display reflects "potential feeling," not as fully repressed as would be the case were there no incongruent nonverbal affective cues at all.

The reason patients sometimes fail to experience the feeling usually associated with their NEB has to do with being more attuned to their internally subjective mind set: when the external and the internal are discordant they see the internal as "real" (in a manner diametrically opposed to the perspective of the observer).

Although this was not true of the two patients presented in this paper, there are occasions when patients interpret the nonverbal affective display as simply a defensive facade and nothing more. They may insist, for example, that their smiling just represents a feeble attempt to either hide their true feelings from themselves and others or, more radically, that it actually stands for or is the equivalent of another internally experienced emotion. Hence, it is not uncommon for people to say, "I always smile when I am nervous or embarrassed," implying that this constitutes a fully adequate explanation of their facial expression.

LAUGHTER, SMILING, AND HUMOR AS DEFENSE

In addition to tempering anxiety (nervous laughter), or covering up hostility (turning it into sarcasm or a form of teasing [Greenson 1977]), humor also can attenuate depression (laughing through one's tears). Nonetheless, we may be too quick to assume that we understand everything there is to know about humor, perceiving that it is a tendentious strategy that permits us to distract ourselves from or modify some other less tolerable affective state.

Observable affect is most parsimoniously conceptualized, not as defense, but first and foremost, as the external signifier of a given "emotion" with which it is congruent.

Even though the comic may sometimes screen the tragic, the two are not synonymous. Once patients accept this, they are then in a position to confirm that, in addition to whatever else they may be feeling, their laughter signifies that they are amused.

A factor that facilitates defensiveness about one's laughing and smiling is that frequently it is not entirely apparent why something is funny in the first place. Not knowing makes it easier to rationalize.

The Amusing Situation or Joke

It can be readily understood how an individual in a dangerous circumstance might imagine he will be injured and, therefore, feel anxious or how a person who suffers a loss might, in recognizing this, feel sad. However, it is not as clear what reality factors predispose a person to laugh or smile. This is because one of these factors is the degree to which that reality has embedded within it subliminal cues that suggest an initially hidden dialectic.

The amusing situation or joke constitutes a complicated circumstance where conventionally moral, logical, or standard thinking is overtly reinforced while highly antithetical ideation and/or imagery is covertly suggested, thereby leading to the seemingly spontaneous emergence of ego-alien material into consciousness. Since this involves mental processing outside the awareness of the subject, analysis of such potentially confusing material is best handled in a highly methodical fashion.

The Basic Cognitive Transaction

All events, regardless of whether they are conceptualized as occurring within or outside of the human mind, can be dealt with in psychotherapy by adhering to the format of a particular five-step approach derived from Beck's Daily Record of Dysfunctional Thoughts.

Step I: Delineating the Given

It is obvious that very frequently people do not find the same witticsm or potentially humorous life situation amusing. A person will not "get the joke" if antithetical intrapsychic imagery, for whatever reason, is not spontaneously brought to mind. Discovering what this intrapsychic imagery or ideation is delineates the given.

In the case of M.P., although coming late was the potentially humorous life situation, it was the outrageous, highly antithetical, true idea of "getting a kick out of being late" that constituted the given triggering M.P.'s humorous response.

In the case of F.M., his illness could be taken as the potentially humorous life situation that provoked the spontaneous morbid ideation, that is, the "pseudosuicidal" imagery or black humor. It was these "silly" ideas that directly provoked his rather constant smiling.

It should be noted that in both instances the life situation need not be one that most people would find humorous or much of a joke.

Step II: Eliciting the Feeling

The therapist should keep in mind that even if highly antithetical or ego-alien ideation does come to mind, unless one entertains certain highly specific cognitions, one will still not be amused. This observation is perfectly consonant with another central cognitive tenet: it is not the event or given that most immediately determines or is linked to the affective response, but rather what one thinks about what has occurred.

Assuming that someone admits to being tickled by a joke or funny situation, having elicited a feeling (that is, having completed step II) the therapist is then in a position to ask what those cognitive determinants or automatic thoughts most immediately associated with the cited state of amusement are.

Step III: Determining the Automatic Thoughts

If a person is to feel amused, the conjectured antithetical ideation must excite three kinds of cognitions. The denial or absence of any one part of this network of beliefs will be associated with emotional states at variance with that of finding something funny.

Freud (1905) felt that the release of energy in laughter was due to an economy of effort reflecting the rapid processing of an idea by the unconscious. Freud, seminal thinker that he was, hit upon an important truth. The effortless manner in which the amused individual experiences his deviant ideation is due to his being unconscious of how this ideation has been suggested to him, that is, the manner in which the stimulus has been processed or worked over to come up with the antithetical ideational "product."

Irresponsibility (Unaccountability).   The first cognitive schema or attitude that amused persons need to entertain about the humorous "given" is an insistence that it is ego-alien. Because the antithetical ideation really has been engineered by their minds outside of their own awareness, these individuals convince themselves that it is something for which they bear no responsibility.

M.P. generally had a very conventional critical view of coming late. He had, in fact, repeated on many occasions that people were supposed to come on time. He had no idea when chuckling that therapeutic permissiveness implicitly encouraged him to articulate his wish to be unconventional. Hence, he did not at all understand how he could be held responsible for his grossly narcissistic musing about his lateness.

F.M. also was mystified by the recurrent imagery of his throwing himself out the window. It had nothing to do with his conventionally life-affirming philosophy. He almost felt as if the antithetical imagery had been visited upon him from without.

Incongruity.   Nerhardt (1976) has convincingly argued that an appreciation of incongruity is another significant component of humor. Should people not be struck by the incongruous nature of the antithetical intrapsychic event, that is, should they not believe that the spontaneous ideation is outrageous in respect to their usual train of thoughts, they will, most likely, find their ego-alien thinking boring or burdensome.

In respect to the clinical examples, as already suggested, both M.P. and F.M. were convinced that whatever "popped into their minds" was absurdly deviant and nothing like their usual way of thinking about either tardiness or suicide, respectively.

Inconsequentiality. Rothbart (1973) demonstrated that children only laugh and smile when aroused by funny provocative situations that they judge to be safe. The idea of fun or inconsequentiality is the third component.

If, in either of the cases presented, the patients had seen their spontaneous, incongruous ideation as consequential they would not have been laughing and smiling. Left to their own devices they would have most probably been very uncomfortable. The trivialization of the antithetical imagery allowed them to escape these troubling emotions and accounts for the defensive aspect of humor that has already been discussed.

As demonstrated, the patients also defended against understanding the positive implications of their unconventional thinking because they then might have been seduced into more destructive acting-out of the ideation.

Clinical Relevancy of Increased Understanding of the Humorous Response

If a therapist knows in advance what assumptions or beliefs are likely to be associated with any particular affect that has been elicited, he is forearmed when confronting the patient's most predictable resistances.

Foreknowledge of schemata associated with finding something funny is particularly useful. This is because the therapist cannot rely on those who are feeling amused to be able to readily "articulate their automatic thoughts" (Step III). Unless they are extremely insightful, explanations tend to be inchoate due to the fact that, as stated, the humorous response is one that necessarily involves a significant participation of mental processing outside the individual's own awareness.

Step IV: Formulation of a Rational Response

The question the therapist ultimately gets amused patients to consider is the degree to which their spontaneous ideation is truly incongruous and inconsequential.

M.P., after reflecting only a few minutes, realized that the idea of his enjoying coming late was not that ego-alien or unusual. Once he hit upon the truism that a person need not be consistent, he was then also able to confirm that he wanted to be impolite and that this was not an idea that sprang to mind without any participation on his part.

M.P. also ultimately understood that this small bit of behavior was not inconsequential, but that it had an important symbolic meaning pertaining to the actualization of his wish and right to be free.

Similarly F.M. discovered that his entertaining pseudosuicidal ideation was consonant with a habit he had as an executive of exploring all possibilities, and working through a variety of very different scenarios in his mind. F. M. had hit upon a cost-efficient way of considering alternatives that was neither incongruous nor grossly absurd.

Step V: Making the Outcome Explicit

In the process of correcting their network of beliefs, M.P. and F.M. began to smile and laugh less. They both became more seriously hopeful. In fact their affective display of amusement, once made explicit and, therefore, no longer somewhat dissociated was almost immediately tempered by internal states of guilt and impotency, which were, themselves, reciprocally lightened by the patients' now more fully integrated sense of humor.

Making a state of being amused explicit and analyzing it leads not necessarily to its elimination but rather to a healthier sense of humor. This is because "many a truth is said in jest." The process of forever emancipating ourselves from the tyranny of conventional thinking by integrating spontaneous ideation that originally seems absurd is what links humor and creativity (Hilgard and Atkinson (1967).

Other matters that have a bearing on humor in psychotherapy were not touched upon in this paper. They have to do with the social aspect of laughing and smiling. As with many forms of nonverbal expressive behavior, particularly yawning (Marcus 1973), laughing and smiling are highly contagious. This was not discussed, as the paper focused primarily on techniques connected with directly modifying dysfunctional thoughts.

Shared smiling and laughter can be an important nonspecific aspect of cure. (The therapist's laughing and smiling as a psychotherapeutic stratagem is beyond the scope of this paper.)

Let it simply be said that insofar as a therapist is indulging in a pathologically humorous attitude reflecting his own dysfunctional thinking, one might be strongly suspicious of a therapist's joking during sessions (Kubie 1971). Conversely, recognizing that humor, laughter, and smiling can also be highly adaptive, it would be wrong to deprive certain patients of a modeling experience that teaches them one more way of surviving in the face of life's vicissitudes.

SUMMARY

A method of analyzing humor was presented. Patients are first made aware of their being amused by bringing their smiling and laughing to their attention. They can be then be led to see that their external life situation has predisposed them to experience an intrapsychic event—the spontaneous emergence of antithetical ideation into consciousness—which has, in turn, given rise to three beliefs: (1) the irresponsibility, (2) the incongruity, and (3) the inconsequentiality of the production and nature of this ideation.

Two patients were presented to illustrate how foreknowledge of the three beliefs could aid the therapist in working through what might otherwise have been intractable pathology.

The author is generally in favor of a more relaxed attitude about the use of humor and nonverbal expressive behavior, but urges that this material be integrated within the framework of a structured cognitive approach.

REFERENCES

Allport, G. W. (1960). *The Individual and His Religion*. New York: Macmillan.

Beck, A. T., Rush, A. J., Shaw, B. F., and Emory, G. (1979). *Cognitive Therapy of Depression*. New York: Guilford.

Chapman, A. J., and Foot, H. C. (1976). Introduction. In *Humor and Laughter: Theory, Research and Applications*. London: Wiley.

Freud, S. (1905). Jokes and their relation to the unconscious. *Standard Edition* 8.

Greenson, R. (1977). *Technique and Practice of Psychoanalysis*. New York: International Universities Press.

Haig, R. A. (1986). Therapeutic uses of humor. *American Journal of Psychotherapy* 40:543–553.

Hilgard, E. R., and Atkinson, R. C. (1967). *Introduction to Psychology*, 4th ed. New York: Harcourt Brace.

Kris, E. (1952). *Psychoanalytic Exploration in Art*, pp. 217–239. New York: International Universities Press.

Kubie, L. (1971). The destructive potential of humor in psychotherapy. *American Journal of Psychiatry* 128:861–866.

Lane, R. D., and Schwartz, G. E. (1987). Levels of emotional awareness: a cognitive developmental theory and its applications to psychopathology. *American Journal of Psychiatry* 144:133–143.

Marcus, N. (1973). Yawning: analytic and therapeutic implications. *Child Psychotherapy* 2:406–418.

_____ (1985). Utilization of nonverbal communication in cognitive therapy *American Journal of Psychotherapy* 39:467–478.

Mehrabian, A. (1972). *Nonverbal Communication*. Chicago: Aldine Atherton.

Nerhardt, G. (1976). Incongruity and funniness: towards a new descriptive model. In *Humor and Laughter: Theory, Research, and Application*, ed. A. J. Chapman, and H. C. Foot. London: Wiley.

Rothbart, M. K. (1973) Laughter in young children. *Psychological Bulletin* 80:247–256.

Humor in Psychiatric Healing

Bernard Saper

Like some good news–bad news joke, the value of using humor in healing, particularly as the treatment of choice, remains inconclusive. The aphorism that "laughter is the best medicine" is herein examined in the light of reason, experience, and more or less empirical research and limited scholarship. Specifically, three drops in the shower of sometimes extravagant claims regarding its benefits are rather cursorily reviewed: first, the extent to which the positive emotions of joy and laughter influence the physiological components of health and illness such as the immune, respiratory, cardiovascular, and neuroendocrine systems; second, individual differences in the personalities of both the patient and therapist that may or may not enhance the efficacy of humor in the treatment of mental or physical disorders; and third, the wisdom and utility of incorporating humor into the psychotherapeutic aramentarium.

HUMOR AND PHYSIOLOGY

Much has been said of the positive effects of mirthful laughter on human physiology (Godkewitsch 1976, Langewin and Day 1972, Levi 1965, McGhee 1983). One of the most vigorous proponents of this view has been Fry (1977, 1979, Fry and Stoft 1971) who for a score of years has studied its effects on heart rate, oxygen saturation levels of peripheral blood, respiratory phenomena, and so forth. He found that both the arousal and cathartic effects of humor in psychological terms are paralleled in the physiological processes. Moreover, laughter, in contrast to other emotions, involves extensive physical (motor) activity, and thus the results are comparable to that of physical exercise. According to Fry, laughter increases breathing activity and oxygen exchange, increases muscular activity and heart rate, and stimulates the cardiovascular system, the sympathetic nervous system, and the production of catecholamines like epinephrine—all of which in turn stimulate the production in the brain of endorphins, the body's natural pain-reducing enzymes.

The value of exercise in health and fitness has been reasonably documented. But the benefit of joyous laughter in producing physical well-being—especially in the alleged prevention or alleviation of heart disease, cerebrovascular accidents, cancer, depression, and various stress-related conditions that appear to follow such physiological upheaval—has yet to be supported by well-replicated, "clinical trials."

In a recent, well-executed, "good news" study, Dillon and her associates (1985) found that the concentration of salivary immunoglobulin A (IgA) increased significantly after subjects viewed a humorous videotape, but did not change significantly after they viewed a didactic videotape. While enhancement of IgA concentrations was obtained in subjects viewing humorous videotape, these levels declined within minutes after viewing. In the same study, subjects who on a questionnaire perceived themselves as using humor as a coping device more often than those who did not had significantly higher IgA concentrations prior to watching either the humor or didactic tapes. One implication here was that although viewing a humorous videotape may enhance immunity, the effect appears to be short-lived. Nonetheless, longer term effects might be realized by incorporating humor as an ongoing coping style in everyday life. This empirical study suggests that one explanation of the mechanism by which positive emotion may influence disease prevention and cure may be found in its enhancement of the immune system.

But, needless to say, the immune system is enormously complex. Measures of immunological functioning are manifold and include the ability of lymphocytes to kill invading cells (lymphocyte cytotoxicity), the ability of lymphocytes to reproduce when stimulated artificially by a chemical (mitogen), the ability of the lymphocytes to produce antibodies, the ratio of suppressor and helper T cells, the ability of the white cells to ingest foreign particles (phagocytotic activity), and others. Because this system involves so many different types of cell and plasma components, there is a wide variety of potential measures of immunological functioning, not all of which will necessarily relate well to one another. One indicator of immunological functioning may show an effect, whereas another may not.

Borysenko (1987), in an overview of the "complex and sometimes controversial field of psychoneuroimmunology," has concluded with cautious optimism that "we are beginning to understand how [the bidirectional interaction among the immune, nervous, and psychosocial systems] can either set the stage for disease or enhance the prospects of health."

Some other alternative psychophysical procedures—for example, simple relaxation training—can enhance cellular immune function as well or better than laughter. In one study (Ornstein and Sobel 1987), 45 geriatric residents of an independent living facility were taught progressive relaxation and guided imagery techniques three times a week for one month. Relaxation was presented to these residents as a way to gain some control over their world. By the end of the training period the group showed a significant increase in natural killer cell activity compared to a control group and a group that merely had "social contact" visits from a college student. The relaxation group also showed significant decreases in antibodies to herpes simplex virus, possibly because the herpes virus was being controlled better by the immune system. These relaxation-induced improvements in immune function were accompanied by self-reports of less psychological distress.

It may be concluded that a few small but persuasive research studies reveal the good news that laughter *can* enhance the immune, respiratory, cardiovascular, and neuroendocrine systems. The bad news, however, is that a number of other nonhumorous procedures such as medications, relaxation, meditation, exercise, contingency management, diet, systematic desensitization, and power gratification can also achieve the same results. Clearly, many more careful investigations need to be done in order to definitively and scientifically demonstrate the psychophysiological mechanisms by which positive emotions influence biochemistry and physiology, and the role of these processes and mechanisms in healing mental and/or physical illness.

INDIVIDUAL DIFFERENCES AND HEALING

The position that humor can be directly or indirectly effective in promoting health and treating illness has been taken by a number of health professionals, most notably by Fry (1963), Goldstein (1982), Peter and Dana (1982), Robinson (1977, 1983), and Walsh (1928), as well as by noted nonprofessionals such as Norman Cousins (1979). Even more advocates

can be found among mental health professionals, whose views are discussed in the next section.

Indeed, the past decade and a half has witnessed an astonishing
bandwagon effect, in which numerous popular and scientific–professional
books, articles, seminars, workshops, and clinics have promoted the
time-honored notion that humor and laughter and similar positive attitudes
and behaviors are good for what ails you. In a segment (May 17, 1987) of
the CBS "60 Minutes" program, Diane Sawyer presented a strong endorse-
ment of this view. She described the operations of the "wellness" center or
community located in California, which was founded by layman Harold
Benjamin and makes available gratis an opportunity for patients, many of
whom are terminally afflicted with such diseases as cancer, to come
together and "laugh it up" as an adjunct to other types of treatment. In the
same program she interviewed Dr. Lee Burke at Loma Linda University
who has been studying the "psycho-neural-immunology" of disease,
claiming that, if nothing else, these positive feelings can definitely improve
the quality of the patient's life.

But the use of humor is a tricky enterprise. Individual differences in
both the patient and the humor-wielding health professional are bound to
qualify the results. As has already been discussed, differences in the
physical or physiological conditions, the severity of the illness, and the
sociocultural status of patients can easily alter the efficacy of the mirthful
intervention. Similarly, patients with the same illness may have different
personalities, temperaments, coping styles, and appreciations of humor.
Moreover, the therapist—internist, nurse, psychiatrist, clinical psychologist, or social worker—may not be sufficiently adept at wielding humor as
a crucial component of treatment.

Psychologically, positive emotions tend to provide a sense of confidence, a lightened coping style in the face of stress and adversity, a
technique for combating helplessness and hopelessness, and a device for
letting off the steam of pent-up emotions. On the other hand, the notion
that mood, mental state, or personality can promote good health or cause
physical illness has been seriously questioned (Angell 1985).

Aside from the fact that patients may be too gravely ill—too much
in pain, too concerned about dying, too intensely in anguish—to be dealt
with humorously, it must be constantly kept in mind that people
respond differently to humorous stimuli and situations. In addition to
individual differences in sense of humor, there are gender, age, class, and
ethnic differences.

Ziv (1984), for example, has hypothesized that different types of
personality may prefer different types of humor. Health professionals who
set out to use humor even adjunctively in treatment would be well advised
to know themselves, as well as their clients, as thoroughly as possible.

Ziv postulated four personality types that might describe the variety of health professionals as well as clients. The *emotional extroverts* appear as touchy, restless, angry, aggressive, excitable (recognize type A behaviors?), as well as impulsive, active, and changeable (recognize type T—thrill-seeking—behaviors?). Such choleric individuals are apt to be seen as emergency patients in the cardiologist's or surgeon's office. They would rarely be seen for emotional disturbances. According to Ziv, they probably would find aggressive humor most funny.

The *stable extroverts* display sanguine behaviors that might describe a role model for either the patient or the therapist: sociable, outgoing, responsive, easygoing, lively, and carefree. These people would probably laugh most heartily at interpersonal jokes.

The *stable introverts* are rather phlegmatic: passive, careful, inhibited, reflective, controlled. These individuals could seek psychotherapy for self-realization or self-actualization. They tend to have the feeling that life is one grand party to which they were not invited. Intellectual humor would be most likely to get a laugh from them.

The *emotional introverts* would be considered the most typical of the kind of individuals who seek psychiatric help. They are moody, pessimistic, unsociable, anxious, rigid, and cheerless. These melancholic persons would appear to derive less enjoyment from humor than any of the other types of personality in Ziv's scheme. To put it another way, they are the kind of people who have to be pushed into temptation, and once there they do not enjoy it anyway.

Just about all humor-using health professionals have taken pains to warn us that regardless of individual differences, humor that humiliates, deprecates, or undermines self-esteem, intelligence, or well-being is *never* proper. Unfortunately, therapists are too often adept at rationalizing their mirthful inputs as potentially beneficial to the patient.

Goodman (1983) distinguishes between laughing "with" and laughing "at." The former can be used for constructive purposes, and includes "going for the jocular (rather than the jugular) vein . . . based on caring and empathy, . . . builds confidence, . . . is supportive," (p. 11). His numerous recommendations, while they are delightfully amusing and appear "therapeutic" on an intuitive basis, are in need of scientific validation.

The question that needs to be asked: Is the clinic, hospital, or psychotherapy office the best or even proper place in which to introduce humor?

Would humor be better provided outside of the formal treatment situation, in perhaps more popular, efficient, and immensely cheaper places and forms? How much better, if at all, is seeing a zany movie like *Beyond Therapy* or tuning in Dr. Ruth or Dr. Art Ulene of the "Today

Show" or reading *The Laughter Prescription* by Peter and Dana (1982), or regularly viewing funny movies (as did Cousins) or situation comedies like "Night Court," or partaking" of a Dial-a-joke, or attending a three-day workshop on putting "smileage" into our lives, conducted by humor salesman Joel Goodman (1983)? Should an internist, surgeon, or psychiatrist be required to train in the comic arts before they undertake to apply humor?

In a word, the bad news is that more and better empirical research is needed in behavioral or holistic medicine to determine under what conditions positive emotions such as humor and laughter work best, if at all, with what types of patients, what severity of illness, and what kinds of jokes.

Responding to a query of an ex–medical student of his about a new "wonder" drug that had come on the market, the sage old professor advised: "Prescribe it for as many patients as you can as often and quickly as you can, before it is proved to be worthless."

HUMOR AND PSYCHOTHERAPY

Although, as in the case of medical treatment, very little systematic empirical research is available to support conclusively the contention that humor in, as, or with psychotherapy is beneficial, the past 15 years or so have witnessed a burgeoning advocacy of its use. Nonetheless, deliberately bringing together humor and psychotherapy is not without its risks (Kubie 1971, Kuhlman 1984, Mindess 1976, Salameh 1983, Saper 1987). As in the case of copulating porcupines, such a marriage should be consummated very, very carefully.

But first the good news. "Provocative therapy," identified as a humor-applied variant of the client-centered approach was developed by Farrelly and his associates (Farrelly and Matthews 1981). As the name implies, the therapist tries to be provocative and self-disclosing. Humor plays a central role in this therapy. Among the techniques used by the therapist are exaggeration, mimicry, ridicule, distortion, sarcasm, irony, and jokes. These presumably help to amplify clients' maladaptive behaviors while simultaneously expressing their worst thoughts and fears about themselves. These tactics deprive clients of their usual defensive ploys.

Another humor-based psychotherapeutic approach is O'Connell's (1981) "natural high therapy." This therapy uses psychodramatic and empty-chair techniques, role playing by both client and therapist, dialogue with significant others, guided imagery, exercises to develop optimism, and meditation techniques using breath-focusing and contemplation.

Humor is incorporated into these procedures because it is "the royal road" toward actualization. O'Connell has conducted workshops and has developed a therapeutic technique, called "humordrama."

A growing number of therapists have reported using humor in their practice when they deem it appropriate. Among the better known is Ellis (1977), who in his rational-emotive therapy employs absurdity and humor including puns, sarcasm witticisms, and shocking language as one of his "disputing interventions" to challenge the clients' false and irrational belief systems. He believes that human disturbance largely consists of exaggerating the significance or seriousness of things. The ripping up of such exaggerations by humorous counterexaggeration is one of the main methods of his therapeutic attack. Lamb (1980), within the frame-work of logotherapy, employs a technique called "paradoxical intervention" in which clients are encouraged to exaggerate their symptoms to the point of absurdity. He claims that this develops their ability to laugh at their neurotic maneuvers, which in turn permits divestment and extinction of symptoms.

Greenwald (1975) focuses on the clients' ridiculous life decisions, and by mirroring or exaggerating their maladaptive behavior, they are provided a chance to explore new and perhaps better choices. Grotjahn (1971a, b) makes jokes, thereby signaling that his clients in psychoanalysis may adopt a similar emotional freedom.

Mindess (1971, 1976) is probably the chief exponent and most efficient practitioner of the careful and judicious use of humor in psychotherapy. He has employed apt jokes, situationally generated wit, teasing, and kidding—naturally introduced. He believes that the therapist—if a basically funny person, prone to wit, flippancy, and clowning—can serve as a model. Such "fun" presumably frees the client to emulate the therapist. Indeed, such a sense of humor could also save a therapist from making a pompous ass of himself.

A number of other therapists have also reported the successful use of humor in behavior therapy (Ventis 1973, 1980), in counterconditioning (Smith 1973), and in self-management (Lamb 1980).

Corey (1986) has reported that Adlerian therapists often employ humor in their therapy. He himself subscribes to this position, stating that:

> Although therapy is a responsible matter, it need not be deadly serious. Both clients and counselors can enrich a relationship by laughing. I have found that humor and tragedy are closely linked and that, after allowing ourselves to feel some experiences that are painfully tragic, we can also genuinely laugh at how seriously we have taken our situation. . . . The important point is that therapists recognize that laughter or humor does not mean that work is not being accomplished. There are times, of course,

when laughter is used to cover up anxiety or to escape from the experience of facing threatening material. The therapist needs to distinguish between humor that distracts and humor that enhances the situation. [p. 380]

A balanced discussion of humor and psychotherapy is provided by Kuhlman (1984), who does not appear to have as big a good-news axe to grind as Farrelly, O'Connell, Ellis, Mindess, Greenwald, and others. The premise upon which Kuhlman's book is based is that humor in psychotherapy has short-term and long-term effects that can be distinguished. The short-term effects are signaled by tension reduction, mirth, and other emotional responses that are the immediate consequences of any effective humor.

As was suggested in the previous section, different forms of humor serve different functions depending on the different components of the therapeutic process into which it is introduced.

Even without adducing the rather meager and bleak results of careful empirical research on outcome, conducted over the past decade and a half (cf. an extended discussion in Saper 1987), a number of practitioners and theorists have been warning us about the dangers of employing humor in psychotherapy. Kubie (1971) has been one of the most vehement in pointing up its destructive potential. He insists, not without good reason, that humor can mask hostility. The patient may perceive the therapists' humor as heartless and cruel. In psychoanalytic treatment, the patient may be diverted from free associating productively. The patient may get to wondering if the therapist is really serious or merely joking. If the patient uses humor as a defense, the therapist who uses humor might inadvertently reinforce the defense. The patient is essentially a captive audience, and the therapist may be self-aggrandizingly parading his wit. If the patient happened to be a victim of cruel joking in early life, the use of humor could serve to hinder progress in therapy. Patients may resent the fact that the therapist is lighthearted in the face of their suffering. Humor could undermine the therapist's leverage of objectivity. And, finally, Kubie insists that beginning and inexperienced therapists really do not know how to handle humor properly.

A similar dissenting opinion was given by Parry (1975), who warned that joking may be appropriate in education, when it could be used to emphasize a point. Jokes, however, are never appropriate in psychotherapy. The therapist should not joke with clients nor respond to jokes made to them. If the client accuses the therapist of being cold and humorless, such a statement could express some negative transference feelings. If a client presents a serious problem in the form of a joke, the therapist should always examine such a communication in the light of "true words are often spoken in jest."

More moderate and balanced views have been taken by others. Mindess and Turk (1984) have suggested a ranking procedure to maximize the abuses of humor. The worst approach they feel is to *plant* a joke that is contrived, forced, and inappropriately pulled into therapy from nowhere without adequately preparing the client. A somewhat better technique would be teasing or kidding the client naturally in a context of sufficient rapport and trust. This method may initially provide a double take followed by laughter or (if done improperly in an atmosphere of mistrust) by anger. The best technique is for the therapist to provide a role model for the client, letting the good humor spill over, as it were, into the therapeutic transaction.

Salameh (1983), in an excellent even-handed summary of the status of the "alliance" between humor and therapy as reflected in the current theories and existing research, has presented a promising system for rating the levels of therapist humor. This five-point Humor Rating Scale, which appears to have methodological significance and research potential, rates the therapists' input in the following terms: destructive humor, harmful humor, minimally helpful humor, very helpful humor, and outstandingly helpful humor. Salameh also lists a dozen "therapeutic humor techniques," with definitions and examples, which also may prove useful in future research.

According to him, therapeutic humor has an educative, corrective message; promotes cognitive-emotional equilibrium; attacks behaviors while affirming the essential worth of the client; and acts as an "interpersonal lubricant." On the other hand, harmful humor exacerbates the client's problems, thwarts cognitive-emotional equilibrium, undermines personal worth, and leaves a deleterious "bitter aftertaste."

Salameh has pulled together the more useful techniques into a list, including definitions and examples, as follows: "surprise, exaggeration, absurdity, the human condition, incongruity, confrontation/affirmation humor, work play, metaphorical mirth, impersonation, relativizing, the tragi-comic twist, and bodily humor."

The bad news is that when the definitions, illustrations, and examples of Salameh's techniques were presented informally to clinical psychology students, psychotherapists, and other health and mental health professionals who attended the author's classes, seminars, and workshops they generated considerable debate regarding their suitability and funniness. Salameh himself admits to this problem of lack of agreement about what is funny and, more important, therapeutic.

In sum, the infusion of humor into psychotherapy is good news for some therapists (e.g., Ellis, Farrelly, Levine, O'Connell) but bad news for others (e.g., Kubie, Parry). The balanced views of a number of two-armed appraisers (e.g., Kuhlman, Mindess, Salameh) are acknowledged. Alas, psychotherapies are not automobiles, and are unfortunately never recalled because of defective parts. Indeed, the premature adoption of humor in psychotherapy may be unilaterally and partially gratifying—like premature ejaculation—but it could in the long run surely prove disastrous for the total enterprise.

REFERENCES

Angell, M. (1985). Disease as a reflection of the psyche. *New England Journal of Medicine* 312(24):1570–1572.

Averill, J. R. (1969). Autonomic response patterns during sadness and mirth. *Psychophysiology* 5:399–414.

Borysenko, M. (1987). The immune system: an overview. *Annals of Behavior Medicine* 9(2):3–10.

Borysenko, M., McClelland, D. C., Meyer, D., and Benson, H. (1983). Academic stress, power motivation, and decrease in secretion rate of salivary secretory immunoglobulin A. *The Lancet* 5:1400–1402.

Corey, G. (1986). *The Theory and Practice of Counseling and Psychotherapy*, 3rd ed. New York: Brooks/Cole.

Cousins, N. (1979). *Anatomy of an Illness*. New York: Norton.

Dillon, K. M., Minchoff, B., and Baker, K.H. (1985). Positive emotional states and the enhancement of the immune system. *International Journal of Psychiatry in Medicine* 15:13–17.

Ellis, A. (1977). Fun as psychotherapy. *Rational Living* 12:2–6.

Farrelly, F., and Matthews, S. (1981). Provocative therapy. In *Innovative Psychotherapies,* ed. R Corsini, pp. 678–693. New York: John Wiley.

Fry, W. F. Jr. (1963). *Sweet Madness: A Study of Humor*. Palo Alto, CA: Pacific Books.

——— (1977). The respiratory components of mirthful laughter. *Journal of Biological Psychology* 19(2):39–50(b).

——— (1979). Humor and the human cardiovascular system. In *The Study of Humor*, ed. H. Mindess, and J. Turek. Los Angeles: Antioch University.

Fry, W. F. Jr. and Stoft, P. E. (1971). Mirth and oxygen saturation levels or peripheral blood. *Psychotherapy and Psychosomatics* 19:76–84.

Godkewitsch, M. (1976). Physiological and verbal indices of arousal in rated humor. In *Humor and Laughter: Theory, Research, and Application*, ed. A. J. Chapman, and H.C. Foot. London: Wiley.

Goldstein, J. H. (1982). A laugh a day: Can mirth keep disease at bay? *The Sciences* 22:21–25.

Goodman, J. (1983). How to get more smileage out of your life: making sense of humor, then serving it. *Handbook of Humor Research* 2:1–22.

Greenwald, H. (1975). Humor in psychotherapy. *Journal of Contemporary Psychotherapy* 7:113–116.

Grotjahn, M. (1971a). Laughter in psychotherapy. In *A Celebration of Laughter*, ed. W. M. Mendel, pp. 61–66. Los Angeles: Mara Books.

_____ (1971b). Laughter in group psychotherapy. *International Journal of Group Psychotherapy* 12:234–238.

Kubie, L. S. (1971). The destructive potential of humor in psychotherapy. *American Journal of Psychiatry* 127:861–866.

Kuhlman, T. L. (1984). *Humor and Psychotherapy*. Homewood, IL: Dow-Jones-Irwin.

Lamb, C. S. (1980). The use of paradoxical intention: self-management through laughter. *Personnel and Guidance Journal* 59:217–219.

Langewin, R., and Day, H. I. (1972). Physiological correlates of humor. In *The Psychology of Humor*. ed. J. H. Goldstein, and P. E. McGhee. New York: Academic Press.

Levi, L. (1965). The urinary output of adrenalin and noradrenalin during pleasant and unpleasant emotional states. *Psychosomatics and Medicine* 27(1):80–85.

McClelland, D. C., Alexander, C., and Marks, E. (1982). The need for power, stress, immune function, and illness among male prisoners. *Journal of Abnormal Psychology* 91(1):61–70.

McGhee, P. E. (1983). The role of arousal and hemisphere lateralization in humor. In *Handbook of Humor Research*, vol. 1, ed. P. E. McGhee, and J. H. Goldstein, pp. 13–35. New York: Springer Verlag.

Mindess, H. (1971). *Laughter and Liberation*. Los Angeles: Nash.

_____ (1976). The use and abuse of humor in psychotherapy. In *Humor and Laughter: Theory, Research, and Applications*, ed. A. J. Chapman, and H. C. Foot, pp. 331–341. London: John Wiley.

Mindess, H., and Turk, J. (1984). Humor in psychotherapy. In *Abstracts, the Fourth International Congress on Humor*. Israel: University of Tel Aviv. p. 63.

O'Connell, W. E. (1981). Natural high therapy. *Innovative Psychotherapies*, ed. R. Corsini, pp. 554–568(b). New York: Wiley.

Ornstein, R., and Sobel, D. (1987). The healing Brain. *Psychology Today* 21(3):48–52.

Parry, R. A. (1975). *A Guide to Counseling and Basic Psychotherapy*. New York: Churchill Livingstone.

Peter, L. J., and Dana, B. (1982). *The Laughter Prescription*. New York: Ballantine Books.

Robinson, V. M. (1977). *Humor and the Health Professions*. Thorofare, NJ: C. B. Slack.

———— (1983). Humor and health. In *Handbook of Humor Research*, vol. 2, ed. P. E. McGhee, and J. H. Goldstein, pp. 109–128. New York: Springer-Verlag.

Salameh, W. A. (1983). Humor in psychotherapy. In *Handbook of Humor Research*, vol. 2, ed. P. E. McGhee and J. H. Goldstein, pp. 61–88. New York: Springer Verlag.

Saper, B. (1987). Humor in psychotherapy: Is it good or bad for the client? *Professional Psychology: Research and Practice* 18:360–367.

Smith, R. E. (1973). The use of humor in the counterconditioning of anger responses: a case study. *Behavior Therapy* 4:576–580.

Ventis, W. L. (1973). Case history: the use of laughter as an alternative response in systematic desensitization. *Behavior Therapy* 4:120–122.

———— (1980). Humor in behavior therapy. In *The Study of Humor*, ed. H. Mindess and J. Turk, pp. 16–23. Los Angeles: Antioch University.

Walsh, J. J. (1928). *Laughter and Health*. New York: Appleton.

Ziv, A. (1984). *Personality and Sense of Humor*. New York: Springer.

III

INNOVATIVE APPLICATIONS

Humor as an Intervention Strategy

Frank J. Prerost

The psychological literature presents a near unanimous agreement on the beneficial influences of humor. Allport (1961), Maslow (1961), Rogers (1961) have each acknowledged humor as one attribute manifest among fully functioning persons. O'Connell (1960) has found well-adjusted people to have a well-developed sense of humor. Apparently, an individual with effective coping skills can appreciate the gravity of a serious situation, yet lessen the debilitating anxiety often associated with such events (Allport 1968). Many people have seen how jokes are employed to reduce tensions before important group discussions and meetings. Zillman (1977) has upheld the concept that a sharing of laughter can induce meaningful interactions between individuals and assist toward the completion of the task at hand. Pines and colleagues (1981) have claimed that humor is one of the best coping devices to combat burnout at work.

The individual who is adept at sharing humorous anecdotes or who can direct attention toward humorous incidents in the surrounding environment often receives special attention and enthusiasm from others (Ziv 1981). This permits an effective humorist to exert leaderships in groups and enjoy social popularity (Dunphy 1969). The humorist becomes a person enjoyed by others while he or she accepts a special connectedness to people (Goodchilds 1972). This mutual relationship provides significant rewards for the humorist. An expansion of self-esteem and social interest accrues to the person promoting humor (Cassel 1974). Whenever laughter is produced and social interactions are enhanced, the humorist's self-worth can grow and develop. Self-knowledge is enhanced as the social involvement of the humorist creates opportunities to receive feedback. The information received from others is critical for improved self-awareness and knowledge. The feedback proffered by others stimulates the expansion of self-esteem and psychological growth. Thus, not only does the humorist enjoy the rewards of significant social exchange, he or she can experience personal growth and increased self-awareness (Greenwald 1977).

A number of theorists have stressed the relationship between humor and healthy adjustment including Kris (1938) and Freud (1905). O'Connell (1977) discussed the role of humor in the self-actualizing process. In his view, the humorist rediscovers the euphorias of childhood, gaining access to innate sources of self-worth and inherent belonging. These liberating qualities of humor have been extensively discussed by Mindess (1971) who conceives of humor as an escape from inhibitions and restrictions. The overconcern about conformity robs people of spontaneous and flexible behavior, and impedes personal growth and development. Humor reduces the demands toward conformity and permits the free exchange of information or feelings between persons. For Mindess, liberation and personal growth are fundamentally intertwined. The true humorist can function in life at a pace conducive to personal development while avoiding the demands of conformity.

Children possess the outlook of the humorist before they are coerced to conform to the dictates of the adult world (Mindess 1971). The healthy child enjoys playing with the endless possibilities of nonsense and absurdity available in the world. Examination of the emotionally healthy child's fantasy reveals the wide variety of pleasurable nonsense experienced by the child (Wolfenstein 1954). McGhee (1979) describes how cognitive growth in childhood occurs concurrently with the basic nonsensical aspects of humor appreciation. Personal psychological development becomes slowed when social expectations suppress the fantasy life of these absurdities. The child or person who is punished or discouraged from maintaining a humorous outlook on life, runs the risk of falling into a life of restrictive functioning and constricted psychological health (Prerost 1984). When excessive conformity, or concern for it, totally replaces the playful qualities of humor, personal emotional adjustment can suffer. A limited view of life creates a limited opportunity for meaningful social exchange and gathering of personally relevant information. While the true humorist can enjoy enhanced self-esteem, the person devoid of healthy humor can become trapped in a spiral of self-inhibition (O'Connell and Cowgill 1970).

The disturbance in humor appreciation usually manifests along the dimension of either excessive and inappropriate laughter, or the complete absence of humor (Duchowny 1983). Extreme laughter seems out of proportion to the stimulus event, and the person laughing appears beyond control of the response. Other forms of excessive laughter usually revolve around aggressive and sexual themes. The inappropriate humor accompanying displays of aggression and/or sadistic sex should not be considered healthy expressions of humor (Harrelson and Stroud 1967). These expressions of humor lack the social qualities inherent in the behavior of the true humorist. Excessive and inappropriate humor responses can result for suspect psychological adjustment and are signals for possible professional concern.

When humor is significantly diminished in a person's functioning, the path toward psychological growth is slowed (Greenwald 1977). The losing of one's sense of humor signals the retreat from social exchange and a blocking of feedback from others. When a person encounters stress that is not effectively dealt with, a withdrawal into oneself may take place. In what may be a protective retreat, the individual risks fewer humorous exchanges than before the stressful circumstances, and emotional isolation begins to solidify. Events and situations that were previously rewarding become potential sources of rejection or failure. Since humor is a basic social exchange, the sharing of humor diminishes as social interactions are limited.

The use of humor during therapy can serve two significant functions. First, the enjoyment of humor could lift a depressed mood state and alleviate the anxiety present. Second, humor can assist in resolving the threatening aspects or conflicts surrounding a stressful circumstance. The beneficial aspects of humor in the psychotherapeutic process have been identified by numerous therapists (e.g., Greenwald 1975, Hershkowitz 1977, Levine 1977, Ziv 1981). These writers agree that when appropriate laughter is triggered in a patient, it usually signals therapeutic progress. The comments used by these therapists are designed to promote laughter in their patients. Bloomfield (1980) has written of the importance of intuitively knowing when to make a humorous remark. Unfortunately, this often leads to a nonsystematic and inconsistent use of humor during therapy. Some therapists (e.g., Kubie 1971) have written of the potential dangers of using humor in this fashion during psychotherapy. Without the proper care, a humorous remark can be destructive to the patient or the professional relationship, if the comment is interpreted in a negative fashion. The danger of the patient feeling he or she has been belittled by the therapist is an ever-present danger of using humor in a nonsystematic fashion during therapy. Although humor is viewed as a way to establish warm relations with clients and reduce anxiety, the danger for the professional arises because of the ease with which humorous remarks can be generated during treatment (Rosenheim 1974). The therapist can see the illogical nature of the patient's behavior quickly during treatment and use it to develop humorous remarks.

In order to avoid pitfalls cited above, this author developed a method to systematically induce humor during psychotherapy. To provide a safe yet therapeutic vehicle for the use of humor the author developed the Humorous Imagery Situation Technique (HIST) (Prerost 1981). This method formalizes the use of humor in therapy by combining imagery techniques as a companion for humor in therapy. The directed daydream technique forms the foundation of the HIST. The directed daydream has been used to permit persons with conflicts to confront them in a safe and nonthreatening fashion (Scheidler 1972). The HIST expands on the ideas of Schorr (1972) who devised an imagery method in which the individual's own fantasy reveals major problem areas. The patient becomes involved with a series of interactions at the fantasy level that are helpful in alleviating causes of stress. When anxiety producing situations are confronted at the imaginal level, they can be faced without the emotional turmoil often present when difficult issues are explored verbally. The HIST utilizes the advantages of an imagery technique while promoting humor appreciation. Once humor can be reinstated in a patient at the imagery level, an expansion of positive affect to daily functioning can occur. The confronting of distressing life events with humor during imagery scenes can permit an outlet for feelings of apprehension. A major goal of using HIST with patients is to break any self-perpetuating cycle of withdrawal and safely release anxiety. The experience of anxiety can have a debilitating effect on humor appreciation in everyday functioning (Prerost 1980, Prerost and Brewer 1980). Once HIST reduces the presence of anxiety, humor should be restored in daily activity.

METHOD

The Humorous Imagery Situation Technique (HIST) begins with the patient seated in a comfortable reclining chair. Once the client feels comfortable and closes his/her eyes, a state of relaxation is induced through mental exercises. The suggestions of bodily weight and warmth are combined with deep breathing exercises. Keeping the client isolated from extraneous noises and distractions, together with dim lighting, aids in the relaxation procedures.

Once the client has achieved relaxation, practice in visualization of imagery scenes can begin. A fantasy is suggested to the client by the therapist who serves as a guide. During the initial imagery experience, the client is guided through scenes familiar or common to most individuals.

The scenes used are adaptations of those used by a number of therapists who employ imagery techniques (e.g., Schorr 1974). The patient is moved through such scenes as walking across a meadow, exploring an empty house, hiking in a forest, and lounging on a beach.

After the client can visualize him- or herself in one of the scenes, descriptions of the experience are requested by the therapist. Facets of the scene that are spontaneously suggested by the client are accepted and discussed. The client is given practice moving through the imagery scenes and encouraged to interact with the characters, events, and situations encountered. The client has the opportunity to become comfortable with clarifying the imagery experience and permitting the mind's eye to function.

Once the client can achieve vivid images on a consistent basis, the first step in the HIST can begin. Use of the HIST requires development of imagery situations in consultation with the client. Imagery scenes are then constructed by the therapist that reflect areas of concern for the client and have a role in the client's emotional state. The fantasies formulated by the therapist incorporate life experiences that are potentially stressful for the client or elicit avoidant responses. The actual imagery scenes used in HIST can vary from person to person depending upon the client's problem areas.

The HIST begins when the fantasies developed specifically for each patient are used in the guided daydreams. Although therapeutic benefit can arise from the standard guided imagery scenes, the focus of treatment for the HIST is on the personal imagery scenes. It is the humor that is promoted during personalized humorous imagery scenes that effects the maximum curative changes.

When using the scenes to elicit humor, the therapist suggests and guides the client through familiar situations. The client, who draws upon personal information and remembrances, typically can construct a mental scene rich in detail and vividness. Once the client's fantasy is crystallized in vivid detail, the therapist begins the use of two procedures. First, the therapist introduces humor into the fantasy by focusing the client's attention on humorous reactions of others in the scene. Characters in the daydream are seen laughing and/or interacting with one another in a playful fashion. Questions are provided to elaborate on the mental image and include such remarks as: "What is causing the laughter?" "Are these people enjoying the laughter?" "What is being said or done to create the laughter?" "Do you feel like joining in the laughter?" "Can you say or do anything to contribute to the enjoyment and laughter?" The goal of the directions is to involve the client in the expression of humor present in the scene and eventually allow the client to generate reasons for the humor.

The second procedure requires the therapist to interject factors into the fantasy that can elicit humor responses from the client. The therapist provides directions that introduce incongruous elements into the fantasy scenes. The significance of incongruity and its resolution in the creation of humor responses has been documented by numerous investigators (e.g., Rothbard and Pien 1977). Incongruity in the stimulated laughter involves the conflict between what is expected and what actually occurs. When a person is confronted with a situation demonstrating incongruous elements, the potential for laughter exists. Some incongruity can produce laughter by its very existence, for example, a distinguished scholarly person who suddenly slips and falls while giving a serious speech. But some incongruity requires resolution in order to produce laughter. Resolution of incongruity necessitates an explanation or "logical" reason for the incongruous elements to appear together. Riddles provide a common example of when resolution of incongruity promotes laughter. Once a person engages in some mental exercise and hears the unexpected answer, the incongruity is resolved and laughter can take place. The potential power of incongruity to produce laughter is used in the HIST. Once a client is involved in a guided daydream, the therapist must be prepared to direct the client's attention toward incongruity in the scene. Familiar characters need to act in unexpected ways or behave in a fashion that violates the client's expectations about them. For instance, the business associate known for her sartorial perfection can be seen in extremely mismatched colors and designs, or the boastful supervisor could be portrayed in a humbling fashion. When the therapist has worked at generating appropriate incongruities for the client's areas of concern, the potential for laughter exists. The incongruous elements must thoroughly populate the imagery scenes. Some attempts will be more successful than others in producing humor. It is important to try numerous possibilities of incongruity during the fantasies until those most effective with the client are identified. The inquiries made to the client when observing laughter in the imagery scenes should assist the therapist in recognizing the factors the client enjoys and associates with laughter. Thus, the importance of both the observation of humor in the fantasy scenes, and the introduction of incongruity to stimulate humorous reactions are interrelated. In addition, the observing of humor encourages the social exchange opportunities available in humor responses. The resolution of incongruity can be used to reflect on personal apprehensions and permits the client to cope with stress during the fantasy experience. The appreciation of jokes reflecting on areas of concern empirically has been found to be an effective method to release tensions and aggressions (Prerost 1976, Prerost and Brewer 1977).

DISCUSSION

The combination of standard guided daydreams and client-specific scenes allow for the generation of humor that instills a positive affective outlook among clients. Any withdrawal or lack of interest present during depressed moods or during periods of anxiousness can be overcome through uses of HIST. The underlying cognitions nurturing conditions of depression or anxiousness can be resolved at the imaginal level and replaced with a humorous outlook. Any suppression of the humorous perception of life's difficulties is overturned during HIST, and the client can once again enjoy the benefits, both emotional and social, from enhanced humor enjoyment.

The appropriate scope for the use of HIST is still untested, but it is hoped that continued work will provide beneficial results among a wide range of emotional problems. The skill of the therapist in developing appropriate client-specific imagery scenes is paramount in the successful employ of the HIST. Practice in recognizing and understanding the nature of humorous incongruity is central to the HIST. Before this technique can be used effectively by a therapist, a working understanding of the theories of humor must be attained. The HIST is not a series of jokes told by the therapist; rather, the professional must be knowledgeable in setting up the situations for humor to spontaneously occur. The client must be guided toward humor responses through direction to the elements underlying laughter. As a therapist understands the antecedents to humor, he or she can begin to integrate this knowledge with the standard methods of guided fantasy. The therapist becomes both a script writer and director in the therapeutic endeavor.

REFERENCES

Allport, G. W. (1961). *Pattern and Growth in Personality*. New York: Rinehart & Winston.
_____ (1968). *The Person in Psychology*. Boston: Beacon.
Bloomfield, I. (1980). Humor in psychotherapy and analysis. *International Journal of Social Psychology* 26:135–141.
Cassel, S. L. (1974). The function of humor in the counseling process. *Rehabilitation Counseling Bulletin* 17:240–245.
Duchowny, M. S. (1983). Pathological disorders of laughter. In *Handbook of Humor Research*, vol. 2, ed. P. McGhee, and J. Goldstein. New York: Springer-Verlag.
Dunphy, A. C. (1969). *Cliques, Crowds, and Gangs*. Melbourne: Cheshire.
Freud, S. (1905). Jokes and their relation to the unconscious. *Standard Edition* 8.
Goodchilds, J. D. (1972). On being witty: Causes, correlates and consequences. In *The Psychology of Humour*, ed. J. H. Goldstein, and P. McGhee. New York: Academic Press.

Greenwald, H. (1975). Humor in psychotherapy. *Journal of Contemporary Psychotherapy* 7:113–116.

———— (1977). Humour in psychotherapy. In *It's a Funny Thing, Humour*, ed. A. Chapman, and H. Foot. Oxford: Pergamon Press.

Harrelson, R. W., and Stroud, P. S. (1967). Observation of humor in chronic schizophrenics. *Mental Hygiene* 51:458–461.

Hershkowitz, A. (1977). The essential ambiguity of, and in, humor. In *It's a Funny Thing, Humour*, ed. A. J. Chapman, and H. C. Foot. Oxford: Pergamon Press.

Kris, E. (1938). Ego development and the comic. *International Journal of Psychoanalysis* 19:77–90.

Kubie, L. S. (1971). The destructive potential of humour in psychotherapy. *Journal of Psychiatry* 127:861–866.

Levine, J. (1977). Humor as a force in therapy. In *It's a Funny Thing, Humour*, ed. A. J. Chapman, and H. C. Foot. Oxford: Pergamon Press.

Maslow, A. (1961). *Toward a Psychology of Being*. Princeton: Van Nostrand.

McGhee, P. (1979). *Humour: It's Origins and Development*. San Francisco: W. H. Freeman.

Mindess, H. (1971). *Laughter and Liberation*. Los Angeles: Nash.

O'Connell, W. E. (1960). The adaptive function of wit and humour. *Journal of Abnormal and Social Psychology* 61:263–270.

———— (1977). The sense of humour: actualizer of persons and theories. In *It's a Funny Thing, Humour*, ed. A. J. Chapman, and H. C. Foot. Oxford: Pergamon Press.

O'Connell, W. E., and Cowgill, S. (1970). Wit, humour, and defensiveness. *Newsletter for Research in Psychology* 12:32–33.

Pines, A., Aronson, E., and Kafry, D. (1981). *Burnout: From Tedium to Personal Growth*. New York: Free Press.

Prerost, F. J. (1976). Reduction of aggression as a function of related humour content. *Psychological Reports*. 38:771–777.

———— (1980). The effects of high spatial density in humour application: age and sex differences. *Social Behavior and Personality* 8:239–244.

———— (1981). The application of humorous imagery situations in psychotherapy. In *Imagery: Concepts, Results, and Application*, ed. E. Klinger. New York: Plenum.

———— (1984). Evaluating the systematic use of humor in psychotherapy with adolescents. *Journal of Adolescence* 7:267–276.

Prerost, F. J., and Brewer, R. E. (1977). Humor content preferences and the relief of experimentally aroused aggression. *Journal of Social Psychology* 103:225–231.

———— (1980). The appreciation of humour by males and females during conditions of crowding experimentally induced. *Psychology* 13:15–18.

Rogers, C. R. (1961). *On Becoming a Person*. Boston: Houghton Mifflin.
Rosenheim, E. (1974). Humor in psychotherapy: an interactive experience. *American Journal of Psychotherapy* 28:584–591.
Rothbard, T., and Pien, D. (1977). A theoretical synthesis of incongruity resolution and arousal theories of humor. In *It's a Funny Thing, Humour*, ed. A. J. Chapman, and H. C. Foot. Oxford: Pergamon.
Scheidler, T. (1972). Use of fantasy as a therapeutic agent in latency age groups. *Psychotherapy: Theory, Research and Practice* 9:299–302.
Schorr, J. (1972). *Psycho-imagination Through Imagery*. New York: Thieme-Stratton.
_____ (1974). *Psycho-imagination Through Imagery*, 2nd ed. New York: Thieme-Stratton.
Wolfenstein, M. (1954). *Children's Humor*. Glencoe, IL: Free Press.
Zillman, D. (1977). Humour and communication: an introduction. In *It's a Funny Thing, Humour*, ed. A. J. Chapman, & H. C. Foot. Oxford: Pergamon.
Ziv, A. (1981). Facilitating effects of humor on creativity. *Journal of Educational Psychology* 68:318–322.

The Laughing Game: An Exercise for Sharpening Awareness of Self-Responsibility

Daniel I. Malamud

In the course of developing an experiential Workshop in Personal Growth at New York University's School of Continuing Education, I have created a large repertoire of self-confrontation exercises in which members are encouraged to involve themselves with an attitudinal blend of playfulness and curiosity. In designing such activities I aim at experiences so novel that students' customary responses will be bypassed, and they will have an opportunity to see themselves from a surprising perspective (Malamud 1955, 1960, 1971, 1974; Malamud and Machover 1965).

Some years ago I began to explore the selective application of such self-confrontation procedures with patients in therapy, moving beyond the usual patterns of verbal exchange and inviting them to participate during the session in one or another simple but challenging task, "game," or experiment (Malamud 1973, 1976). My evolution as a therapist in this direction was deeply reinforced and influenced by my personal experiences with Fritz Perls and his Gestalt therapy methods. In this paper I describe in detail one such exercise, the Laughing Game.

I developed the Laughing Game as an antidote to the passive orientation of many group members who lack a deeply felt sense of the extent to which they contribute to the creation of their own experiences, and, therefore, tend to see themselves as the passive receivers of pressures and demands from the outside world, or, in the extreme, as helpless victims to whom things happen. This exercise has been used with apparent effective ness in groups ranging in size from eight members to over 100, in therapy groups, two-hour convention workshops, and in the Workshop in Personal Growth where it was first developed. Through their own experiences in the game and through later reflection on these experiences, most participants become more intensely aware of their automatic sets, assumptions, and behavior patterns, and of their responsibility for the ways in which they interpret and respond to outside events.

PROCEDURES

I ask the group to break up into quartets. Then I say, "Pair up with somebody in your quartet. Decide who of the pair will be A and who will be B. Member A will share his or her thoughts and feelings on a specific theme for 3 minutes while B listens as deeply and acceptingly as possible without interrupting. The theme is 'The Role of Play in My Life.' When I call time, you will reverse roles: B will share his or her thoughts and feelings about this same theme for 3 minutes while A listens receptively without interrupting." (If there is an odd person without a partner, he or she is instructed to observe silently one of the pairs and to make sure that he or she gets a partner in the next interaction.)

After each member of the pair has had an opportunity to share reactions to the first theme, I ask members to form new pairs with others in their quartets and to repeat the sharing and listening process described above, this time focusing on the theme "The Role of Competition in My Life."

The above procedure is repeated a third and final time with the theme "Taking Responsibility for my Life."

I then distribute $8\frac{1}{2} \times 11$ sheets of paper to the group. I ask each member to tear his or her sheet into 16 equal-size paper tokens. Following this, each member finds a partner he or she has not paired up with before (that is, with somebody outside his or her quartet).

I ask each pair to decide who will be A and who B. I then give the following instructions to the A's: "A's, your task is to make B smile or laugh as frequently as possible within 1 minute. You can tell jokes, voice odd noises, make funny faces, or get into ridiculous postures. You can do anything to stimulate laughter with one exception: you may not tickle your partner. Each time you stimulate a smile or a laugh your partner will give you one of his or her tokens. The merest trace of a smile counts as a full smile, and you are the final judge as to whether such a trace of a smile occurred. Each token you receive is yours for keeps."

I next address myself to the B's: "B's, do not speak to A at all throughout your 1 minute interaction with him or her. Give A a token promptly each time you smile or laugh, and then immediately resume a serious, sober expression on your face, so that A can make a fresh attempt to stimulate you.''

I then give the following instructions to both A's and B's: ''At my signal, A will reverse roles with B, and B will attempt to stimulate A to smile or laugh as often as possible for a minute. There will be four such 2-minute rounds with four different partners. Each of you is starting off with an equal number of tokens. After the fourth round I will ask you to add up your tokens to see how many you have ended up with.''

In response to questions about the purpose of the game or how one should play it, I simply repeat one or another relevant instruction without elaborating, or I say, ''It's up to you!''

I start off the group's first round by announcing in a playful tone of voice, ''Get ready . . . set . . . go!'' At the end of a minute I call a halt to the action: ''Please stop, everybody. Now A and B will reverse roles, and B stimulates A to smile or laugh. Get ready . . . set . . . go!''

Immediately at the end of the first round (that is, after both A and B have had opportunities to play the role of smile-stimulator) I ask members to close their eyes and to maintain absolute silence. I say: ''Please imagine as vividly as you can that your mother has been present in this room and has been watching you for the last few minutes as you've been playing this game. Now see her walking over to you. Hear her saying something to you. She is giving you a one-sentence reaction to what she has observed. Listen, and in your mind's ear, hear what she says to you.''

After about half a minute of silence I ask partners to open their eyes, convey nonverbal goodbyes to each other, and find new partners with whom they have not as yet paired up.

I start off the second round as before. At the end of the second round I ask the members to close their eyes and this time to imagine that their fathers have been watching them and to ''hear'' their one-sentence reactions.

Members then find new partners for a third round. At the end of the third round I announce, ''The next round will be the last one. Please add up the number of tokens you have now and share this number with your partner. Do not exchange any comments about these figures. Simply share them, then express your nonverbal goodbyes, and find a new partner for your last round.''

After the fourth round I request members to add up the final number of tokens they have in their possession. I then ask members to line up in the order of the number of tokens each one has, with the person having the most tokens placing himself at the end of the line, and the one having the least, at the beginning. Each person in turn then calls out his total so that the group can learn its range of "scores." (When the group consists of more than twenty members, instead of having them line up, I simply ask individuals who ended up with more tokens than they started with to raise their hands. Then I make the same request of members who ended up with fewer tokens.)

Next members are requested to return to their original quartets to discuss the following questions: How do I feel about my rank order in the group as far as token totals are concerned? What assumptions was I operating on during this game, and do any of these assumptions operate in my everyday life? Who was responsible for my smiling and laughing? What did my parents say to me, and what influence, if any, did their statements have on my subsequent feelings and performance? Who was responsible for this influence?

After about 15 to 20 minutes of discussion I call for the group's attention: "I imagine that many of you have wondered about the point of this game, so I would like to tell you that I designed it with the intent of drawing your attention to the meanings that you yourself created as you went about playing it. The game process in and of itself is meaningless. There is no intrinsic reason for A to try to make B laugh, or vice versa. The paper tokens are simply pieces of paper. Acquiring more tokens than you started with is not an intrinsically superior outcome to ending up with fewer. It was you who brought your own meanings into these and other aspects of the process. I made up the rules of the game, but it was you who decided what the point of these rules was, and once made, this decision shaped your ways of seeing, thinking, feeling, and behaving in the events that followed. You decided what this game was 'really' all about, and then you reacted to the requirements, pressures, and demands of this 'reality' as if it were the only reality, a given imposed upon you from the outside rather than a 'reality' you yourself invented or projected.

"People can play this game in any number of ways, and from my point of view, no one way is intrinsically better than another. For example, some of you assumed that the point of this game was to acquire as many paper tokens as possible, and you really threw yourself into the competition. On the other hand, some of you, not caring about winning, just focused on entertaining and being entertained. So some of you created a world of competition, others a world of play, and then you unwittingly became the effects of these worlds you created, either relishing the competition or distressed with the pressure of it, or enjoying opportunities to have fun.

"And now let me put some questions to you, and with each question notice what thoughts and especially what feeling reactions occur in you. Are you ready? What if life, indeed the whole universe, is like this game—full of events and processes, apparently operating according to certain rules and lawful sequences, but with no intrinsic meanings and values other than those we ourselves define, based on our inborn physical equipment and learned conditioning? What if all of life is a process in which absolute objectivity about anything is impossible except for those consensual agreements humans make that shift and change from one culture and historical period to another? How does my raising such questions affect you as you listen to them? Please share your reactions, thoughts, and feelings with your group for the next 10 minutes."

TYPICAL PARTICIPANT EXPERIENCES

The main responses to the game tend to constellate around three different nuclear themes:

1. The point of the game is to win, and one should acquire as many tokens as possible in order to do so. Some members take to the perceived competition with relish, either for the sheer pleasure of winning, or as a satisfying opportunity to exercise their powers of control, be it over themselves or others. (Some in this subgroup realize with dismay that they pursued their ambitions at the price of missing out on simply having fun and some pleasurable social contacts.) Others experience "having to" compete as an anxiety-producing or burdensome pressure to "prove" themselves, either as persons who can make an effective impact on others or as self-disciplined persons who can control their emotional reactions.
2. It is more important to avoid hurting, embarrassing, or frustrating one's partners than it is to win. Members of this subgroup make a point of laughing readily in response to their partners' antics whether they feel like it or not.
3. The game is an enjoyable opportunity to socialize in a context of playful fun.

Reports exemplifying some of the above themes follow.

I enjoyed the competition and was determined to win. It was important to me to get more tokens than I gave out, and I was very good at maintaining a poker face.

I ended up with the most papers, but I envied those who let themselves laugh and have fun. Me, I was tense throughout. And for what? A bunch of useless paper and a puffed up ego!

I felt very pressured. I told myself to think of jokes, try to be funny, like a dating situation where I have to constantly think of things to say. The burden was on me to produce, and to prove to myself that I have a sense of humor and can make others warm up to me.

I would laugh just to appease my partner. I didn't want them to suffer or feel completely defeated. Fulfilling my "good guy" image again!

I didn't consciously try to collect so many tokens, but rather saw the exercise as a nice way to meet my classmates. Making my partners laugh was fun and gave me momentary warm, personal contacts.

Imagined parents' statements are usually negative and critical. For example: "Why are you making such a fool of yourself?" "Shmuck! Can't you control your giggles?" Parents' statements often come as a surprise and provoke considerable introspection about the influence of such internalized messages not only on how participants performed in the game, but on how they live their lives as well:

I originally felt that I found no significance to the game, but when I told my group that my mother laughed at me for not being "mature" and that my father gave me a mean look and walked out of class, I realized that what my parents "said" did influence my behavior. From a laughing, jovial individual in the first round, I changed to a competitive one, lacking humor, being very serious for the last three rounds, the same effect my parents had on me in my youth. I am seeing more and more that my mother is generally rigid, uptight, and controlled, and that I have acquired some of her rigidity, making it hard for me to let go in life.

Participants often experience emotionally charged realizations as they observe themselves in action:

I've always considered myself a noncompetitive person. But I found myself counting my tokens repeatedly. The less tokens I had, the more frantic I got in trying to make the other person laugh. Toward the end I found myself acting compulsively, in trying to obtain as many tokens as possible. What I found out about myself is that I hate to lose!

I felt that I was responsible if I laughed, yet if my partner didn't laugh, I felt I had failed and was to blame for the outcome. On the other hand, if my partner did laugh, I didn't really take credit, but I extended to them the responsibility of their making themselves laugh. I was amazed at how I distort in order to place blame on myself and deprive myself of credit.

My partner used no words, only grimaces, movements, and nonverbal coaxings to make me smile. She clarified how one-dimensional were my ways of stimulating laughs with words alone. There were so many other ways I had not tried, but they had never occurred to me! I'm wondering why not?

My ways of relating to the two sexes were surprisingly different. Instead of saying silly things to the men (as I did with the women), I found myself getting sort of cute in tone and expression and began to ask them to, "Come on, do it for me."

As members share their reactions to the game, they cannot help but be impressed by the sheer diversity of their experiences, and they realize with high intensity (sometimes with a sense of shock) the degree to which they created their own "realities" and that to an unknown extent they may be living by unrecognized projections. One student, for example, reported:

This "meaningless" game turned out to be a very powerful experience for me. The idea that the world is an inkblot, subject to many different interpretations, became an intensely lived experience. It came as a shock— the fact that other people didn't have any "rules," that they were not that worried with my own worries and not expecting the same things. I felt a bit scared. I ask myself: if I'm always projecting my own needs and feelings and creating my own reality, how can I be in contact with "real" reality, and what if I never can be?

CLOSING STATEMENT

The Laughing Game may be seen as a real life analogue. Its structure is sufficiently open to elicit a wide variety of reactions, and the utter simplicity of the task throws members' motives, perceptions, and coping styles into bolder than usual relief. Participants are stimulated to recognize assumptions and biases that were formerly seen as givens, to glimpse some origins of these habitual sets in past relationships with parents, and to become more open to the existence of orientations other than their habitual ones. As participants come to see themselves more as the authors and producers of their own life-scripts, there is an increase in felt incentive to take responsibility for what and how they experience and to be in charge of their own lives.

Variations of this game suggest new and intriguing possibilities to be explored. For example, what if, after the game was played and discussed, I were to ask the participants to play several more rounds, but with a new orientation in attitude or behavior, one as different as possible from their initial pattern? Or what would happen if I asked members to use pennies, dimes, or quarters instead of paper tokens? Or what if, after each occurrence of laughter, B were instructed to give A either a hug or a token, depending on A's preference?

REFERENCES

Malamud, D., *A Participant–Observer Approach to the Teaching of Human Relations*. Chicago: Center for the Study of Liberal Education for Adults.

———— (1960). Educating adults in self-understanding. *Mental Hygiene* 44:115–124.

———— (1971). The second-chance family: a medium for self-directed growth. In *Confrontation: Encounters in Self and Interpersonal Awareness*. ed. M. Gottsegen, G. Gottsegen, and L. Blank. New York: Macmillan.

———— (1973). Self-confrontation methods in psychotherapy. *Psychotherapy: Theory, Research and Practice* 10:123–130.

———— (1974). Self-confrontation in the second-chance family. *Journal of Humanistic Psychology* 14:19–39.

———— (1976). Expanding awareness through self-confrontation methods. In *Emotional Flooding*, ed. P. Olsen. New York: Human Sciences Press.

Malamud, D., and Machover, S. (1965). *Toward Self-Understanding: Group Techniques in Self-Confrontation*. Springfield, Il: Charles C Thomas.

The Application of Joy in Group Psychotherapy for the Elderly

Shura Saul and Sidney R. Saul

Joy: this three-letter word carries a powerful sweet punch to the emotional solar plexus. Webster's definitions all elicit images of pleasure, feelings of warmth, and the glow of gladness to mind and heart. "Joy . . . from the Latin . . . *gaudia* a jewel: to gladden, to make or possess with pleasure, . . . the cause of happiness." Synonyms are noted as "delight, gladness, rapture, ecstasy, happiness, exultation" (*Webster's New Universal Unabridged Dictionary*, 2nd edition, 1979).

It is a common human desire to experience these feelings as deeply and as often as possible. One might say that the ability to experience these feelings is an important dimension of normal living. One might say further that enabling or assisting an individual to "enjoy the feelings of joy" is one of the significant goals of psychotherapy.

Like group psychotherapy for all ages, the use of this modality for elderly people seeks to help them cope with the stresses of this stage of their lives and to enable them to function in a manner that is satisfying and acceptable to them.

This process is nurtured through such group techniques as interaction, experience, insights, and conceptualization; through enabling group members to experience the full range of human emotions, and to understand their impact on intrapsychic and social functioning.

Often, it is the loss of the ability to experience these emotions that has brought the person to therapy in the first place. Depression—in its various forms often unrecognized, unacknowledged, and undiagnosed—may well be a common denominator for members of a therapy group (Zarit 1980). Some type of depression may be the basic cause of a person's inability to enjoy life, even its everyday activities. The ability to sleep through a night with pleasure in the sweetness of rest, to awaken in the morning with a reasonable and relevant response to one's immediate surroundings, to anticipate the day and its responsibilities with a healthy, individually acceptable outlook, to interact with a range of diverse individuals in a range of diverse situations and to perform these and other tasks with patience, appropriateness, health, and humor—these are the small acts of daily living that signify normalcy.

Yalom's (1975) listing of "curative factors" reflects the uses of group therapy for restoring to group members their potential for healthier, more acceptable, and pleasurable functioning. He lists these factors as the instillation of hope, universality, imparting of information, altruism, the corrective recapitulation of the primary family group, development of socializing techniques, imitative behavior, interpersonal learning, group cohesiveness, catharsis, and existential factors.

The emotion of joy is inherent in these factors, and the planned use of joyful experiences becomes a booster to their curative powers.

The aging process challenges individuals to cope with the stress of change and the losses that it may bring. These may be summarized as physical changes, for example, in appearance, health, strength, and competence in particular areas; changes in role, status, and relationships (work, family, social); changes in economic status, altered opportunities for satisfying interaction, and altered patterns of daily living. For many elderly people, these changes may be accompanied by feelings of loss of control over one's life, and by an intensification of the dependence–independence struggle. A person's long-established mechanisms of ego defense and methods of coping may have become dysfunctional. There are fewer opportunities for self-actualization and life satisfaction (Saul 1983).

Some of the psychological and emotional responses to such losses include depression (in its many expressions), depletion, a sense of loneliness, isolation, and/or despair, fearfulness, anxiety, suspicion, and anger (Cath 1965).

Depression and joy are pretty much at the opposite extremes of the spectrum of human emotions. Minimizing the former and maximizing the latter may well be a common goal for individuals in group therapy. The model presented here suggests the structuring of joyful group experiences but does not overlook the significance of the other human emotions in the therapeutic process. Unless one recognizes and understands sorrow, one may well not recognize joy.

It is not suggested here that all group sessions be joyful, but that selective use of joyful group experiences has a place in planning group treatment.

The possibilities for the occurrence of joyful experiences within the group are limitless. However, some descriptive categories may be suggested as relevant to the goals of group therapy and congruent with Yalom's curative factors. They may be summarized as:

1. The joys of finding oneself—the twin factors of identity and belonging.
2. The joys of relationship, of sharing ideas, tears, pleasures (relates to belonging above).
3. The joys of loving, and of being loved through a range of relationships of varying intensity (suggested in 2, above).
4. The joys of self-actualization, of achieving, feeling powerful, and in control (relates to 1, above).
5. The joys of helping and being helped.
6. The joys of touching—physical, spiritual, symbolic.
7. The joys of discovery, of rediscovery, and insights.
8. The joys of creating and of experiencing creativity.
9. The joys of laughter and sharing laughter.
10. The joys of feeling alive, the joy of living.

All of these categories are readily identifiable as components of healthy human existence. One of the remarkable aspects of group treatment is that several different emotions can be experienced simultaneously, by each group member, and by all. One inherent advantage of group treatment lies in this phenomenon, for those who are willing and able to participate.

A few examples, drawn from group sessions, will illustrate these facets of joy as they were developed in the group. Most of incidents illustrate more than one "category" of joy.

The joy of finding oneself involves a renewed emphasis on one's identity (Erikson 1959). During the aging process, the older person may feel the loss of some dimension(s) of self. It is a source of joy to find oneself again within the group, to realize that one is still "the same person," even though changed in some ways because of the different challenges of time and life. ("There's life in the old bones yet!") Along with this insight is the joy of discovering new dimensions of one's self, of recognizing how one has changed, and how one may need to change further to meet life's challenges. Butler (1975) notes that "human beings need the freedom . . . to invent and reinvent themselves a number of times throughout their lives" (p. 103).

Mrs. S. had joined a group of blind elderly women. She was terribly distraught over her visual loss and the loss of self that it represented to her. Although she was a very verbal person, for the first few sessions she listened and spoke only when addressed directly. At the fourth session, she suddenly took the floor and in her melodious voice told the group that until this day she had thought she had lost herself entirely . . . could never find herself again . . . would never be herself again. In this group, however, she realized that she is still the same Mrs. S. and can go on with her life.

Her brief, emotional little speech was offered with a lovely smile and flowed from her heart in rhythm to the tears that flowed from her eyes. Her joy and her grief commingled.

The twin to the pleasure of finding oneself is the joy of belonging. So much of the individual's identity stems from participation in a range of reference groups. The older person loses contact with a number of these, such as groups in the workplace, the social, spiritual, and cultural worlds, finally, perhaps, even the world of his or her own family. Each of these losses cuts away another strand of the person's connectedness to a vital aspect of living.

Membership in a therapy group can regenerate the joy in belonging through participation in the significant and exciting group process.

The joys of relationship, of sharing ideas, tears, and pleasure: inherent in the joy of belonging are the relationships that develop through the group's atmosphere of trust and caring. These are important especially for those elderly persons who have lost important people in their lives, such as a spouse, family members, friends, even elderly children.

Loneliness and isolation can be alleviated within a group. Especially poignant is the following, which illustrates the joys both of belonging and of relationships.

Mr. D., a patient in an early stage of Alzheimer's, joined an outpatient treatment group and was ecstatic to find peers who did not reject him. After the first week of participation in a daily group treatment program, he wrote a poem at home during the weekend entitled "My New Friends." His joy is very clear. He wrote, in part:

I am grateful and proud to be *able* to be proud
To be able to acknowledge fellows
You are happy, I am happy . . .
I am grateful to be happy, so grateful to have fellows like you
I know I shall never forget you . . .
I hope to be one of you
To all with full heart I hail you that I am one of you.

Loving and being loved are experiences that exist along the continuum of human relationships. The desire for affectionate relationships is identified by Maslow (1970) as the third common human need in his hierarchy. In the therapy group there occurs a strong positive mutual transference between therapist and group members and among the group members. This is a positive emotion in the force field of love and an open conduit for a flow of trust.

The following poem was developed with a group of blind women, in the course of discussing their loss. It expresses the profound significance to them of the important loving relationships they found in the group (Saul 1983):

When I lost my vision, when I became blind
The shock of it exploded in my mind
And left a smoky haze behind
Beclouding intellect and thought

And now, here we sit, talking together a little bit
Sharing the woe that this explosion brought

Here within the group I find, I'm freed somewhat from fear
The talk is warm, the newfound friendship dear
And softly, gently now—the haze begins to clear.

[p. 110]

Self-actualization: Maslow (1970) puts the need for self-actualization at the peak of the hierarchy of human needs. In order to attain this state, there has had to be fulfillment of the prioritized needs (physical needs, safety, love, and esteem). When these are met, one is enabled to fulfill the need for becoming "all that one is . . . all that one hopes to be." *All* is a global word, and must be experienced, by most of us, in partial phases as life develops. It is achieved in segments that may add up to a major "chunk" of feeling the power of one's self and one's achievements, whatever they may be. The joy of reaching this point can be experienced and identified within the group.

The joys of helping and being helped: Yalom (1975) writes of altruism and its attendant joys. Heaven, in the Hassidic story he cites, is the place where people have learned to feed each other. Both literally and symbolically, the nurturing that occurs in group therapy is a source of joy for the members. Older people who may have lost their social and familial roles can find fulfillment in sharing and in feeding each other in the group.

When the group is intergenerational, as it may well be, the opportunity to help younger people restores some sense of familial interaction as well.

> Mr. E. was fairly new in the group. In introducing himself, he told us that since adolescence he had lived alone. He'd been in a mental hospital once, and after that no one he knew wanted to associate with him, not even the members of his family. He told us that the next week would bring his thirty-fifth birthday, and he had no one to celebrate with. In fact, he said, he did not ever recall having had a birthday party.
>
> At the next session, Mr. Z., a retired baker, came to the group carrying a large box and announced that he had baked a birthday cake for Mr. E. so that the group could celebrate his birthday. Glowing with pleasure and with tears of joy, Mr. E. served a small piece of cake to each member. While telling everyone how much he appreciated this thoughtful event, he slowly finished eating the entire remaining half of the huge cake!
>
> The therapist and the group noted his hunger with silent understanding.

In this incident, it is important to note that the plan was initiated by an elderly group member, and not by the therapist. Mr. Z. was reflecting the milieu of the group as a place like "Heaven, where people feed each other." Everyone grows in such an encounter: the joy is felt no less by the helper than by the one helped, and is shared with the entire group.

The joys of touching: Isolation and loneliness bring the deprivation of human contact—physical, spiritual, and symbolic.

Older people are often treated as physical "untouchables" and suffer from this loss. Normal, socially appropriate touching, such as holding hands, hugging, kissing, and other forms of contact, underscore the warmth of the relationships. Opportunities for such contact should not be overlooked, as they are "naturals" in the group situation. (One caveat here: some folks just do not like to be touched casually. The therapist must be sensitive to this, and for such a person, touching must be symbolic.)

The therapist notes how often, while discussing such matters as family relationships, death, friendships, losses, sexual problems, and needs, some group members reach out to hold hands or touch shoulders. When there is laughter and joking, there is often also hugging and back-slapping.

At a group for confused, disoriented residents of a nursing home, the therapist routinely ended the session with an individual goodbye and warm handshake with each person. Within a very short time, this became an exchangeof hugs as the group members said goodbye to each other and to the therapist.

Warmth and affection within the group also encourage the sharing of problems of intimacy.

Mr. and Mrs. F. were regular in their attendance at the group sessions. Mrs. F. was always shy and withdrawn. Mr. F. was open, outgoing, and friendly. Following an earlier session during which another couple had discussed their sexual difficulties, Mr. F. asked the group if they would be willing to help him with a problem. He disclosed that he had very strong sexual desires that his wife was reluctant to accept. Mrs. F. shyly admitted to feeling overwhelmed by her husband's advances. Finally, she admitted to the group that she had only lately read and learned about female orgasm.

Turning to the women, she asked them what they knew about it. They responded openly, sharing their knowledge. She was amazed. "I never felt like that!" she exclaimed. That group suggested that the couple might use some help from the therapist, separately as a couple. They did this for a few sessions.

About three weeks later, the couple returned to the group all smiles. Mrs. F., blushing, reported: "It's unbelievable! Where was I all these years?" Mr. F. was equally ecstatic.

The joys of discovery, rediscovery, and insights: The rediscovery of self and the joy of renewed identity are integral to the additional discoveries that are sources of joy to group members. The discovery of beauty in past and present relationships; of beauty in one's physical surroundings; the discovery of pleasures in activities, old and new—these are limitless.

Insights are a special kind of discovery and rediscovery—and when the group helps a member to understand himself better, a new level of pleasure is realized.

Mr. B., an elderly depressed patient and a diagnosed paranoid schizophrenic, participated in a group session in which the patients requested and received definitions and descriptions of their diverse diagnoses. A discussion ensued and at one point, Mr. B. began to shout angrily about the people around him, accusing them of being "out to get him." The group became very silent. Aware of this, Mr. B. stopped shouting, began to smile, turned to the therapist, and said, "That was my illness talking, wasn't it?" It became part of his treatment in the group that, whenever he became inappropriate, he was reminded that his "illness was talking." The feeling of power and control that ensued was a source of elation to Mr. B.

The insights that result from group experiences can relieve earlier pressures, correct mistaken ideas, ease "leftover" anger, and release positive energies toward greater satisfactions.

The joy of creativity: Solving and resolving life's problems is a constant demand on a person's creative capacities (Taylor 1975). Successful older people are extremely creative in adapting to change. When group discussions focus on the sharing of successful coping methods by individual members, creative energy is released for all the members (Barsky 1985).

The arts, in particular, are remarkably effective media for planned therapeutic experiences that are joyful and creative. Poetry reading and writing elicit considerable emotion, insight, and joy (Saul 1988, pp. 223–230):

> The reading of Edna St. Vincent Millay's "Renaissance" to a group of women, all over 80, resulted in a profoundly emotional discussion about losses, and the rebirth of oneself when coping with the severe challenges of aging. Their discussion culminated in a group poem emphasizing the joy of creativity . . . "Creating—that means living!" they wrote. They left the group that day in a state of exultation sensing a power in themselves that had developed in this session.

Reminiscing is another powerful tool:

> The therapists brought a bouquet of flowers to be distributed. What emotions would this simple plan evoke? What memories?
>
> Each person chose his or her own flower and some time was spent in the sensual enjoyment of each. The group members were truly delighted!
>
> The therapist asked, "What does the flower bring to your mind? What memories? What feelings?"
>
> The answers flowed. Tears and smiles mingled with memories of other times, other occasions when there were flowers, and of the people who shared them. The group closed with feelings of warmth and joy—of which their tears had been a significant dimension.

Laughter and humor: These are well-known therapeutic agents to help alleviate depression and anxiety. Often a well-placed, tasteful pun, or an appropriate joke, can set the stage for a constructive and productive session.

> On this afternoon, the group presented as surly and unwilling to discuss anything of substance. The members were negative and critical of each other and the therapist. "And what the hell is a therapist for anyhow!" exclaimed Mr. A.
>
> The therapist grabbed at this lifeline and said, "Well, we know that a neurotic builds castles in the sky" (everyone gets interested).
>
> "We also know that a psychotic moves into that castle" (smiles).
>
> "Well, the therapist collects the rent! Now, won't you help me collect my rent?"
>
> There was general laughter and the group was freed to attend to its therapeutic tasks.

Laughter eases tensions that otherwise may set the climate for an unproductive session. A good laugh can, and often does, reverse negative energy. The sharing of laughter develops a camaraderie that enhances group cohesiveness.

The joy of living, of feeling alive: "Feeling alive" suggests that an individual can and does experience the full gamut of human emotions, from sad to joyful. Group therapy offers opportunity for such diversity. The sharing of sad situations is also a form of joy. Tears shed in an empathetic climate release tensions, open expression, cement relationships, and warm the atmosphere. The older person who enters a therapy group is often characterized by an emotional numbness, an inability to express feelings, by inappropriate or dysfunctional responses, by behavior destructive to his or her own happiness or life satisfaction. To relearn and reexperience the ability to feel the fullness of one's life in all its dimensions, to be in tune with all phases of one's life, to respond and behave in a humanly appropriate way, is to be healthier, more competent, and in control—and therefore to feel a greater joy in one's existence.

The group member who has developed to this point has achieved some zest in living and is ready for discharge. He or she leaves the group with hope, and to the great joy of the therapist who has helped guide this person to this goal.

REFERENCES

Barsky, M. (1985). The creative powers within us. In *Creative Arts with Older Adults*, ed. N. Weisberg, and R. Wilder, pp. 145–154. New York: Human Sciences Press.

Butler, R. N. (1975). The creative life and old age. In *Successful Aging: A Conference Report*, ed. E. Pfeiffer, pp. 97–109. Durham, NC: Duke University Press.

Cath, S. H. (1965). Some dynamics of the middle and later years. In *Crisis Intervention*, ed. H. Parad, pp. 174–192. New York: New York Family Service Association of America.

Erikson, E. (1959). Identity and the life cycle. In *Psychological Issues*, vol. 1, no. 1. New York: International Universities Press.

Maslow, A. H. (1970). *Motivation and Personality*. 2nd Ed. New York: Harper & Row.

Saul, S. (1983). *Aging: An Album of People Growing Old*. New York: Wiley.

_____ (1988). The poetry group. In *Group Therapies for the Elderly*, ed. B. W. MacLennan, S. Saul, and M. B. Weiner, pp. 223–231. Madison, CT: International Universities Press.

Taylor, I. A. (1975). Patterns of creativity and aging. In *Successful Aging: A Conference Report*, ed. E. Pfeiffer, pp. 113–118. Durham, NC: Duke University Press.

Yalom, I. D. (1975). *The Theory and Practice of Group Psychotherapy*. New York: Basic Books.

Zarit, S. H. (1980). *Aging and Mental Disorders*. New York: Free Press.

Humor as Metaphor

Don-David Lusterman

A metaphor is a word or figure of speech that compares one thing to another by speaking of the one as though it were the other. Unlike its cousin, the simile, a metaphor does not use any word of comparison, such as "like" or "as," and therein lies its special power. If a man says of his work, "Everyday I go off to do battle," he is speaking metaphorically, and the metaphor says volumes about his experience of work. In fact, metaphor touches us at such a deep level because it avoids the logical, sequential thinking of the simile, which merely equates one thing with another.

The power of metaphor is that it traverses boundaries. It is a form of linguistic and experiential transformation. In fact, the two Greek words that form the word metaphor are *meta* (to go over, or beyond) and *pherein* (to carry, or bear), suggesting that the power of metaphor is that it can carry us beyond our immediate level of perception.

Metaphor has a disarming quality. If one compares two things, that is to say, makes a simile, it is easy enough to challenge the comparison on the basis of its imperfection. "An apple is like an orange" may elicit the response, "Yes, but one is red, the other is orange," or, "One is a citrus fruit, the other is not." A simile, then, may promote, "Yes—but" thinking. One frequently notes the dangers of simile in family or couples therapy, where one person often accuses the other of being "just like your mother [brother, father, etc.]." Clearly, such similes tend to invite disqualification.

A metaphor, on the other hand, goes beyond simple logic, and therefore is less likely to call forth logical defenses.

Milton Erickson was particularly noted for his use of metaphor. A famous example is that of a purportedly psychotic patient who claimed to be Jesus. "I hear you are a carpenter," said Erickson. "Will you help me build some shelves?" (Haley 1973). Soon Erickson had his patient so overburdened with various carpentry assignments that he not only refused to continue his woodworking, but he also ceased claiming that he was Jesus. Erickson's metaphoric thinking is effective because it transcends logical limits (how can I convince this man that he is not Jesus) and instead continues the patient's own metaphor, merely intensifying it by moving to the thought, "If he is Jesus, he is a carpenter." If one accepts that he is Jesus, it is irrefutable that he is a carpenter, and quite unlikely that, as Jesus, he would refuse the request to help someone in need.

Madanes (1981) has pointed out that systems can themselves be viewed as metaphors. "For example," she writes, "a wife who vomits compulsively may be expressing disgust at her husband." This sensitivity to the metaphoric nature of the symptom can lead the therapist to new and slightly altered metaphors that challenge the metaphor by which the system is operating. Bateson and colleagues (1956) published a ground-breaking paper, "Towards a Theory of Schizophrenia." With the benefit of hindsight, it is now generally accepted that, while they believed they were theorizing about the etiology and treatment of schizophrenia, their major contribution was instead to sensitize us to the nature of communication, and particularly to the power to metaphor.

I mentioned earlier the disarming quality of metaphor. This is true either if the metaphor is presented to a person or system, as happens in the therapeutic encounter, or if a particular metaphor has come to dominate the life of a person or system. It is important to remember that the power of metaphor cuts both ways—the power to hurt or to help. The early work of Selvini-Palazzoli and her group in implementing the theorizing of Bateson and his group is well-known. The general term *paradoxical thinking* has become a kind of shorthand symbol for all those theorists who struggle to find ways to rescue their patients from the grip of the often destructive metaphors by which they live.

Humor, like metaphor, has a disarming quality. Although laughter is such an important part of life, it has received relatively scant attention in the psychological literature. Mahrer and Gervaize (1984), however, under-took a comprehensive review of the issue of strong laughter in therapy. They concluded that laughter that is a singular, discrete event in the session and is marked by strength, high energy, and intensity is a welcome and desirable event. Such laughter is valuable for several reasons. It may indicate a positive shift in the patient's self-concept or self-perspective. It may heighten feelings. It may move the patient toward healthier goals. It may also strengthen the patient–therapist relationship through increased warmth and reduced emotional distance. They then list a number of therapeutic methods for eliciting strong laughter. Curiously, the telling of a joke is not included.

The use of jokes may have important functions in helping patients to be released from the grip of oppressive metaphors. Such jokes, of course, find their way into therapy because the therapist feels that they are evocative of the oppressive metaphor, and may produce change. The telling of a joke in therapy is akin to storytelling as practiced by Erickson and colleagues (1976). It is playful, tends to catch the listener unawares, and because it is unexpected in the context of therapy, may increase alertness, thus encouraging some interruption of the existing cognitive frame.

A mother and father in their late fifties came to therapy with their 26-year-old son, who was still living at home. He had dropped out of some of the best colleges, and had lived at home since the age of 20, never holding a job for more than a few days, and frequently unemployed. After a number of sessions in which the family had demonstrated quite well how much they could stick together in disqualifying one rational suggestion after another on my part, I suddenly found myself very bored and uninterested. As I listened to them drone on, an old joke came to my mind. I found myself inquiring if they had ever heard the story about Mrs. Cohen.

> One day Mrs. Cohen pulled up to a plush hotel in Florida. As she went to the desk, she was greeted by the manager, who noticed that her chauffeur had gone to the back seat of her limo, picked up her very handsome son, and deposited him on a chair in the lobby. "What a handsome young son you have, Mrs. Cohen," said the manager, "and how sad it is that he can't walk." "What do you mean, can't walk?" replied Mrs. Cohen. "Thanks to God, he doesn't have to."

There was general laughter, followed by silence. The family began to play with the story. Mother, at first, laughed and said that she couldn't see what was so terrible about that—he was in the lap of luxury. The young man did not think it was so funny. He wondered what life would be like for the young man as he got older. If the legs weren't used for long enough, he thought, wouldn't they begin to atrophy? The father said he felt kind of like the chauffeur. Having enjoyed a good laugh, we went on with the session.

Interestingly enough, the family returned to the theme of this joke frequently in subsequent meetings. The young man said to his mother one day, "Don't Mrs. Cohen me." Sometimes she would herself allude to the "Mrs. Cohen fallacy." Father wondered when the boy would regain the use of his legs. After a few months, the young man got a full-time job, and a bit after, an apartment of his own. A follow-up call revealed that, after a year, he was maintaining his newfound independence.

A young couple in their early thirties entered therapy because of marital problems. He was a rather demanding and perfectionistic mate, although he felt that he was very empathic and supportive. His approach to the marriage was very serious, and she stolidly resisted his pleas for lengthy conversations about their relationship, where it was going, why it wasn't better than it was, and so forth. The more he would pursue her with requests for heart-to-heart talks, the more she would distance herself. He felt extremely put-upon, because he believed he was trying so hard to make things work, and she so frequently rebuffed him. I asked if I had ever told them about Moish.

> Moish was a good and a God-fearing man. His religion demanded that he pray three times a day, but Moish prayed constantly. Moish did many good deeds. Nonetheless, tragedy continually dogged him. His business failed, the dog died, he got boils, and developed a bad case of gas. One day, he cried out to the Lord. "What is it with you? I do nothing but good deeds. I think only of others. You ask me to pray three times a day, and I pray constantly. What is wrong?" The voice of the Lord replied loud and clear: "Moish, you 'noodge' [harass] me too much."

The couple was much amused by this story. Curiously, the husband did not become defensive, but began to observe the effect of what they began to call his "Moishisms" on her distancing behavior. Again, the story became a new part of the couple's interaction, a new metaphor that helped them to reconstruct their own reality in a more productive way. One of her observations was that it made her nervous to be put in the position of God, and this caused her to feel even more distant. They began to focus instead on what was good in their marriage, and in particular, what good friends they were. Both agreed that sharing what they each liked about the marriage was much more enjoyable than endless attempts to analyze it. Both agreed that intimacy increased.

I have cited two examples of the use of jokes in therapy, and described jokes as a particular type of metaphoric intervention. I am in no way suggesting that there is a need for a new therapeutic modality henceforth to be known as joke therapy. It is simply useful to remember that an appropriate joke, growing out of the patient, couple, or family's metaphoric bind, may be a useful way of introducing therapeutic change.

As with any intervention, there are certain qualifications to be met. First, the therapist must enjoy telling jokes. Second, the therapist should be sure that the joke is, indeed, motivated by the therapeutic situation, and not by a personal need for attention on the part of the therapist. Finally, the patient, or the system, may or may not find the joke funny, or may not find it helpful. Good comics know that if you have to explain it, it isn't funny. The same holds true for jokes in therapy. If they are not responded to, that is fine, too. But if their message is belabored by the therapist, they may have precisely the reverse of the desired effect. They may be turned from metaphor to simile, and engender the very resistance that we would like to avoid.

REFERENCES

Bateson, G., Jackson, D., Haley, J., and Weakland, J. (1956). Toward a theory of schizophrenia. *Behavioral Science* 1:251–264.
Erickson, E., Rossi, E., and Rossi, S. (1976). *Hypnotic Realities*, p. 225. New York: Irvington.
Haley, J. (1973). *Uncommon Therapy: The Psychiatric Techniques of Milton H. Erickson: M. D.*, p. 214. New York: W. W. Norton.
Madanes, C. (1981). *Strategic Family Therapy*, p. 32. San Francisco: Jossey-Bass.
Mahrer, A., and Gervaize, P. (1984). An integrative review of strong laughter in psychotherapy: what it is and how it works. *Psychotherapy* 21:510–516.

16

The Place of Humor in Psychotherapy

Warren S. Poland

In a 1971 contribution to the technique of psychotherapy Kubie (Chapter 8, this volume) spelled out cautionary advice concerning the destructive potential of humor in psychotherapy. From a technical viewpoint his warnings are well taken; certainly this is especially so if one recognizes his allowing slight leeway for the occasional and specific use of humor.

It is my feeling that humor may also be used quite constructively in making a therapeutic intervention and that recent advances in psychoanalytic ego psychology and the theory of countertransference enlighten us as to the significance of such humor.

Because Kubie made the point that most therapists avoid presenting examples of their therapeutic use of humor, I will present two case reports from my work in psychoanalysis. My entire experience in recent years has been in psychoanalysis; although the situation in analysis is different from that in the briefer therapies, it has some advantage due to the opportunity for more intensive follow-up on the effect of humor. While the following comments may seem flat in a printed article, they were experienced by the patients and me as funny, eliciting laughter.

CASE REPORTS

Case 1. This patient was a 43-year-old woman who was in her second year of psychoanalysis with me. At the beginning of one hour, the patient recounted with great anger how her father had guarded her from seeing books that he considered to be too adult because of their sexual or aggressive content. As a child, whenever she asked to see such a book, he dismissed her with the comment, "No, that's a man's book!"

The patient then went on to speak of her current complaints about her husband, whom she bitterly resented for not being giving enough. She spent the next 20 minutes complaining about men in general. After this she spoke of her dissatisfaction with her analytic work with me, particularly in terms of how little she was getting from me. She went on to say that she had heard a good deal about Karen Horney and was very interested in learning something of Horney's advice on self-analysis (presumably so that she could try to provide herself with what she had not obtained from me).

At this point the patient noticed on my bookcase a copy of Horney's collected papers. She asked me for permission to borrow the book, to which I answered, "No, that's a man's book!"

The patient's initial response was to laugh and to suggest that I said this to try to make her laugh. The subsequent work then had to do with sorting out the distortions of her father transference.

The patient experienced my point as a reinforcement of my alliance with her, using the laughter to move to a position of greater observation from one of simply reliving earlier experiences. That is, the patient experienced the joke as one in which she and I were able to re-ally ourselves in order to view a transferential ghost, and the therapeutic regression was brought more directly into the service of her ego.

The obvious danger in such a case is that the joke could have been experienced as gratification of an erotic longing for her father. Considerably later in analysis this matter did come up. However, this risk did not seem to interfere with the therapeutic utility of my intervention nor to function as a parameter that was not subsequently analyzable.

Case 2. This patient is the 40-year-old professional man referred to in Chapter 1 who had a "Yes, but" character. See pp. 20–21.

DISCUSSION

The above two examples here, like all interventions, are complex in the mixture of what they simultaneously clarify and obscure. In terms of subsequent work with these patients I am satisfied that it led to the further opening of associations rather than to closure.

I am not suggesting that humor is without attendant dangers, as described by Kubie (1971). Some of the dangers I have encountered in other instances with my patients have been the use of humor to act out in the transference–countertransference some erotic interaction on a symbolic level; the use of humor to act out and to gratify, thus obscuring, sadistic aggressive impulses; and the use of humor to obscure frustration by obtaining narcissistic gratification.

It is my impression that the most crucial criterion the therapist can use to evaluate the usefulness of humor is the state of the therapeutic alliance. Where the alliance is weakened because of the extensiveness of the conflictual sphere of the patient's ego or of the regression leading to this, then the greatest likelihood exists that the therapist will use humor as an aggressive tool against the patient. These are situations that Racker (1957) has described as instances of the analyst's complementary identification, rather than concordant identification, with the patient.

> The concordant identification is based on introjection and projection . . . this part of you is I, and . . . this part of me is you. . . . The complementary identifications are produced by the fact that the patient treats the analyst as an internal (projected) object, and in consequence the analyst feels treated as such; that is, he identifies himself with this object. [p. 312]

Racker considered empathy to be similar to concordant identification and added: "To the degree to which the analyst fails in the concordant identifications and rejects them, certain complementary identifications become intensified" (p. 312).

In this light we can now consider the useful potential of humor in psychotherapy. Those who practice psychoanalytically oriented psychotherapy, as well as those who practice primarily classical psychoanalysis, often find that their resistance to resonating with the psychology of the patient are greater problems than the acting out of neurotic countertransference distortions. To put it differently, Kubie's warning against the expression of humor by the junior therapist must be paralleled by its corollary—a warning against the fear of experiencing and using humor by the therapist. In the cases described here, the humor was spontaneous and was appreciated by both patient and therapist.

Spontaneity

By "spontaneous" I do not mean to suggest that the impulse expressed in wit is not digested by the ego prior to expression. However, much of the processing done by the therapist's work ego is done unconsciously.

There is a distressing myth concerning perfectionism in psychotherapy, which, unfortunately, is often identified with psychoanalysis. This suggests that every intervention the analyst or psychotherapist makes must be absolutely autonomous from conflict. This totalistic view of course ignores the concept of the continuum of secondary autonomy and leads to behavioral stereotypes that approach the absoluteness of death and would be more appropriate for the role of the mortician than for that of the therapist.

Consensus

We are all aware of the many problems in trying to assess the actual validity of an interpretation in the presence of a doctor–patient consensus of validity. What is relevant in evaluating validity is the subsequent course of the patient's associations. I have presented two examples, without going into the follow-up, where I believe that the patients' subsequent course demonstrated not only the validity but the usefulness of the partial interpretations made by humor. I am especially impressed with the usefulness of humor in cases like these since it demonstrates the therapist's striking concordant identifications with the patient.

The abstinence principle, which recommends that the therapist frustrate the patient's wish for transference gratification, can only apply when the patient and therapist are together, when there is something that can be genuinely frustrated. Silence, distance, and detachment are not necessarily evidence of employing the abstinence principle in a useful way. The abstinence principle is relevant only to the extent that it promotes further psychologic work by the patient. It can, like humor, be used to act out sadistic impulses toward the patient. As Anna Freud (1954) pointed out in the context of analysis, technique was not devised for the defense of the analyst.

Integrated, appropriate, spontaneous humor is indicative of a high degree of alliance between the patient and the therapist and is thus informative of the presence of the patient's observing ego. The fact that humor cannot, and should not, be a major tool of the therapist does not mean that it must always be avoided.

Wit can provide a very useful mode for the therapist's intervention and can be indicative of the state of the therapeutic alliance and of the patient's observing ego. That it can often be misused and can be highly charged with unneutralized conflictual feeling ought not lead to a therapist's resisting its possible constructive use in psychotherapy.

REFERENCES

Freud, A. (1954). Problems of technique in adult analysis. *Bulletin of the Philadelphia Association for Psychoanalysis* 4:44–70.

Kubie, L. S. (1971). The destructive potential of humor in psychotherapy. *American Journal of Psychiatry* 127:861–866.
Racker, H. (1957). The meanings and uses of countertransference. *Psychoanalytic Quarterly* 26:303–357.

17

Jokes Psychoanalysts Tell

Margot Tallmer and Joseph Richman

Although psychoanalytic case histories in the literature often contain reports on what made a particular patient cry, the corollary is rare: we seldom learn what made a patient laugh. Even less frequently do accounts surface of what makes analysts laugh. As is well-known, Freud included about 200 puns, jokes, and anecdotes in "Jokes and Their Relation to the Unconscious," and he also told Fliess in 1897 that he was collecting Jewish jokes (a collection Freud later destroyed). Freud clearly had great affection for jokes and used them as a part of his presenting self. Although he did not write of the jokes and witticisms of his patients, he did use jokes when analyzing (Lowenstein 1958) and as illustrations of psychological theories. For example, to illustrate the continued importance of infantile egoism, he told of the married couple, one of whom said to the other, "If one of us dies first, I shall move to Paris."

HUMOR AS A PSYCHOTHERAPEUTIC TOOL

Today, the question of whether to use humor as a psychotherapeutic tool is only ambivalently answered. Many articles in the psychoanalytic literature cite a particular idiosyncratic use of humor and the beneficial results attained, but generally with the caveat that humor must be used *very* selectively. Rosenheim (1974) sees humor in an interpersonal framework, broadening patients' self-awareness and providing a corrective experience. Heuscher (1980), urging a judicious use of humor, stresses the need to assess carefully the genuineness of the relationship between therapist and patient. Humor can force an opening into a wider world, enticing the patient to forsake a monotonous, repressed existence and to confront and integrate a different, more intimate reality. The patient's rigid world design is at least temporarily modified. But the quality of the interpersonal interaction, the relevance of the joke, and the patient's receptivity to the use of humor must be taken into account as well as the monitoring of transferential and countertransferential aspects. Humor is a helpful technical device, a therapeutic tool that can be learned, but its effectiveness also depends on the artistic and stylistic talents of the analyst (Rose 1966). Kubie (1971) and Reik (1964) warn of the possible destructive effects of using humor in psychotherapy. Poland (1971) suggests a clear appraisal of the therapeutic alliance to potentiate possible benefits. He further notes the corollary to all these warnings—the therapist's fear of experiencing and utilizing humor. What would the analyst's use of humor reveal?

The senior author (M.T.) has employed humor, but not always to the particular advantage of the patient. Some time ago, a patient was referred to me, after many years of treatment with a Dr. Thorne. The patient consistently compared me most unfavorably to the former analyst, reiterating that my therapeutic efforts had made him ill; even now in the session he was experiencing a lot of soreness of his lower abdomen. In lieu of inspecting or even acknowledging my rage, narcissistic hurt, and frustration at the patient's constant carping, I quipped, "Perhaps you now have a thorn in your side!"

Despite this lamentable illustration, it must be acknowledged that jokes are as important in analysis as any other intrapsychic production, revealing as they do underlying meaningful material. In many ways they are analogous to dreams, for both jokes and dreams employ primary-process thinking and make use of displacement, illusions, conversion to the opposite, condensation, and magical thinking (Freud 1905). Dreams are an asocial phenomenon, of interest primarily to literary or psychoanalytically inclined persons, while jokes are, by definition, interpersonal, requiring as they do a listener and a teller. They both are by analogy royal roads to the unconscious.

THE PURPOSE OF HUMOR

What purpose, then, do jokes serve? Popular notions of the uses of humor include the expression of sexuality and the adaptive, active defense against melancholy. From this latter idea has developed the stereotype of the sad clown. Zolotow (1952) describes Bert Lahr as a "melancholy clown." W. C. Fields was a notoriously heavy drinker; Mark Twain was rumored to suffer from persistent bouts of sadness, and Sid Caesar has been referred to in newspapers and magazines as a depressed, pessimistic man.

S. J. Perelman believed that humor was basically an expression of anger, its purpose to deflate pretentiousness and expose man's follies. He once said, "Generally speaking, I don't believe in kindly humor—I don't think it exists." Robert Gottlieb, who was Perelman's editor for a time, agreed that anger was an essential element of the writer's work. Perelman, he said, was "very charming and very affable and a wonderful raconteur . . . but in my view, a deeply involved, selfish and angry person, like many great humorists" (Richler 1987).

In Freud's (1905) view, the function of humor is to liberate our forbidden, inhibited thoughts and allow us to suddenly, abruptly voice them. The joke technique diverts attention, momentarily relaxing our internal censor. The unwelcome content, of id derivation, slips past the superego—the customs officer has failed to notice the contraband. The energy that is usually required to repress the inhibited underlying thoughts and the associated affect has now become superfluous. This successful circumvention affords us a deep pleasure, pleasure that is then discharged in laughter. Pain has been converted into enjoyment. Psychic economy has been achieved by a mature ego. The successful resolution of the incongruity inherent in humor is ego-enhancing, leading to a feeling of achievement, competence, and mastery.

Like dreams, jokes allow the expression of such repressed desires as denigration of a respected figure, rejection of morals, an attempt at seduction, even an attack on reason, all made acceptable and pleasurable. Freud differentiated between tendentious jokes—jokes that have a point to make—and nontendentious jokes, such as puns. Tendentious jokes have the greatest intrapsychic importance for the listener and the teller and, not incidentally, are more likely to lead to outbursts of laughter.

Humor offers us a creative discharge, a safety valve against unchecked aggression; it is closely related to the unconscious (Schwarz 1972). Certainly, humor does provide psychic economy. When a long-suffering, obedient person says he has been freed of his "forbidinal" impulses, interpretation is facilitated. Or, when a female patient claims to have consistently loved her mother, even during the "reproachment" period, we can easily examine her ambivalence. Humor is an adaptive mechanism of a high order, a victory of the ego in the face of an objective stress situation. It can illuminate conflict, permit an expression of id impulses, and serve as a socially acceptable interpersonal communication. Nor is humor confined to impulses. Jokes can assist in mastery of the anxiety and stress engendered by major critical life cycle experiences.

JOKES TOLD BY PSYCHOANALYSTS

Although there have been a large number of jokes about psychoanalysis, we know of no previous study that examined the jokes *told* by psychoanalysts. Therefore, in a very behavioral-scientist way, we proceeded to ask a group of analytic trainees and practicing psychoanalysts ($N = 160$) for their age and gender and their favorite joke. Each joke was then analyzed for major themes, for the butts of the stories, and for the main characters. We also sought to find any differences, by sex or age of the analyst, in the types of jokes reported. The major themes are discussed in the following sections.

Aspects of the Psychoanalytic Situation

A small but significant number of jokes reported deal with loneliness and an implicit dread of separation. The basic message is that we need each other and that interpersonal contact is essential. Here are two examples:

A Jewish woman requests cremation. In response to her persistent pleading, the rabbi, although horrified, reluctantly agrees. She then asks that her ashes be scattered over Bloomingdale's. "Why?" asks the rabbi. The woman answers, "That way, at least I'd be sure of seeing my daughter once a week!"

The value of being bisexual is that you have twice as much chance of being alone on a Saturday night.

This second example is an interesting offering, for the actual joke, a Woody Allen line, suggests that bisexuality would offer twice as much chance for a date.

In most of these jokes, loneliness is seen as the result of one's own doing. However, in one—"What's yellow and eats alone? Yoko Ono"—loneliness occurs as a result of victimization. Because John Lennon was killed by a mental patient, we may ask if there is a buried fear in this joke of the results of working with emotionally disturbed persons, or of getting nourishment alone.

Psychoanalytic Techniques

The method of confronting patients is also an important theme; in their jokes the analysts debate the value of direct, dramatic confrontation versus long-term, slow, unfolding interpretation in making the unconscious conscious. Kindness and reassurance may, in fact, be cruel. An older woman analyst, now relocated in a distant continent, sent in this example:

> Situation: Aboard a U.S. Destroyer, World War II. Sailor Fitch sits peacefully on a scaffold. The sky is blue, the sea calm, the air balmy. Suddenly, over the bullhorn two feet from Fitch's ear, comes the bellowing voice of the first mate: "Now hear this, now hear this: First announcement—Seaman Fitch's mother has died, repeat, Seaman Fitch's mother has died. Second announcement . . ." But Fitch never hears the second, for the shock has caused him to faint dead away, fall off the scaffold, and break his leg. The captain, advised of the circumstances of the mishap, summons the first mate. In a towering fury, he roars, "Mister, of all the stupid, insensitive ways to tell a man he's lost his mother, this is the worst. The next time you do a thing like that you'll get punished so you'd better find a better way." Inevitably, a few weeks later, a similar situation arises. The captain hears the crew being summoned on deck for roll call at an unusual time and goes out on the bridge to see what's up. There stands the first mate, roster in hand, bawling out to the assembled crew, "Now when I call your names I want all of you whose mothers are living to take two steps forward!" He proceeds to call the roll. When he gets to Abercrombie and Abercrombie starts to step forward, the first mate bawls out, "Not so fast, Abercrombie!"

The need to be tactful and considerate, and the fear of being destructive, is addressed in a different way by the following joke, also contributed by a female analyst, aged 53:

> A man was sitting in an airplane next to a woman holding a baby in her arms. When she drew the blanket away from the child's face, the man became convulsed with laughter. His laughter became uncontrollable and he pointed to the child exclaiming, "That is the ugliest baby I ever saw . . . What an ugly baby." He rose from his seat and walked to the back of the plane, still convulsed with laughter. The mother sat, stunned and weeping. A stewardess approached and said, "Madam, I'm so sorry to see you so distressed; is there anything I can get you? A pillow? A cup of coffee? A banana for your monkey?"

The jokes caution us not to abruptly remove symptoms, but to concentrate on ego defenses and strengths. (Other possible themes of this joke include hostility to mother and infant, sibling rivalry, and the importance of appearance.)

The following, submitted by a male, aged 60, may reveal a persistent interest in oedipal problems, but also evidences a stress on retaining fantasy life:

A lady comes to a psychiatrist complaining that she cannot sleep. She is married, a mother, yet she dreams of a fancy young man who makes love to her. She gets anxious and has insomnia. Pills are prescribed. She returns to the doctor and reports that the pills work okay, but she wants to give them back. The psychiatrist asks why and she says, "I am kind of missing my young man!"

The Psychoanalyst as a Person

Analysts laugh at the pomposity, the assumed profundity and expected wisdom of our profession. They caution therapists to stick to the rules:

Patient: "Doctor, doctor, kiss me."
Doctor: "Technically, I shouldn't even be on the couch."

and poke fun at the discipline of psychology:

A man, having completed a memory course based on remembering through associations, runs into a familiar face: "I know you—I met you in 1980 at the corner of Madison and 81st—you were wearing a blue and brown suit and your name is . . ." The familiar face stares. "Are you crazy? I'm your brother Charlie!"

It is noteworthy that this last example was sent to us in the mail by a middle-aged male analyst who had relocated to another part of the country. Are personal concerns of being remembered a factor in this particular story?

Many of the jokes acknowledge that shrinks are beset by their own problems and that their authority must be questioned, since they are beleaguered by their own intrapsychic struggles.

Four clergymen were sitting on a park bench sunning themselves on a warm spring day. One of them said, "Since we're here alone, let's talk about our own problems." The first minister said that he had an alcohol problem and drank uncontrollably. The second confessed that he was addicted to gambling and often used congregational funds. The third said he had designs on one of his married women parishioners. And then the fourth, who had not spoken, was asked what would be his most troubling problem. He hesitated and then said, "I am an incurable gossip."

With such a fellow, patients would be foolish to open up. Priests (and/or analysts) have sexual, monetary, and impulse problems just as everyone else does, making us at one with our patients.

En passant, it should be noted that most of these jokes, all sent in by psychoanalysts, deal with psychiatrists, rather than analysts, social workers, therapists, or psychologists. Thus not only is our profession projectively teased but the M.D. is specifically targeted.

> A man went to a psychiatrist seeking treatment for depression. "I cry a lot. I can't sleep. I am very unhappy. I don't enjoy anything. My life is totally miserable. Can you help me?" The psychiatrist replies, "I can cure your depression, but what's the use?"

Despite the stress on the psychiatrist or therapist as the subject, the jokes maintain that patients are still the most important persons in the analytic relationship. A 51-year-old female psychoanalyst writes:

> Joe claimed to know everyone in the world. His wife, Helen, didn't believe it. "You don't know Governor Cuomo," she said. They went to Albany and the governor greeted them warmly. "Okay," said Helen, "but you don't know President Clinton." Off they went to Washington, D.C. Clinton came to the door of his office. "Joe, my old friend!" he exclaimed. "Okay," said Helen, "but you don't know the Pope." They went to Rome and visited the Vatican. Helen stayed below in the courtyard. Joe told her, "In ten minutes the Pope and I will appear at the balcony." Indeed, they did. At that moment, an old woman tapped Helen on the shoulder. "Tell me," she said. "Who's that man up there with Joe?"

Male Versus Female Humor

Frequent themes of jokes told by analysts include Talmudic and/or analytic reasoning, being the recipient of arcane, mysterious knowledge, the unhelpful helper, and therapeutic enterprise. Since jokes are commonly employed to demonstrate one's superiority, ethnic jokes abound in our sample and are used to criticize therapeutic endeavors.

The issue of status leads us to a consideration of male versus female humor, for herein social power is also addressed. Traditionally, women are expected to be respondents to male initiators of humor. Humor is associated with dominance, aggression, and assertiveness, all traditionally male purviews. A female clown is a deviant and, empirically, women tell demonstrably fewer jokes than men in social situations, in group therapy sessions, and in personnel training groups. In terms of power, higher status is generally correlated with making others, rather than the self, the butt of jokes. For example, executives laugh at junior staff, who in turn ridicule those lower on the career ladder. Women, often more sensitive than men in social situations and more affected by the responses of others, do not use others as targets in their jokes. While it is commonly assumed that sex and aggression are topics more popular with men than with women, this is not true of our sample. Nor do women in our group prefer jokes in which women are victimized, another commonly held assumption.

In looking at any interpretation, the lens of the interpreter must be examined. The two authors of this paper, one female and one male, differed in their interpretation of the following story, told by a 58-year-old woman:

> When a beautiful, talented, brilliant woman working as a prostitute was asked what she was doing in this whorehouse, her reply was, "Guess I'm just lucky."

Humor is in the "I" of the beholder: The female author heard the stereotypic theme of victimization and the putative pleasure women take in such a state. The male author resonated to the nonsexual symbolism of vocational choice and its satisfaction—just as the prostitute who told a difficult client, "It's a business doing pleasure with you" was responding to the vicissitudes of troublesome clients, whatever the profession. His analysis saw the above joke as expressing an appreciation of her vocational choice, which involves the gratification of the total personality—the intellectual, the libidinal, and the interpersonal. The prostitute is "lucky" for these reasons, and not because she is a victim.

Even taking into account variances in interpretation, there are clear differences between the jokes contributed by men and those sent in by women. Interestingly, the main character of the joke and the butt of the humor is male in *both* cases. The main identification in the joke is also with the male. From the women, though, nearly all the jokes are about sex, with male inadequacy as a frequent theme. A 33-year-old female analyst writes:

> An elephant sees a naked man and says to him, "How can you breathe through *that*?"

Direct teasing of males and masculine interest is revealed in the following story, told often in many versions:

> A retired man puts all his energies into golf. One day he asks his priest, "Do you think there are any golf courses in heaven?" The priest agrees to ask St. Peter. Next day, the priest returns and says, "Well, I've got good news and bad news. The good news is that there are wonderful golf courses in heaven. The bad news is that you tee off tomorrow at seven."

In jokes contributed by men, oedipal themes are in evidence, as well as avoidance of growing up and hostility toward women. All are present in the following joke, one of a large number dealing with mothers bragging about their sons:

> The first mother says her son sends her flowers every day, the second says her son buys all her clothes, the third says hers sent her a TV set and VCR, but the fourth claims that her son goes to an analyst five times a week and talks only about her.

Besides conflict with the mother, who is nearly always presented within an oedipal plot, there is other conflict with women, as in this example:

> Two cannibals, after walking several hours in the jungle, stop to eat. One says, "I just can't stand my mother-in-law." The other replies, "Well then, just eat the vegetables."

Men in our sample also joked about aging and sibling rivalry more often than the women.

DISCUSSION

The humor of psychoanalysts is of a high order, reflecting the special characteristics endemic to our profession; psychoanalytic work demands a long incubation, a training period that is, in a sense, never completed. An analyst is dependent upon intellect leavened by artistry, and that intellect is persistently concerned with introspection. The interpersonal field is fairly well controlled. The analyst is self-employed and reaps monetary rewards, rewards that are seen as making treatment meaningful for the patient. Further, analysts are not free to say whatever they may wish to, must exercise control of impulses, and are vigorously opposed to exploiting patients for narcissistic gratification. (These strictures are largely true for most professionals, but analysts must scrutinize their behavior regularly.) Finally, psychoanalysis is often a lonely profession. Analysts eschew outside contacts with patients, work with a limited number of persons, and subscribe to the obligation not to discuss daily analytic work directly with others. All these issues emerge in the jokes of psychoanalysts.

These jokes are not offensive to our profession, but rather demonstrate the importance of our work to all of us. Comedy, even more than tragedy, points out flaws and targets for correction. In tragedy, there is one fatal flaw; in comedy, all is flawed.

We should not feel defensive but rather pleased by these jokes, for they tickle the toes of pomposity and arrogance and affirm our common humanity. The true mark of humor is the ability to laugh at oneself. Our sample has this in abundance. We psychoanalysts do deal with the nitty gritty of existence every day in our work. We cannot constantly be elevated to an exalted position.

Finally, the authors must acknowledge that analysts also poke fun at researchers who study humor:

Q: Why do some condoms come filled out with a little ink reservoir at the tip?
A: So that if you can't come, you can at least write.

REFERENCES

Freud, S. (1905). Jokes and their relation to the unconscious. *Standard Edition* 8:3–245.

Heuscher, J. (1980). The role of humor and folklore themes in psychotherapy. *American Journal of Psychiatry* 137(12):1546–1549.

Kubie, L. S. (1971). The destructive potential of humor in psychotherapy. *American Journal of Psychiatry* 127:861–866.

Lowenstein, R. M. (1958). Remarks on some variations in psychoanalytic techniques. *International Journal of Psychoanalysis* 39:202–210, 240–242.

Poland, W. S. (1971). The place of humor in psychotherapy. *American Journal of Psychiatry* 128(5):635–637.

Reik, T. (1964). *Listening with the Third Ear*. New York: Pyramid Books.

Richler, (1987). The road to dyspepsia. *New York Times Book Review* August 9.

Rose, G. J. (1966). *King Lear* and the use of humor in treatment. Paper presented at Western New England Psychoanalytic Society, New Haven, March, 1966.

Rosenheim, E. (1974). Humor in psychotherapy: an interactive experience. *American Journal of Psychotherapy* 28(4–5):584–591.

Schwarz, B. E. (1972). Telepathic humoresque. Presented at the 125th Annual Meeting of the American Psychiatric Association, Dallas, Texas.

Zolotow, M. (1952). Broadway's saddest clown. *Saturday Evening Post* 224:34–35.

Classical, Object Relations, and Self Psychological Perspectives on Humor

Roberta Satow

The meaning of jokes and humor in treatment seems to have been explained by Freud to everyone's satisfaction until recently when English object relations theory and self psychology have gained much wider acceptance in psychoanalytic circles. Hence, it makes a great deal of sense to reconsider the role of humor in therapy—particularly group therapy, where the possible uses of humor are so much greater than in individual treatment.

Until now, humor, laughing, or jokes in treatment seemed to be inextricably linked, in theory, to the structural model. From that theoretical point of view, laughter is the release of repressed hostility. There's nothing more to be said.

But in practice, we all know that there is much more to be said:

1. Humor encourages the observing ego.
2. Humor points out themes most anxiety provoking.
3. Humor can be an excellent way of making an interpretation that bypasses resistance.
4. Humor can strengthen the working alliance.
5. Humor can enhance group cohesion.
6. Humor can be used for scapegoating.
7. Humor can be an expression of spontaneity, mastery, and strength.

How we understand humor, jokes, or laughter depends to a large extent on our theoretical perspective. Different clinical interventions depend on the theoretical perspective of the therapist.

If we think in terms of the structural model, we will tend to be cynical about humor in group or individual treatment. We tend to look for the hostile and defensive aspects of laughter when used by the analyst or the patient. If the therapist uses humor more than very occasionally, we might wonder if this isn't a way of expressing countertransferential hostility to the patient or if it isn't an expression of the therapist's narcissism.

On the other hand, for the patient to tell a joke or engage in humorous banter is seen as a type of resistance that requires interpretation of its defensive function. Greenson (1967, p. 386) points out, for example, that attempts to engage in humorous exchanges during treatment may signify the patient's resistance to acknowledging hateful feelings toward the analyst. Patients may cover up hostility with humor or teasing in the hope that it will escape notice. But Greenson warns that we must be vigilant in seeking out the negative transference. Although Greenson says that the best therapists do seem to possess a sense of humor and a ready wit and to enjoy story telling, the analyst must always be careful that it is not exhibitionist, entertaining, or disguised sadism.

If we think in terms of object relations theory, we will tend to focus on the object relationship that is being repeated or defended against. What self representation is in play and what object representation is being projected in the humorous exchange? Is the patient playing the object representation and the group being treated as the self representation or vice versa?

If we are self psychologists, we will look for the adaptive and mastery-building aspects of laughing. Humor might be used by the patient in group as a way of maintaining self-esteem or as a way of maintaining boundaries while sharing some threatening feelings. The self psychologist would look for the two aspects of the transference—the repetitious one and the selfobject function. This therapist would focus on what was developmentally needed and try to legitimate the child's needs as expressed in the laughing, humor, or joke.

Let me give you a vignette from a group to illustrate my point. Jane came into group and sat down. She is an extremely moody borderline patient. The members of the group are often scared of her moods. She had been feeling extremely positive during the last few group sessions, but this time she sat in a fetal position with her legs up and did not respond to the group. The therapist chose to let it go and let the group deal with it. After 20 minutes, John asked her what was going on. She said she didn't want to be there. The group went off in other directions, ignoring her. Then, 15 minutes before the end of the session, Jane jumped up and said, "Okay, I will tell everyone what's wrong with me." Everyone started to laugh. John said he never saw anything so funny in his life. Jane laughed along with the rest of the group.

From a classical perspective, the group's laughter could be seen as a relief from the tension caused by the group's rage at Jane's behavior. John, who was most hurt and angry at Jane's withholding, was the group member who found it most funny. Jane's laughing with them can be seen in the same way—a harmless expression of her own hostility that she had been sitting with all session.

However, the therapist did not view it that way. She understood it from an object relations perspective. Jane came from a family in which she was treated as very fragile. There was an overemphasis on her unhappiness. There was no humor in that house, no relief of tension. Her mother responded to her moodiness by responding to her as if she were a troubled, crazy person.

By leaving her alone, the therapist and the group were saying: "We're not so worried about you. You're not so crazy." It was through their *not* taking her so seriously that she got to the point of wanting to tell them what was going on. And when they all laughed, she experienced it as their saying she isn't so sick and crazy and bad. She does not have to be taken so seriously; she's not so fragile.

From the object relations point of view, Jane's being able to join the group in laughing at herself reflected her increasing ability to observe herself and appreciate the absurdity of her own behavior.

I think this example points out an important difference between individual and group treatment. In a recent talk, Priscilla Kaupff pointed out that group is often more useful with character disorders because the group can say things that the analyst can't. In this case, the therapist in an individual session would have had to sit silently while Jane sat silently. Or the analyst might have tried to engage Jane, which would have been a repetition of her mother treating her as fragile and disturbed. Or the analyst might have interpreted that Jane was trying to re-create her experience with her mother as the fragile, disturbed little girl, which probably would have gotten "Just leave me alone" or anger or silence.

It would have been much more difficult to let her be. And it would have been downright inappropriate for the analyst to start laughing at her if she decided to share what was bothering her, although the analyst might feel the same angry tension the group did.

The group did not get drawn into a repetition by her projective identification. This reflects well on the group because there is a pressure exerted by the projector on the recipient group members to experience her and behave in a way that is congruent with the projective fantasy (induced feeling). The psychological processing of the projection by the group members and the reinternalizion of the modified projection by the projector is referred to by different theorists as "containing," "processing," "metabolizing," etc.

If the recipient group members can deal with the feelings projected into them differently than the patient does, a new set of feelings is generated that can be viewed as a "processed" or "digested" version of the original ones. The reinternalizion of the processed feelings offer the projector/patient a new way of handling a painful set of feelings.

From the self psychologist's point of view, the group's letting her be while she was in her fetal position was performing a self–object function. She was welcome; they would be receptive if she wanted them, but they were not overly anxious about her unhappiness the way her mother was. Because the group served that positive self–object function, Jane was eventually able to join them, that is, decide to share with them what was bothering her. When they laughed, she was able to join them because their selfobject function had created a bond with the group. The laughing was a further bridge that she could take advantage of because she was already soothed.

Another example is a patient who came to a session and said to the group, "Unfortunately, our session was very helpful." Everyone laughed. From a classical perspective, the humor is related to the hostility. "You helped me but I hate you for it." A classical analyst might respond by pointing out the anger.

Melanie Klein (1977) would point out the anger at the envy of the good breast that comes along with the gratitude. Non-Kleinian object relations analysts would not necessarily focus on the anger, although it is clearly there. The focus might be on how difficult it is for the patient to feel helped because it sets off his wishes to be taken care of by the group, which he defends against so strongly.

The self psychologist would try to put him- or herself into the subjective shoes of the patient. What is this person feeling along with the anger? The self psychologist would reflect back on both sides of the person's inner experience and affect—the feeling that he was given to and fed, and the anger that he was hungry in the first place. In other words, the self psychologist would articulate both the good news and the bad news.

I hope this brief discussion has made clear that how we understand and deal with humor, laughter, and jokes in treatment is based on our general theoretical perspective about psychological development and what brings about healing.

REFERENCES

Greenson, R. (1967). *The Technique and Practice of Psychoanalysis*, vol. 1. New York: International Universities Press.

Klein, M. (1977). *Envy and Gratitude and Other Works: 1946–1963*. New York: Dell.

The Use of Humor in Psychotherapy

Harry A. Olson

One extremely potent, yet apparently little recognized tool in psychotherapy is humor. By humor, I am referring to something positive that brings mutually shared enjoyment and pleasure; that which is philosophic rather than belittling. Humor as a therapeutic tool must build instead of knock down, and therefore excludes sarcasm and cynicism, which aggrandize the self at the expense of others.

Positive humor is potent because it is a universal means of relationship-building. Those who laugh together soon forget their differences as humor provides a common bond for mutually shared experiences where the participants momentarily drop their guard and relate authentically. It may be said that a good belly-laugh levels all ranks and convinces all of the laugher's humanity. Humor is also a universally accepted indicator of positive mental health, with a sine qua non of emotional adjustment being the ability to laugh at oneself. Regardless of the cultural background and varying definitions of mental disorder, it is generally agreed that as an individual becomes emotionally disturbed, one of the first aspects to become impaired is the positive sense of humor. This becomes eclipsed by a lessening of social interest accompanied by an inordinate emphasis on superiority as opposed to equality. The disturbed person takes himself and his difficulties devastatingly seriously (O'Connell, personal correspondence).

The establishment or return of a positive sense of humor may well be considered a goal, or at least a highly desirable by-product, of psychotherapy, and the degree to which the sense of humor becomes established may be considered one criterion of the success of therapy. The person with a sense of humor is more likely to be flexible and able to take the exigencies of life in stride. Humor can thus become a buffer, without which a person would have to rely on less adaptive means to face the onslaughts of life. Humor becomes a sign of the encouraged person; its absence, a hallmark of discouragement (O'Connell 1975a).

From the Adlerian viewpoint, the overall goal of psychotherapy is to help the client move from a perceived minus situation to a plus situation (Ansbacher and Ansbacher 1956), to recognize and alter his mistaken notions (Shulman 1971), and to develop a more effective, courageous, and egalitarian approach to the tasks of life. In short, this is the process of encouragement. As a part of the therapeutic relationship, humor becomes encouraging and serves many purposes. Its use early in therapy takes the "edge" off the client's anxiety regarding the awesomeness of the therapist and the therapy process. With the appropriate use of humor, the therapist demonstrates his humanness, that he, is a "regular guy" who need not be feared (O'Connell 1975a). In my own practice I have found that humor also facilitates trust and the cementing of the therapeutic alliance. After all, someone who jokes with you can't be *all* bad. I was treating an emotionally immature, highly discouraged, and dependent 14-year old boy with very poor eyesight and poor coordination. He was picked on by his peers at school and had only one neighborhood friend. He was a teacher's pet and a tattletale, and displayed a very superior attitude with his peers. Initially, it was difficult for him to talk with me in therapy, so at the beginning of each session we swapped jokes and had some good laughs together. This was an effective icebreaker and led to the establishing of a relationship more rapidly than would have been possible otherwise.

Humor helps demonstrate acceptance and respect for the client, and also helps put the course of therapy in a positive direction. Although the therapist takes the client and his problems seriously, humor lets the client know that the therapist entertains hope and does not feel overwhelmed by the difficulties the client presents (O'Connell 1975b). Humor is contagious, and usually the client will respond positively to it.

In the analysis phase of therapy (Dreikurs 1967), humor allows the client to see, as Adler did, that everything can be something else as well, and that the client's problems have more facets than he originally anticipated; that problems may be redefined as opportunities for growth (O'Connell 1975b).

In the interpretation phase, which bleeds into that of reorientation/ reeducation (Dreikurs 1967) humor becomes a marvelous technique for allowing the client to see some of the useless things he is doing without becoming offended (O'Connell 1975b). Again, humor takes the edge off and lessens resistance. I have found that when some of my strongest interpretations are presented with a glint in my eye or phrased in a humorous way, they have had better results with a higher degree of acceptance by the client. The therapist's message becomes, "This is what you're doing to louse yourself up, but I still like you anyway." One of the most difficult things for many clients to do is to develop and maintain a truly positive (not bravado) sense of self-worth while finding out something about themselves that does not fit their self-ideal. The acceptance of self-worth, as a given apart from actions, must be learned in the process of therapy.

As the client begins to laugh with the therapist, he grows in his feelings of self-control over his problems. This is especially true in depression, as depression cannot survive a state of humor. When the client can bring himself to laugh, he vividly demonstrates to himself that he, not his symptoms or moods, is in control of his life. A true realization of this fact is often the turning-point from which earnest improvement can develop.

Since humor is contagious, usually the client will become encouraged by the therapist's encouraging outlook, and will use the therapist's sense of humor as a model for his own. Modeling is an important therapeutic responsibility (O'Connell 1975a) and is one of the fastest ways for the client to develop a positive sense of humor. Like responsibility, humor cannot be taught didactically, but must be observed and personally experienced to be mastered. Contrary to the opinion of some, a discouraged therapist will find it difficult at best, if not impossible, to encourage a discouraged client.

Although humor is an effective therapeutic tool, certain conditions must prevail. First, the humor must be genuine on the part of the therapist. If it is not, the client may feel conned and may back off through heightened resistance. Second, humor must never be at the client's expense. This discourages and is the antithesis of effective therapy (O'Connell 1975b). Third, the therapist must know his client and must understand what kind of humor is appropriate, the degree of subtlety necessary and when it should be used. Although generally very effective with depressives, using the same humor with a highly paranoid client, especially early in therapy, may prove disastrous. Common sense, clinical sensitivity, and skill are essential in the use of humor. Then, humor in therapy becomes a backdrop against which a variety of techniques are used, a part of the peculiar style of the clinician who employs it (O'Connell 1975b).

The poets can usually say things more tersely than those of us who resort to prose. Jack Point, the jester in Gilbert and Sullivan's *The Yeoman of the Guard*, succinctly sums up the use of humor in psychotherapy.

When they're offered to the world in merry guise
   Unpleasant truths are swallowed with a will.
For he who'd make his fellow-creatures wise
   Should always gild the philosophic pill!

REFERENCES

Ansbacher, H. L., and Ansbacher, R. R. (1956). *The Individual Psychology of Alfred Adler*. New York: Harper and Row.

Dreikurs, R. (1967). Goals in therapy. In *Psychodynamics, Psychotherapy, and Counseling*, ed. R. Dreikurs. Chicago: Alfred Adler Institute.

O'Connell, W. E. (1975a). The humorist: an ideal for humanistic psychology. In *Action Therapy and Adlerian Theory*, ed. W. E. O'Connell. Chicago: Alfred Adler Institute.

_____ (1975b). The humorous attitude: Research and clinical beginnings. In *Action Therapy and Adlerian Theory*, ed. W. E. O'Connell. Chicago: Alfred Adler Institute.

Shulman, B. H. (1971). Confrontation techniques in Adlerian psychotherapy. *Journal of Individual Psychology* 27:167–175.

Therapeutic Laughter:
What Therapists Do to Promote
Strong Laughter in Patients

Patricia A. Gervaize, Alvin R. Mahrer, and Richard Markow

The focus of this research is the patient who breaks into singularly strong, discrete, hearty laughter. The main audience to whom this paper is addressed is psychotherapists for whom such an event is a welcomed and desirable occurrence. The clinically relevant finding is that by examining a large number of instances of strong laughter in patients seen by professional psychotherapists, and by careful investigation of what these psychotherapists did just prior to the occurrence, it seems that there is a small set of actual interventions that precedes the strong laughter.

Not all therapeutic approaches regard this event as welcomed and desirable. In large measure, psychoanalytic clinicians consider this kind of laughter as perhaps pathognomonic of serious disturbance (Levine 1976, Noyes and Kolb 1963), as a dangerous expression of unconscious impulses (Bergler 1956, Freud 1905, Grotjahn 1970, Harman 1981, Plessner 1970), and as a defensive avoidance against threat (Ansel et al. 1981, Kubie 1971, Zuk 1966). In contrast, the large family of experiential approaches identifies such strong laughter as an expressly valuable therapeutic event (e.g., Bugental 1976, Farrelly and Brandsma 1974, Jackins 1965, Mahrer 1983, Perls 1970, Pierce et al. 1983, Polster and Polster 1973). It is held as an expression of therapeutic experiencing, positive movement, freeing of feeling, and the opening of deeper processes.

A comprehensive review of strong laughter in psychotherapy (Mahrer and Gervaize 1984 [Chapter 21, this book]) found no research on the question of antecedent therapist statements, but reported a rich clinical literature that was organized into eight categories of therapist statements held by practicing psychotherapists as directly instrumental to the occurrence of strong laughter in patients. A research design was built around an extensive library of audiotaped therapy sessions conducted by professional psychotherapists. By examining therapist statements antecedent to actual instances of strong laughter, and by comparing these with therapist statements antecedent to no laughter and mild/moderate laughter, the hypothesis could be examined that there were distinctive identifiable therapist statements that were followed by such strong laughter in patients.

METHODOLOGY

Data Pool

The data pool consisted of approximately 280 hours of audiotaped individual psychotherapy sessions conducted by fifteen professional therapists with seventy-five adult patients. The therapists were drawn from a variety of approaches and a variety of professional contexts. Most of the sessions were of the middle phases of therapy, and were illustrative of each therapist's actual work rather than selected as exemplar or demonstration sessions.

Identification of Strong Laughter, Other Laughter, and Non-laughter

In order to study strong laughter occurring as a singular, discrete event, rather than as a characteristic style of the patient, sessions that contained at least twelve instances of any kind of laughter were excluded from further study. In order to examine antecedent therapist statements, laughter events that occurred within the first three patient statements in the session were also excluded.

Strong laughter and other laughter were identified by means of a procedure used by Nichols (1974) and Nichols and Bierenbaum (1978) for identifying strong feeling moments in therapy sessions. A doctoral student in clinical psychology went through the entire pool of 280 hours of audiotaped therapy, and identified sixty-four instances of strong laughter and thirty of other (mild or moderate) laughter. Following this, two other doctoral students in clinical psychology were given a training audiotape containing descriptions and sample examples of strong laughter and mild or moderate laughter. These two kinds of laughter events consisted of those identified by both judges. Non-laughter instances were randomly selected from sessions indicated by both judges as containing instances of strong laughter.

Content Analysis Systems for Therapist Statements

The unit of study was the complete therapist statement, defined as including all the words spoken by the therapist, preceded and followed by the words spoken by the patient. In order to identify the kinds of therapist statements antecedent to instances of strong laughter, other laughter, and non-laughter, the content analysis system was taken from the eight categories of therapist statements proposed by Mahrer and Gervaize (1984) from a review of the clinical literature as instrumental to the occurrence of strong laughter:

1. *Directed interpersonal risk behavior.* The therapist directs the patient to carry out a risked interpersonal behavior. The behavior is to be carried out immediately in the therapy session, within the context of an imagined or fantasied scene including a significant other. The behavior is risky in that it is threatening, tension-producing, anxiety-engendering, impulse-related, unusual, or atypical for the patient.
2. *Defined risk behavior by patient or other.* The therapist describes in concrete detail a risk (threatening, deep-seated, dangerous, shocking, defended-against) behavior as if it were carried out by the patient or significant other.
3. *Ridiculous explanation/description of patient.* The therapist offers an explanation or interpretation of the patient in a way that is ridiculous, that is, burlesqued, unrealistic, farfetched, exaggerated, absurd, outrageous, playfully caricatured.
4. *Instruction to carry out affect-laden behavior with heightened intensity.* The therapist instructs the patient to carry out affect-laden behaviors repeatedly and with increasing feeling. This may consist of instructions to "say it again, louder," to scream and yell affect-laden words, to hit, kick, pound with increasing feeling expression.
5. *Carrying out risk behavior as/for the patient.* The therapist carries out or acts out a behavior that is risky (impulse-related, wicked, tabooed, exciting, outlandish, unusual) for the patient, and does so as/for the patient.
6. *Risked being of other person or entity.* The therapist instructs the patient to "be" (take the role of, be the identity of, speak as) some

other person or entity, for example, the grandfather, taxi driver, spouse, or one's own stomach, voice, or clenched fist.

7. *Excited pleasure over risked behavior*. The therapist responds with excited pleasure immediately following the patient's expression of a risked behavior. The therapist's response includes expressed excitement, approval, welcoming pleasure.

8. *Directed risk behavior toward the therapist*. The therapist directs the patient to carry out a risk behavior toward the therapist herself or himself, for example, to hit, hug, push, squeeze, hold, or slap the therapist.

9. *Other*. Therapist statements that do not fall within the above eight categories.

In order to enable identification of additional "target" categories and therapist statements falling in the "Other" category, it was determined to use a standard backup category system. The selected instrument was the Hill Counselor Verbal Response Category System (Hill, 1978) consisting of fourteen nominal, mutually exclusive categories: minimal encourager, approval-reassurance, information, direct guidance, closed question, open question, restatement, reflection, nonverbal referent, interpretation, confrontation, self-disclosure, silence, and other.

Judges

Two teams of three judges were used, one for the target nine categories and one for the Hill Counselor Verbal Response Category System. Judges included three professional clinical psychologists, two postinternship doctoral students in clinical psychology, and one honors student in psychology, each with extensive experience in using category systems for rating psychotherapy transcripts.

Procedure

Data to be judged consisted of excerpts containing the three therapist statements preceding each instance of strong laughter, other laughter, and non-laughter identified by the two doctoral students, together with the intervening patient statements. These were presented in transcript form to eliminate any cues as to whether the excerpt was one of strong laughter, other laughter, or non-laughter. The immediately following patient statement including the strong laughter, other laughter, or non-laughter was not included in the excerpt. Finally, the three kinds of excerpts were randomized. Since both sets of judges were ignorant of the purposes of the study, and were instructed only to place the therapist statements in one of the categories in the system, the data were regarded as reasonably unbiased.

Each set of three judges was given a 10-hour training program that was satisfactory to attain a criterion level of 90% agreement on fifty therapist statements not included in the present study. The training program was begun with an introduction and discussion of the nine target categories for one set of judges, and of the fourteen categories in the Hill Counselor Verbal Response Category System, for the second set of three judges.

Following the 10-hour training program, each set of judges was given the three therapist statements (and intervening two patient statements) to be placed into a single category of the system used by the judging team. Since the study focuses upon the therapist statement immediately preceding the strong laughter, as compared with other laughter and non-laughter, the "hard" findings will include only the immediately preceding therapist statement. However, the two penultimate therapist and patient statements were also included to provide "soft" indications of therapist statements that may also serve to contribute to the consequent occurrence of strong patient laughter.

Reliability was assessed by means of kappas (Tinsley and Weiss, 1975), and also by intermixing therapist statements that failed to reach criterion on the initial judging with an equal number of therapist statements that attained criterion agreement. Criterion agreement was set at 67% among the three judges. Therapist statements that failed to reach criterion on rejudgment would be deleted from further study.

Given this design and procedure, the hypothesis is that a significantly higher proportion of therapist statements falling under the eight target categories will occur immediately antecedent to strong laughter, as compared with the proportion occurring antecedent to other laughter and non-laughter. The design and procedure also allows for exploration of the two penultimate therapist statements.

Results

From the total pool of 280 hours of therapy, the first doctoral student identified sixty-four instances of strong laughter and thirty of other laughter. Of these, a pair of judges independently agreed on sixty of the sixty-four strong laughters, and all of the thirty other laughters. Accordingly, data consisted of sixty instances of strong laughter, thirty instances of other laughter, and thirty instances of non-laughter, randomly selected from the strong laughter sessions.

The sixty instances of strong laughter were distributed unevenly over ten therapists from the total pool (chi-square 21.28, df $= 9$, $p < .02$ and $> .01$), with three therapists having only two instances each, and two having eleven and twelve instances. Nevertheless, in view of the relative low frequency of the target event, the decision was to retain the sixty instances rather than even out the distribution and sacrifice frequency.

Immediately Preceding Therapist Statements

A separate set of three judges categorized the 120 therapist statements immediately preceding sixty instances of strong laughter, thirty of non-laughter, and thirty of other laughter. On initial judgment of the 120 therapist statements into the eight target categories and the "other" category, 112 (93.3%) reached criterion agreement. The eight remaining therapist statements were intermixed randomly with eight therapist statements that attained criterion, and all sixteen reached criterion on rejudgment, with category confirmation on all of the latter eight therapist statements. In terms of kappas, interrater reliabilities for all pairs of judges were 0.76–0.79, and were deemed adequate. Each of the eight randomly selected therapist statements was reconfirmed at or above criterion level of agreement. While the criterion level of interjudge agreement was set at 67%, the more stringent nine-category actual mean agreement level was 86.4%. In general, reliability was deemed satisfactory.

Looking at the eight target categories of immediately preceding therapist statements as a group, of the sixty strong laughter events, forty-four (73.3%) fell within the eight target categories. Of the thirty non-laughter events, only 1 (3.3%) fell in the eight target categories, and of the thirty other-laughter events, only three (10%) fell in the eight target categories.

A comparison of the frequencies of therapist statements falling in the eight target categories immediately preceding strong laughter, compared with the frequencies preceding non-laughter and other laughter, yielded a chi-square of 55.6 (df $= 1$, $p < .001$). Independent comparisons of the strong laughter and non-laughter distributions yielded a chi-square of 39.18 (df $= 1$, $p < .001$) and other laughter a chi-square of 32.31 (df $= 1$, $p < .001$).

A closer inspection of the eight target categories indicates that category 6 (Risked Being of Other Person or Entity) had 0 frequency antecedent to strong laughter, non-laughter and other laughter. Of the forty-four therapist statements immediately antecedent to strong laughter, none fell in category 6, three in category 1 (Directed Interpersonal Risk Behavior), and three in category 4 (Instruction to Carry Out Affect-Laden Behavior by Patient or Other). It appears that the higher load was carried by the remaining five categories, and this is also indicated by a comparison of the actual frequencies with an expected even distribution across the eight categories (chi-square 10.68, df = 1, p <.01).

A separate group of three judges placed all 120 therapist statements in the "backup" Hill Counselor Verbal Response Category System. Using the same 67% interjudge agreement level, two of the Hill categories occurred with significantly greater frequencies preceding strong laughter as compared with non-laughter and other laughter. One was Hill's Direct Guidance (chi-square 11.64, df = 1, p <.02 and >.01), and the second was Hill's Other category (chi-square 13.32, df = 1, p <.01). While these results provided some confirmation of the main findings, they shed little additional light on categories of therapist statements preceding strong laughter as compared with other laughter and non-laughter. It is interesting that of the sixteen therapist statements falling in the All Other category of the main findings, most likewise fell in Hill's Other category.

Penultimate Therapist Statements

While the therapist statements occurring two and three statements before the strong laughter were not independent events, the findings also allow a comparison of the proportion of therapist statements falling in the eight target categories antecedent to strong laughter, non-laughter, and other laughter.

Of the sixty therapist statements occurring two statements before strong laughter, twenty-two fell in the eight target categories. Of the thirty therapist statements occurring two statements before non-laughter, none fell in the eight target categories. Of the thirty therapist statements before other laughter, one fell in the target categories. These findings yield a chi-square of 23.72 (df = 1, p <.001).

Similar findings were demonstrated with regard to the sixty therapist statements occurring three statements before the strong laughter, thirty statements occurring before non-laughter, and thirty statements occurring three statements before the other laughter. Frequencies within the eight target categories were 23, 1, and 0 respectively. A comparison of these three distributions yielded a chi-square of 25.2 (df = 1, p <.001).

DISCUSSION AND CONCLUSIONS

The main conclusion is that a significantly higher proportion of therapist statements falling under a group of eight target categories occurred immediately antecedent to strong patient laughter, as compared with the proportion that occurred immediately antecedent to patient non-laughter and to patient other laughter.

The findings lend confirmation to the clinical observations of those psychotherapists for whom the occurrence of singular and strong patient laughter is regarded as a welcomed and desirable in-therapy event (Mahrer and Gervaize 1984). On the basis of these clinical observations, eight target categories were placed into a single group that was found to be immediately followed by strong patient laughter. The distinctiveness and power of this group was indicated by its significant absence immediately before non-laughter and even before instances of mild and moderate laughter.

For the working therapist, however, the pragmatic question has to do with which actual categories seemed to be useful, and in what pattern or configuration leading directly to the strong laughter. Here the findings were only suggestive. If the window is opened to include the three therapist statements before the strong laughter, some data-based speculations are warranted on the basis of a closer inspection of the eight target categories before strong laughter as compared with their occurrence before non-laughter and other laughter. The speculated hypothesis is that five categories occur immediately before strong laughter, and also comprise a pattern or configuration in therapist statements occurring one, two, and three statements before the strong laughter. These five categorie, and their numbers, are (2) Defined Risk Behavior by Patient or Other, (3) Ridiculous Explanation/Description of Patient, (5) Carrying Out Risk Behavior As/For Patient, (7) Excited Pleasure Over Risk Behavior, and (8) Directed Risk Behavior Toward Therapist. An interesting "assisting" category seemed to occur in the two penultimate therapist statements but not immediately antecedent to the strong laughter: (4) Instruction to Carry Out Affect-Laden Behavior with Heightened Intensity.

In the light of the findings, and having studied sixty vignettes in which patients move from non-laughter into strong laughter, we are inclined to propose the following conditions that culminate in strong laughter: (a) The patient is in the near vicinity of being or behaving some way that is risky: ordinarily blocked or avoided, excitingly threatening, wickedly impulsive. (b) The therapist's feelinged reception to this way of being and behaving is welcoming, playful, sharing, pleasurably enjoying, with a demonstrated appreciation of the comic, the absurd, the ridiculous, the wholesale letting go. (c) The therapist carries forward the risky behavior into concrete and specific action, rendering the behavior alive and real, immediate and expressed. (d) Together with the patient, the therapist does this by promoting its repetition with heightened feeling, by defining the specific nature of the risk behavior, by exaggerated attribution of it to the patient, by carrying it out, excitedly welcoming its occurrence, and directing its occurrence here and now in the therapeutic interaction. The following is a representative sample of the process:

Pt: (Hesitantly, describing what she would like to occur with her adolescent son) He could come home on time, and clean his room and . . . and take those damned posters off the wall.

T: (With pleasant high energy) Again! Say it again, and with real feeling. "Take those damned posters off the wall!"

Pt: Oh, I couldn't. I'd get a headache. He'd die if I talked that way to him.

T: (Playfully) OK, let's see if I got it. You order the little bastard to take those damned posters off the wall, and he clutches at his heart, slumps against the wall, and dies, right on the spot!

Pt: He'd only do that to torment me! And the damned posters would still be on the wall!

T: Before you crap out, take the damned posters off the wall!

Pt: (Bursting into strong laughter) I think he'd die of shock! So would I!! The worm turns! I'd love it! Love it!

Not all therapies value the singular occurrence of such strong laughter. However, for those therapies that regard such laughter as a welcomed and desirable event, it seems that there are identifiable sets of therapist statements that are followed by strong laughter as compared with non-laughter and with mild or moderate other laughter.

REFERENCES

Ansell, C., Mindess, H., Stern, E. M., and Stern, V. (1981). Pies in the face and similar matters. *Voices: The Art and Science of Psychotherapy* 16 (4):10–23.

Bergler, E. (1956). *Laughter and the Sense of Humor*. New York: Intercontinental Medical Book Corporation.

Bugental, J. T. (1976). *The Search for Existential Identity*. San Francisco: Jossey-Bass.

Farrelly, F., and Brandsma, J. (1974). *Provocative Therapy*. Fort Collins Co.: Shields.

Freud, S. (1905). Jokes and their relation to the unconscious. *Standard Edition* 8.

Grotjahn, M. (1970). Laughter in psychotherapy. In *A Celebration of Laughter,* ed. W. M. Mende. Los Angeles: Mara Books.

Harman, R. L. (1981). Humor and Gestalt therapy. *Voices: The Art and Science of Psychotherapy* 16(4):62–64.

Hill, C. E. (1978). Development of a counselor verbal response category system. *Journal of Counseling Psychology* 25:461–468.

Jackins, H. (1965). *The Human Side of Human Beings*. Seattle: Rational Island.

Kubie, L. S. (1971). The destructive potential of humor in psychotherapy. *American Journal of Psychiatry* 127:861–866.

Levine, J. (1976). Humor as a form of therapy. In *Humor and Laughter: Theory, Research and Application,* ed. A.J. Chapman, and H.C. Foot. London: John Wiley.

Mahrer, A. R. (1983). *Experiential Psychotherapy: Basic Practices*. New York: Brunner/Mazel.

Mahrer, A. R., and Gervaize, P. A. (1984). An integrative review of strong laughter: What it is and how it works. *Psychotherapy: Theory, Research, and Practice* 21:510–516.

Nichols, M. P. (1974). Outcome of brief cathartic psychotherapy. *Journal of Consulting and Clinical Psychology* 42(3):403–410.

Nichols, M. P., and Bierenbaum, H. (1978). Success of cathartic therapy as a function of patient variables. *Journal of Clinical Psychology* 34 (3):726–728.

Noyes, A. P., and Kolb, L. C. (1967). *Modern Clinical Psychiatry,* 6th ed. Philadelphia: W. B. Saunders.

Perls, F. (1970). Four lectures. In *Gestalt Therapy Now*, ed. J. Fagan, and I. L. Shepherd. Palo Alto: Science and Behavior Books.

Pierce, R. A., Nichols, M. P., and Dubrin, J. R. (1983). *Emotional Expression in Psychotherapy*. New York: Gardner.

Plessner, H. (1970). *Laughing and Crying: A Study of the Limits of Human Behavior*, 3rd ed. Evanston: Northwestern University Press.

Polster, E., and Polster, M. (1973). *Gestalt Therapy Integrated: Contours of Theory and Practice*. New York: Brunner/Mazel.

Tinsley, H., and Weiss, D. J. (1975). Interrater reliability and agreement of subjective judgements. *Journal of Counseling Psychology* 22:358–376.

Zuk, G. H. (1966). On the theory and pathology of laughter in psychotherapy. *Psychotherapy: Theory, Research and Practice* 3(5):97–101.

What Strong Laughter in Psychotherapy Is and How It Works

Alvin R. Mahrer
and Patricia A. Gervaize

While laughing has been studied from such perspectives as anthropology and social psychology (e.g., Bergler 1956, Chapman and Foot 1976), there are no reviews of patient laughter in psychotherapy. Our purpose is to review the conceptual, research, and clinical literature organized around two questions: (a) Is strong, hearty laughter regarded as a welcomed and desirable event by various therapeutic approaches? Our review indicates that a broad array of therapeutic approaches regards the singular discrete occurrence of strong, hearty, high-energy patient laughter as a welcomed and desirable event in psychotherapy. (b) In those therapeutic approaches, how do therapists help to bring about the occurrence of strong laughter? A review of the literature supports the use of eight therapeutic methods linked with the consequent occurrence of strong laughter.

STRONG LAUGHTER AS A DESIRABLE IN-THERAPY EVENT

Conceptual and Clinical Foundations

Within the field of psychotherapy, some hold that laughter, especially strong laughter, is psychodynamically meaningful but not always especially welcomed or desirable. It is sometimes understood as pathogno-monic of serious disturbance (Levine 1976, Noyes and Kolb 1967), as an expression of dangerous unconscious processes (Bergler 1956, Freud, 1905, Grotjahn 1970, Harman 1981, Koestler 1964, Plessner 1970), and as a defensive avoidance against internal or external threat (Ansell et al. 1981, Kubie 1971, Zuk 1966). According to this view, strong laughter may or may not be a therapeutically welcomed event. One must take into account its psychodynamic meaning and the nature of the concomitant feelings. In a closer look at strong laughter that may be regarded as therapeutically welcomed, four reasons are highlighted.

First, strong, hearty laughter may indicate a desirable shift in the patient's self-concept or self-perspective. This may consist of a shift toward more acceptance of oneself (Farrelly and Brandsma 1974, Mindess 1971, 1976, Perls 1970), a positive shift in personal cognitions and constructs (Viney 1983), or a shift toward seeing oneself along the lines of the therapist's interpretations (Berne 1972, Grotjahn 1966, 1970, Mindess 1971, Poland 1971, Rose 1976). This valuing of strong laughter is found in a broad array of approaches including psychoanalytic therapy, direct decision therapy, Gestalt therapy, provocative therapy, Adlerian therapy, interpersonal therapy, and personal construct therapy (e.g., Greenwald 1975, Kris 1940, Mindess 1976, O'Connell 1981, Poland 1971, Shaw 1960, Sullivan 1957, Viney, 1983).

Second, some approaches regard strong patient laughter as an expres-sion of a valued or optimal state characterized by energy, freedom, zest, openness, awareness, acceptance, mastery, and inner harmony (Berne 1972, Harman 1981, Jackins 1965, Jasnow 1981, Kris 1940, Levine 1976, Mindess 1971, Olsen 1976, Perls 1970, Viney 1983). Indeed, many clinical theorists accept strong patient laughter as an expression of an optimal goal state contained in such constructs as actualization, psychological health, personal growth, integration, authenticity, maturity, adjustment, and healthy life outlook (e.g., Greenwald 1975, Levine 1976, Mahrer 1978, 1983, Mindess 1971, 1976, O'Connell 1981, Shaw 1960).

Third, strong patient laughter is regarded as a welcomed and desirable expression of a positive patient–therapist relationship along the lines of warmth and acceptance, intimacy, and a reduction in emotional distance (e.g., Mindess 1971, 1976, Narboe 1981). This way of valuing strong patient laughter is found in approaches such as feeling-expressive therapy (Pierce et al. 1983), provocative therapy (Farrelly and Brandsma 1974), existential-humanistic therapy (Bugental 1976), direct decision therapy (Greenwald 1975), Gestalt therapy (Polster and Polster 1973), and some psychoanalytic schools (e.g., Grotjahn 1966, Rose 1969, Rosenheim 1974).

And last, in some therapeutic approaches, the central axis of psycho-therapeutic change consists of heightened experiencing, strong feeling-expression, emotional flooding, or catharsis. Strong patient laughter is seen as a welcomed and desirable index of the process of therapeutic change itself (Farrelly and Brandsma 1974, Harman 1981, Jackins 1965, Mahrer 1978, 1983, Nichols and Zax 1977, Olsen 1976, Pierce et al. 1983, Perls 1970). The payoff changes are held as the concomitants and consequences of strong patient laughter.

Research Foundation

There are two domains of research on laughter that shed little if any light on the value of strong laughter in psychotherapy. One domain includes studies on the interrelationships among laughter, physiological variables, and physical health (e.g., Cousins 1979, Mazer 1981, Moody 1978). The second domain includes studies of humor and its relation with such personality dimensions as ego strength (Goldsmith 1973), reality contact (Roberts and Johnson 1957), psychopathology (Levine and Adelson 1959, Levine and Redlich 1960), and empathy (Epstein and Smith 1969, Roberts and Johnson 1957). Both of these domains are tangential to the question of the desirability of strong patient laughter in psychotherapy.

Although strong laughter is acknowledged as a common psychotherapeutic occurrence, only two studies examined this event, and both supported its therapeutic value. Nichols (1974) and Nichols and Bierenbaum (1978) examined the relationships between positive therapeutic outcome and the in-therapy expression of strong feelings, with strong laughter as one of the indices of strong feeling. Using actual psychotherapy patients and therapists, both studies reported significant relationships between positive therapeutic outcomes and in-therapy strong feeling-expression, including laughter. The research, although scant, provides some support for strong patient laughter as a welcomed and desirable in-therapy event.

**Characteristics of Therapeutically Desirable
Patient Laughter**

Both of the above studies express a theme that is upheld throughout the conceptual and clinical literatures—there are identifiable characteristics of the kind of patient laughter that is regarded as therapeutically welcomed and desirable. Two defining characteristics are consistently found: (a) It occurs as a singular and distinctive, low-frequency, discrete event in the session, rather than as a high-frequency stylistic characteristic of the patient's consistent mode of behavior (Ansell et al. 1981, Bugental 1976, Greenwald 1975, Grotjahn 1970, Harman 1981, Kris 1940, Levine

1976, Nichols 1974, Nichools and Bierenbaum 1978, Nichols and Zax 1977, O'Connell 1981, Olsen 1976, Perls 1970, Poland 1971, Polster and Polster 1973, Rosenheim 1974, Shaw 1960, Viney 1983); (b) It is characterized by high energy, strength, saturation and amplitude, and unrestrained expressive openness, rather than low energy and mild expressiveness (Bugental 1976, Grotjahn 1970, Nichols 1974, Nichols and Bierenbaum 1978, Nichols and Zax 1977, Shorr 1972).

A third characteristic is found less consistently, and may vary with the therapeutic approach. Some clinical theorists highlight the psychodynamic significance of the strong laughter. They distinguish between strong laughter that may be therapeutically desirable as opposed to strong laughter that may be defensive, expressive of threatening impulses, or pathognomonic of serious disturbance (e.g., Bergler 1956, Levine 1976, Plessner 1970). Other clinical theorists generally restrict this kind of less-welcomed laughter to that which is mild, and to that which is a high-frequency stylistic characteristic of the patient's therapeutic behavior (e.g., Farrelly and Brandsma 1974, Greenwald 1975, Harman 1981, Jackins 1965).

THERAPEUTIC METHODS OF PROMOTING STRONG LAUGHTER

If strong patient laughter is regarded as a desirable event, what therapeutic methods are used to bring it about? On this question, the conceptual and research literature has little to say. The conceptual literature on patient laughter does not deal with the issue of its promotion through specific therapeutic methods. Neither of the research studies (Nichols 1974, Nichols and Bierenbaum 1978) was designed to identify specific therapeutic methods linked to consequent strong patient laughter.

Accordingly, this section reviews two nested domains of clinical writings. One is explicitly aimed at describing therapeutic methods for promoting discrete strong patient laughter. The second is the domain of clinical writings on therapeutic methods of bringing about heightened feeling-expression or experiencing, with discrete strong patient laughter as one such index (e.g., BarLevav 1976, Bugental 1976, Harman 1981, Jackins 1965, Mahrer 1978, 1983, Nichols and Zax 1977, Olsen 1976, Perls 1970, Polster and Polster 1973, Pierce et al. 1983, Shorr 1972).

Many of the writings in these two domains acknowledge that the bringing about of strong patient laughter requires something more than mere therapeutic technique or method. There is a common ingredient, necessary but not sufficient for promoting strong laughter, and variously described as a humorous outlook on life, a spontaneous playfulness, an appreciation of the ridiculous and the tragic-comic, an ability to stand off and see oneself as silly and foolish, a recognition of the absurd, a welcoming of the burlesqued and the caricatured (Ansell et al. 1981, Ellis 1977, 1981, Farrelly and Brandsma 1974, Greenwald 1975, Grotjahn 1970, Killinger 1976, Mindess 1971, 1976, Narboe 1981, Rose 1969, Rosenheim 1974).

On the other hand, there is only a muted acknowledgment that therapeutically desirable strong laughter may be brought about through standard comic routines such as funny jokes, one-liners, slapstick routines, pitter-patter, and lyrics carried out by funny sit-down comedians (cf. Ellis 1981, Harman 1981).

Our focus is on the actual therapeutic methods that the clinical literature suggests are effective in promoting discrete, strong laughter, and are regarded as therapeutically desirable. It is important to differentiate this target question from others such as the following: (a) What is the conceptual basis for these methods? We are concerned here with the actual methods rather than how and why they may be linked to discrete strong laughter. (b) Do these methods really work? To our knowledge, there is no research on this question. (c) What patient variables affect the likelihood that these methods are related to discrete strong laughter? Our integrative review emphasizes the methods rather than their differential effectiveness as related to patient variables. (d) Are there patternings of therapeutic conditions and factors that affect the effectiveness of these methods? The following summary of therapeutic methods is exclusive of whatever conditions and factors may provide a contextual organizational framework within which these methods are effective.

Directed Interpersonal Risk-Behavior

Strong laughter tends to occur when the therapist directs the patient to carry out a risk-behavior that relates to some significant figure (Jackins 1965, Pierce et al. 1983, Shorr 1972). The therapist directs the patient to carry out the behavior, for example, "Do this . . . say these words . . . carry out this behavior." The behavior is risky: anxiety-engendering, unusual, tabooed, threatening, impulsive. The behavior is within the context of an immediate, imagined, fantasied scene or situation involving a direct interpersonal relationship with a significant other person. For example:

"Imagine holding your mother's face in your hands and scream the most impossible phrase at her" . . . He paused for several minutes and said,

"This is too hard, Joe." I urged him on. Then he let go a scream, "I AM NOT YOUR PUPPET, I AM MY OWN MAN!" He . . . cried for a moment, then he burst into hysterical laughter. [Shorr 1972, p. 74]

With the patient who is just starting to welcome her own toughness, the therapist tells her to imagine telling the abrasive neighbor, "Steve, stick it up your ass!" With the 24-year-old Jewish son who has been defensively masking his homosexuality from his family, and who is describing his discomfort with his grandmother on a recent visit, the therapist directs the patient to attend to her and say, "Grandma Sadie, I gotta tell you. I'm gay! I've been gay for almost ten years! My lover is black and . . . he's not Jewish!" The consequence is strong patient laughter.

Directed Risk-Behavior Toward Therapist

Rather than being aimed at some other person, the risk-behavior is aimed directly at the therapist. That is, strong patient laughter tends to occur when the therapist directs the patient to carry out a behavior that is risky—anxiety-engendering, tabooed, threatening, impulsive, unusual— and is to be carried out toward the therapist. For example, the patient is directed to push or hit the therapist, yell at the therapist, hug or squeeze the therapist, be sexual or aggressive toward the therapist.

After the patient vigorously protests against others evaluating and assessing him, the therapist says, "OK, now reach over, take my hand, look at me, and assess me right now. Give me a thorough evaluation!" With the patient who is starting to be filled with love and closeness, the therapist says, "Now move over here a little, put your arms around me, and give me a good hug!" This method is common to bioenergetic therapy, Gestalt therapy, encountering therapy, reevaluation counseling, and virtually all therapies that aim at the promotion of strong experiencing or feeling-expression. It is expressly described and discussed by Bugental (1976), Whitaker et al. (1959), and others.

Direction to Carry Out Risk-Behavior as Other Person

This method is taken from the Gestalt emphasis on being or taking the role of the other person. However, especially as discussed by Casriel (1972), Finney (1976), Jackins (1965), Malamud (1976), and Moreno (1959), the key element is that of carrying out a behavior that is risky— anxiety-engendering, tabooed, threatening, impulsive, unusual. A portion of the risk is inherent in the sheer being of a threatening other figure, and the remainder of the risk lies in the carrying out of the risky behavior.

With the patient who copes with a deeper authoritarianism, the therapist directs the patient to be the policeman who lords his authority over the lowly drivers in saying, "This is the end of your driving for a while, buddy!" To the mother who is objecting to the nasty, disrespectful way her daughter uses foul language, the therapist directs the patient to be the daughter and to say those words to the mother. The clinical literature indicates that the immediate consequence tends to be strong laughter.

Defined Impulsive Behavior by Patient or Other

Strong laughter tends to occur when the therapist explicitly defines or describes in detail a behavior that is impulsive, risky, threatening, ordinarily blocked or defended against, dangerous or shocking, wicked or devilish, and is defined as being carried out by the patient or by some other person (Close 1970, Farrelly and Brandsma 1974, Shorr 1972).

For example, Close (1970) uses this method to bring about strong laughter in a patient who is telling about refusing to hang up his shirts because the rattling of hangers might disturb the other patients on the ward:

> Look, I'll tell you one way you might be able to get your shirts hung up. If you go out to the TV room and turn the TV up full blast, then you could dash madly back to your room before anybody turned it down, and the TV would drown out the rattling of the hangers. . . . Wait a minute, I've got another idea. If you really wanted to do this right, you could set off the fire-alarm . . . that would get the staff all upset, as well as the patients, and you would have plenty of time to hang your shirts up. [p. 111]

In the same way, the therapist may define an impulsive, risky behavior to be carried out by the other person, as indicated below, following which the patient burst into strong laughter (Farrelly and Brandsma 1974):

> C: (With an air of marked independence) I can do without men! (piously) I'll just become closer to God.
> T: (Reminiscing; off-handedly) Reminds me of a friend, recently divorced. Of course, he had sexual feelings—not like you. But anyway, he said that his divorce had really brought him closer to God. Of course I agreed with him—with one small exception . . . [pause] . . . I just wondered how it was to crawl between the sheets with God. [p. 111]

Ridiculous Description of Patient by Therapist

Strong patient laughter tends to occur when the therapist goes beyond the ordinary meaning of interpretation, and describes the patient in a way that is ridiculous—extreme, highly exaggerated, wild, farfetched, unrealistic, caricatured, and burlesqued. In this method, the therapist may simply tell it to the patient, show it to the patient, or even act it out for the patient. This method is described especially by Ansell et al. (1981), Farrelly and Brandsma (1974), Greenwald (1975), Kopp (1974), Poland (1971), Searles (1963), and Whitaker et al. (1962).

When the patient is in doubt about her grip on reality, the therapist says, "Well, let's face it, Gertrude, you're one slight step from being a complete loony. That's your problem, dearie, you're a nut, deranged, out of your mind. And that's just for starters!" or for the patient who is clinging to a lost youthful appeal, "No doubt about it, you're the sexiest, most vibrant guy on the block. Maybe even in Chickabonga County!"

Repetition of Affect-Laden Behavior with Heightened Intensity

The core of the method is for the therapist to instruct the patient to carry out the identified affect-laden behavior again and again, and with heightened feeling and intensity (Bugental 1976, Jackins 1965, Polster and Polster 1973, Rose 1976). This may consist of simple instructions to say it again, louder, to yell the appropriate words. It may also include physical movements such as hitting, kicking, pounding, beating—again and again, with increasing volume, amplitude, feeling, and intensity.

Carrying Out the Risk-Behavior as/for the Patient

Farrelly and Brandsma (1974), Kopp (1974), and Shorr (1972) are representative of therapists who hold that strong laughter is one consequence of the therapist's taking the role of the patient in carrying out a behavior that is risky—impulsive, threatening, anxiety-engendering, tabooed, wicked, mischievous. Instead of the patient's carrying out the behavior, the therapist assumes the role of the patient in carrying it out. For example, when the patient is undergoing a fantasied encounter with her mother, but cannot quite tell her mother that she is having sex, the therapist says the right words, using the right grammar, and tells it forthrightly and explicitly to the mother (Shorr 1972, p. 80). When the patient recoils against the possibility of a verging seizure, the therapist announces that he/she is also subject to seizures, and produces one on the spot, complete with body shaking, trembling, baring and clenching of teeth (Farrelly and Brandsma 1974, pp. 101–102).

Welcoming Pleasure over Risk-Behavior

When the patient carries out a risk behavior, strong laughter tends to occur when the therapist responds with welcoming pleasure. Described especially by Farrelly and Brandsma (1974), this method consists of sheer delight laced with excited happiness, a genuine welcoming pleasure in the patient's actually carrying out the risked behavior.

Farrelly and Brandsma (1974) describe the patient who begins sessions by meekly entering the office, unsure and confused. The therapist pretends to be equally confused and unsure, even about what chair she should sit in, until she blurts out, "Pt: (Suddenly straightening up, frowning; loudly and forcefully) 'Aw, go to hell? I'll sit where I want!!' " (p. 181). Farrelly excitedly welcomes this risked new behavior, expresses full pleasure in its occurrence, and the patient bursts into laughter.

Here, then, are eight concrete methods that clinical experience suggests are instrumental in the promotion of hearty strong laughter, that is, laughter marked by strength, high energy, and intensity, and is a low-frequency, singular discrete event in a session. For the practitioner who welcomes such laughter, this integrative summary perhaps may serve as a clearinghouse of additional methods that the practitioner may use. But for the clinical researcher, a number of inviting avenues of investigation are set forth. Among these are the following:

- Is hearty strong laughter preceded by these eight methods? Are some of these more prevalent than others? Are there other methods beyond these eight?
- Are there potent patterns, combinations, or sequences of therapist statements that precede such hearty laughter? What are the facilitating context effects that are helpful?
- Once we have a fairly good idea of what kinds of therapist methods actually seem to be followed by such hearty strong laughter, there is a reasonable basis for speculating about why this laughter occurs, and why certain methods or patternings of methods seem to be followed by such laughter.
- Are there defining characteristics of strong laughter as a therapeutically welcomed event as contrasted with strong laughter as a less welcomed therapeutic event?
- Is hearty strong laughter accompanied with or followed by indications of (a) a positive shift in the patient's self-concept or self-perspective, or (b) the development of a patient–therapist relationship marked by warmth and acceptance, intimacy, and a reduction in emotional distance?

- What are the concomitants of such strong laughter? What are patients doing and how are they acting when they are in this state? Proponents of some theoretical approaches hold that when patients are laughing heartily they are momentarily expressing a significant therapeutic change. It is as if the hearty laughing is a window into a welcomed and desirable therapeutic state. Accordingly, it would be valuable to examine what patients are doing and how they are acting in the concomitant vicinity of the hearty laughter, especially in contrast to prior ways of being and behaving.

- What are the relationships between the therapeutic value of such strong hearty laughter and whatever therapy and patient variables are deemed meaningful by the given therapeutic approach: for example, timing in the session(s), phase of therapy, personality characteristics of the patient, psychodiagnosis, content of the relevant immediate material?

CONCLUSION

The clinical, research, and conceptual literature provide a foundation for regarding a particular kind of patient laughter as a welcomed and desirable in-therapy event. This laughter is (a) a low-frequency, singular discrete event in the session, rather than a high-frequency characteristic style of the patient, and (b) is marked by strength, high energy, and intensity.

This kind of laughter is regarded as a welcomed and desirable in-therapy event in therapeutic approaches that especially value such laughter as an index or expression of (a) a positive shift in the patient's self-concept or self-perspective; (b) therapeutic change through the axis of heightened feeling, emotion, expression, or experiencing; (c) movement toward a more valued or optimal goal state; and/or (d) the development of a patient–therapist relationship characterized by warmth and acceptance, intimacy, and a reduction in emotional distance.

With the research literature standing silently by, clinical writings provide a foundation for identifying a set of therapeutic methods for promoting the occurrence of the above strong laughter. These methods include directed interpersonal risk behavior, directed risk behavior toward therapist, direction to carry out risk behavior as other person, defined impulsive behavior by patient or other, ridiculous description of patient, repetition of affect-laden behavior with heightened intensity, carrying out the risk behavior as/for the patient, and welcoming pleasure over risk behavior.

REFERENCES

Ansell, C., Mindess, H., Stern M., and Stern, V. (1981). Pies in the face and similar matters. *Voices: The Art & Science of Psychotherapy* 16:10–23.

Bar-Levav, R. (1976). Behavior change: insignificant and significant, apparent and real. In *What Makes Behavior Change Possible?* ed. A. Burton. New York: Brunner/Mazel.

Bergler, E. (1956). *Laughter and the Sense of Humor*. New York: Intercontinental Medical Book Corp.

Berne, E. (1972). *What Do You Say after You Say Hello?* New York: Grove Press.

Bugental, J. F. T. (1976). *The Search for Existential Identity*. San Francisco: Jossey-Bass.

Casriel, D. (1972). *A Scream Away from Happiness*. New York: Grosset & Dunlap.

Chapman, A. J., and Foot, H. C., eds. (1976). *Humor and Laughter: Theory, Research and Applications*. London: Wiley.

Close, H. T. (1970). Gross exaggeration with a schizophrenic patient. In *Gestalt Therapy Now*, ed. J. Fagan, and I. L. Shepherd. New York: Harper & Row.

Cousins, N. (1979). Anatomy of an illness (as perceived by the patient). In *Stress and Survival*, ed. C. Garfield. St. Louis: C. V. Mosby.

Ellis, A. (1977). Fun as psychotherapy. *Rational Living* 21:2–6.

_____ (1981). The use of rational-emotive humorous songs in psychotherapy. *Voices: The Art and Science of Psychotherapy* 16:29–36.

Epstein, S., and Smith, R. (1969). Repression and insight as related to reaction to cartoons. In *Motivation in Humor*, ed. J. Levine. New York: Atherton.

Farrelly, F., and Brandsma, J. (1974). *Provocative Therapy*. Fort Collins, CO: Shields.

Finney, B. C. (1976). Say it again: An active therapy technique. In *The Handbook of Gestalt Therapy*, ed. C. Hatcher, and P. Himelstein. New York: Jason Aronson.

Freud, S. (1905). Jokes and their relation to the unconscious. *Standard Edition* 8.

Goldsmith, L. (1973). Adaptive regression in humor and suicide. Unpublished doctoral dissertation, City University of New York.

Greenwald, H. (1975). Humor in psychotherapy. *Journal of Contemporary Psychotherapy* 7:113–116.

Grotjahn, M. (1966). *Beyond Laughter: Humor and the Subconscious*. New York: McGraw-Hill.

_____ (1970). Laughter in psychotherapy. In *A Celebration of Laughter*, ed. W. M. Mendel. Los Angeles: Mara Books.

Harman, R. L. (1981). Humor and Gestalt therapy. *Voices: The Art and Science of Psychotherapy* 16:62–64.

Jackins, H. (1965). *The Human Side of Human Beings: The Theory of Re-evaluation Counseling*. Seattle: Rational Island Publishers.

Jasnow, A. (1981). Humor and survival. *Voices: The Art and Science of Psychotherapy* 16:50–54.

Killinger, B. (1976). The place of humor in adult psychotherapy. In *It's a Funny Thing, Humour: International Conference on Humour and Laughter*, ed. A. J. Chapman, and H. C. Foot. New York: Pergamon.

Koestler, A. (1964). *The Act of Creation*. New York: Pantheon.

Kopp, S. (1974). *The Hanged Man: Psychotherapy and the Forces of Darkness*. Palo Alto, CA: Science and Behavior Books.

Kris, E. (1940). Laughter as an expressive process. *International Journal of Psycho-analysis* 21:314–341.

Kubie, L. S. (1971). The destructive potential of humor in psychotherapy. *American Journal of Psychiatry* 127:861–866.

Levine, J. (1976). Humor as a form of therapy: Introduction to a symposium. In *Humor and Laughter: Theory, Research and Applications*, ed. A. J. Chapman, and H. C. Foot. London: John Wiley.

Levine, J., and Adelson, R. (1959). Humor as a disturbing stimulus. *Journal of General Psychology* 60:191–200.

Levine, J., and Redlich, F. C. (1960). Intellectual and emotional factors in the appreciation of humor. *Journal of General Psychology* 62: 25–35.

Mahrer, A. R. (1978). *Experiencing: A Humanistic Theory of Psychology and Psychiatry*. New York: Brunner/Mazel.

_____ (1983). *Experiential Psychotherapy: Basic Practices.* New York: Brunner/Mazel.

Malamud, D. J. (1976). Expanding awareness through self-confrontation. In *Emotional Flooding*, ed. P. Olsen. New York: Human Sciences Press.

Mazer, E. (1981 April). A good laugh is great medicine. *Prevention* 82–86.

Mindess, H. (1971). *Laughter and Liberation*. Los Angeles: Nash.

_____ (1976) The use and abuse of humor in psychotherapy. In *Humor and Laughter: Theory, Research and Applications*, ed. A. J. Chapman, and H. C. Foot. London: John Wiley.

Moody, R. A., Jr. (1978). *Laugh after Laugh: The Healing Power of Humor*. New York: Headwaters Press.

Moreno, J. L. (1959). *Psychodrama: Foundations of Psychotherapy*, vol. 2. Beacon, NY: Beacon House.

Narboe, N. (1981). Why did the therapist cross the road? *Voices: The Art and Science of Psychotherapy* 16:55–58.

Nichols, M. P. (1974). Outcome of brief cathartic psychotherapy. *Journal of Consulting and Clinical Psychology* 42:403–410.

Nichols, M. P., and Bierenbaum, H. (1978). Success of cathartic therapy as a function of patient variables. *Journal of Clinical Psychology* 34:726–728.

Nichols, M. P., and Zax, M. (1977). *Catharsis in Psychotherapy*. New York: Gardner Press.

Noyes, A. P., and Kolb, L. C. (1967). *Modern Clinical Psychiatry*, 6th ed. Philadelphia: W. B. Saunders.

O'Connell, W. (1981). The natural high therapist: God's favorite monkey. *Voices: The Art and Science of Psychotherapy* 16:37–44.

Olsen, P. T., ed. (1976). *Emotional Flooding*. New York: Human Sciences Press.

Perls, F. (1970). Four Lectures. In *Gestalt Therapy Now*, ed. J. Fagan, and I. L. Shepherd. Palo Alto, CA: Science and Behavior Books.

Pierce, R. A., Nichols, M. P., and Durbin, J. R. (1983). *Emotional Expression in Psychotherapy*. New York: Gardner.

Plessner, H. (1970). *Laughing and Crying: A Study of the Limits of Human Behavior*, 3rd ed. Evanston, IL: Northwestern University Press.

Poland, W. S. (1971). The place of humor in psychotherapy. *American Journal of Psychiatry* 128:127–129.

Polster, E., and Polster, M. (1973). *Gestalt Therapy Integrated: Contours of Theory and Practice*. New York: Brunner/Mazel.

Roberts, A. F., and Johnson, D. M. (1957). Some factors related to the perception of funniness in humor stimuli. *Journal of Social Psychology* 46:57–63.

Rose, G. J. (1969). King Lear and the use of humor in treatment. *Journal of the American Psychoanalytic Association* 17:927–940.

Rose, S. (1976). Intense feeling therapy. In *Emotional Flooding*, ed. P. Olsen. New York: Human Sciences Press.

Rosenheim, E. (1974). Humor in psychotherapy: an interactive experience. *American Journal of Psychotherapy* 28:584–591.

Searles, H. (1963). The place of natural therapist responses in psychotherapy with the schizophrenic patient. *International Journal of Psychoanalysis* 44:42–56.

Shaw, F. J. (1960). Laughter: paradigm of growth. *Journal of Individual Psychology* 16:115–157.

Shorr, J. E. (1972). *Psycho-Imagination Therapy: The Integration of Phenomenology and Imagination*. New York: Intercontinental Medical Book Corp.

Sullivan, H. S. (1957). *The Psychiatric Interview*. New York: W. W. Norton.

Viney, L. L. (1983 July). *Humor as a therapeutic tool: another way to experiment with experience*. Paper presented at the 5th International Congress on Personal Construct Psychology, Boston, MA.

Whitaker, C. A., Felder, R., Malone, T. P., and Warkentin, J. (1962). First stage techniques in the experiential psychotherapy of chronic schizophrenics. In *Current Psychiatric Therapies*, vol. 2, ed. J. Masserman, pp. 147–158. New York: Grune & Stratton.

Whitaker, C. A., Warkentin, J., and Malone, T. P. (1959). The involvement of the professional therapist. In *Case Studies in Counseling and Psychotherapy*, A. Burton, ed. pp. 218–257. Englewood Cliffs, NJ: Prentice-Hall.

Zuk, G. H. (1966). On the theory and pathology of laughter in psychotherapy. *Psychotherapy: Theory, Research and Practice* 3:97–101.

Acknowledgments

The author gratefully acknowledges permission to reproduce the following:

Chapter 1: "The Gift of Laughter: On the Development of a Sense of Humor in Clinical Analysis," by Warren S. Poland, in *Psychoanalytic Quarterly*, vol. 59, pp. 197–225. Copyright © 1990 by *Psychoanalytic Quarterly*. Reprinted by permission of *Psychoanalytic Quarterly* and the author.

Chapter 2: "The Analyst's Use of Humor," by Michael J. Bader, in *Psychoanalytic Quarterly*, vol. 62, pp. 23–51. Copyright © 1993 by *Psychoanalytic Quarterly*. Reprinted by permission of *Psychoanalytic Quarterly* and the author.

Chapter 4: "The Oral Side of Humor," by Jule Eisenbud, in *The Psychoanalytic Review*, vol. 50, pp. 57–73. Copyright © 1963 by the *Psychoanalytic Review*. Reprinted by permission of the *Psychoanalytic Review* and the author.

Chapter 8: "The Destructive Potential of Humor in Psychotherapy," by Lawrence S. Kubie, in *American Journal of Psychiatry*, vol. 127, pp. 861–866. Copyright © 1971 by the *American Journal of Psychiatry*. Reprinted by permission of the *American Journal of Psychiatry* and the author.

Chapter 9: "The Use and Abuse of Laughter in Psychotherapy," by Robert A. Pierce, in *Psychotherapy in Private Practice*, vol. 3, pp. 67–73. Copyright © 1985 by The Haworth Press. Reprinted by permission of The Haworth Press and the author.

Chapter 10: "Treating Those Who Fail to Take Themselves Seriously: Pathological Aspects of Humor," by Ned N. Marcus, in *American Journal of Psychother-*

apy, vol. 54, pp. 423–432. Copyright © 1990 by the Association for the Advancement of Psychotherapy. Reprinted by permission.

Chapter 11: "Humor in Psychiatric Healing," by Bernard Saper, in *Psychiatric Quarterly*, vol. 59, 306–319. Copyright © 1988 by The Haworth Press. Reprinted by permission of The Haworth Press and the author.

Chapter 12: "Humor as an Intervention Strategy," by Frank J. Prerost, in *Psychology, a Journal of Human Behavior*, vol. 26, pp. 34–40. Copyright © 1989 by *Psychology*. Reprinted by permission of *Psychology* and the author.

Chapter 13: "The Laughing Game," by Daniel I. Malamud, in *Psychotherapy: Theory, Research, and Practice*, vol. 17, pp. 69–73. Copyright © 1980 by *Psychotherapy*. Reprinted by permission of *Psychotherapy* and the author.

Chapter 14: "The Application of Joy in Group Psychotherapy for the Elderly," by Shura and Sidney Saul, in *International Journal of Group Psychotherapy*, vol. 40, pp. 353–363. Copyright © 1990 by the American Group Psychotherapy Association. Reprinted by permission of the American Group Psychotherapy Association and the authors.

Chapter 15: "Humor as Metaphor," by Don-David Lusterman, in *Psychotherapy in Independent Practice*, vol. 10, pp. 167–172. Copyright © 1992 by The Haworth Press. Reprinted by permission of The Haworth Press and the author.

Chapter 16: "The Place of Humor in Psychotherapy," by Warren S. Poland, in *The American Journal of Psychiatry*, vol. 128, pp. 635–637. Copyright © 1971 by *The American Journal of Psychiatry*. Reprinted by permission of *The American Journal of Psychiatry* and the author.

Chapter 18: "Classical, Object Relations, and Self Psychological Perspective," originally published as "Three Perspectives on Humor and Laughing," by Roberta Satow, in *Group*, vol. 15, pp. 242–245. Copyright © 1991 by Brunner/Mazel. Reprinted by permission of Brunner/Mazel and the author.

Chapter 19: "The Use of Humor in Psychotherapy," by Harry A. Olson, in *Individual Psychologist*, vol. 13, pp. 34–37. Copyright © 1976 by *Individual Psychologist*. Reprinted by permission of *Individual Psychologist* and the author.

Chapter 20: "Therapeutic Laughter," by Patrica A. Gervaize, Alvin R. Mahrer, and Richard Markow, in *Psychotherapy in Private Practice*, vol. 3, pp. 65–74. Copyright © 1985 by The Haworth Press. Reprinted by permission of The Haworth Press and the authors.

Chapter 21: "What Strong Laughter in Psychotherapy Is and How It Works," originally published as "An Interrogative Review of Strong Laughter in Psychotherapy," by Alvin R. Mahrer and Patricia A. Gervaize, in *Psychotherapy in Private Practice*, vol. 21, pp. 510–516. Copyright © 1984 by The Haworth Press. Reprinted by permission of The Haworth Press and the authors.

Index